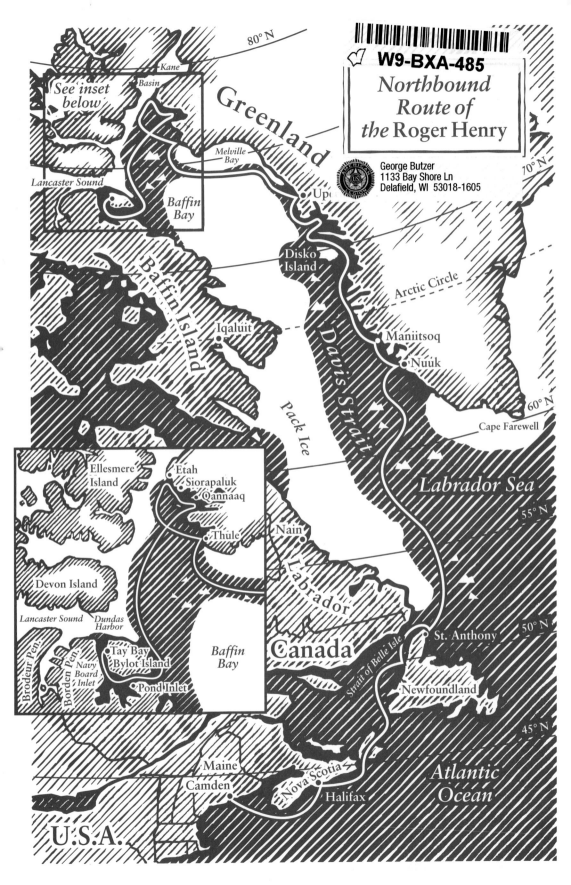

W9-BXA-485

Northbound Route of the Roger Henry

George Butzer
1133 Bay Shore Ln
Delafield, WI 53018-1605

80° N

See inset below

Kane
Basin

Greenland

Melville Bay

70° N

Lancaster Sound

Baffin Bay

Upe

Baffin Island

Disko Island

Arctic Circle

Iqaluit

Maniitsoq

Nuuk

Davis Strait

Pack Ice

60° N

Cape Farewell

Labrador Sea

55° N

Nain

Labrador

50° N

St. Anthony

Canada

Strait of Belle Isle

Newfoundland

45° N

Inset:

Ellesmere Island

Etah
Siorapaluk
Qannaaq

Devon Island

Thule

Lancaster Sound

Dundas Harbor

Brodeur Pen.

Borden Pen

Navy Board Inlet

Tay Bay
Bylot Island

Baffin Bay

Pond Inlet

Maine
Camden

Nova Scotia

Halifax

Atlantic Ocean

U.S.A.

NORTH TO THE NIGHT

North to the Night

A Year in the Arctic Ice

ALVAH SIMON

THE McGRAW-HILL COMPANIES / INTERNATIONAL MARINE

Camden, Maine • New York • San Francisco • Washington, D.C. • Auckland
Bogotá • Caracas • Lisbon • London • Madrid • Mexico City • Milan
Montréal • New Delhi • San Juan • Singapore • Sydney • Tokyo • Toronto

International Marine

A Division of The **McGraw·Hill** Companies

10 9 8 7 DOC 6 5 4 3 2 1

Library of Congress Cataloging-in-Publication Data
Simon, Alvah
North to the night : a year in the Arctic ice / Alvah Simon.
p.   cm.
ISBN 0-07-058052-9
1. Simon, Alvah—Journeys—Arctic Regions.   2. Simon, Diana—Journeys—Arctic Regions.
3. Arctic Regions—Description and travel.   4. Inuit—Social conditions.
5. Explorers—United States—Biography.   I. Title.
G585.S56A3   1998   98-12359
919.804—dc21   CIP

Edited by Jonathan Eaton; Kathryn Mallien
Design by Dennis Anderson, Duluth, MN
Page composition by UG, Atlantic Highlands, NJ
Photographs by Diana White-Simon, with occasional contributions by Alvah Simon
Chapter opener illustrations by Tom Foley, illustration of the *Roger Henry* by Jim Sollers
Endpaper illustrations by Michael Custode

I ONCE READ about an American man of letters who had achieved sufficient acclaim that he felt he owed his adoring audience an auto-biography. Enthusiastically, he produced an enormous pile of messy manuscript, which he turned over to his wife of many years. Her job with this, as with all his work, was to respell it, punctuate it, and beat the text into making some sense.

He waited impatiently for her to finish and then asked confidently, "Well, what do you think?" She said, "Dear, I think it is very good. But I do have one question . . . Did you never marry?"

It seems that our hero was so full of himself that he plumb forgot to mention the spouse who made everything possible. Lest I do the same, I dedicate this book to Diana, who made everything possible. What a gift to have such a companion when the hard winds blow.

THE WORD *ESKIMO* (or *Esquimeaux),* meaning "eater of raw meat"—with derogatory connotation—is a European derivative from the Cree Indian language. In the naming of themselves, the Eskimo generally prefer *Inuit* (*Inuk,* singular), which means simply, The People.

Often the term *Eskimo* is used erroneously to encompass all people native to the Arctic environment. In fact, there are numerous distinct groups spanning the Arctic Ocean shores. The Inuit inhabit Greenland and the eastern and central Canadian Arctic. To their west are the Inuvialuit of the western Canadian Arctic, and to their east are the Saami of Norway and Russia.

PROLOGUE

Tay Bay

JANUARY 1995
ZERO HOURS DAYLIGHT

HEAVY WINDS HOWL off the Inussualuk Glacier, whipping Tay Bay into a winter tantrum, trying to huff and puff and blow my house down. How long has this blizzard blown—two, three days now? What does it matter? The sun vanished months ago, leaving this wasteland cloaked in blackness and lifesucking cold. An hour, a day, a week, they all feel the same to me, huddled in this sleeping bag, sealed in my solo tomb.

When the sound becomes muffled, I know our ice-trapped yacht, the *Roger Henry,* has disappeared completely beneath the drifting snows. If I can, I'll dig my way out when the winds abate. If I cannot . . . well, that takes care of itself. The nerve-shattering shriek of those winds is now only a dull groan. If I could vocalize my aching loneliness, it would sound exactly like that. I have tried so hard to adjust to the darkness and solitude. I even triumphed momentarily, but in the end it was futile. Light and laughter are the core fuels of the human spirit.

Halifax, my calico kitten and only companion, is buried deep beneath my feet. I listen to her breathing, grateful for her company but concerned for her survival.

The mast shudders. I like that; it reminds me of being at sea. I can feel the rumble through the hull and fantasize that I am sailing, all canvas set, heeled in the southeast trade winds, steaming for New Zealand, toward my wife, Diana, her blonde beauty and warm touch. I anchor and run in warm sunlight up the beach to her. I pull my hands from the sleeping bag and rest them on the sweeping curve of her waist, now growing from vivid to virtual in the black void before me. Whiffs of her skin-warmed coconut oil and sweet frangipani lei flood my senses. I pull her toward me . . . but it's no use. I'm pulled back north to stark reality when my hands start throbbing from the cold.

I probe the darkness for the slightest flicker of orange flame in the bowels of the heater, but the snows outside have buried the flue pipe and extinguished my feeble source of warmth. It's probably best, for I am dangerously low on fuel. I can't afford to waste it on personal comfort, which I now define as anything warmer than the outside temperature of fifty degrees below zero.

In seven months the ice will break up, and I will attempt an escape to the south—that is, *if* the ice breaks up this year. If it does not, I will face another year in this frozen wilderness north of Baffin Island. I must be as patient as the Inuit. It is only a year, a finite, even countable three hundred sixty-five days. In the grand scheme of things it's not an awfully long time.

Reluctantly, I crawl out of the sleeping bag into the cavelike cabin. I am driven by extreme thirst, for in spite of its intense cold, the Arctic is a desert, and the dry air sucks the moisture from my lungs. My fingers are stiff and shaking so violently that it's hard to strike a match to light the kerosene stove. I break two matches, exceeding my daily ration. I'll have to make it up later. Finally the burner roars to life, and I huddle over the precious flame for a moment, letting it thaw the ice in my beard, before I slide a pot of ice chips over its warmth.

The sleeping bag beckons, but I should relieve myself while waiting to drink. Fluid in, fluid out. I shuffle to the forepeak where my waste bucket lies. What with food scraps, human waste, and dishwater, I should empty it every other day, but this blizzard has disrupted everything. I turn on my headlamp, and the darkness retreats a few feet, revealing that the bucket is absolutely full. *Damn! Nothing is simple up here, nothing!* I'll have to go outside. It takes ten minutes to dress: mukluks, thick bibs, fur-lined parka, gloves, and goggles. Crawling up the steep, narrow steps, I test the hatch. As expected, it is buried beneath heavy snow. I kneel on the top step and shoulder the hatch like Atlas hefting the earth, pushing slowly with all my strength. At first there is no movement and I fear my injured back will come apart again; then, slowly, the hatch moves away. Being forced to take action now is actually a fortunate turn of events, for I have drifted toward lethargy. Any later might have been too late.

Snow fills the cockpit. The covering tent tarp slats like the crack of rapid rifle fire. I crawl outside, pulling the bucket behind me. Fully exposed now, I push through the frenzied air to the disposal pit. When the heavy cylinder of ice slides out of the bucket, I am caught off-guard and the fierce wind rips the bucket from my hands. It is an essential piece of equipment. Without thinking, I sprint after it as it tumbles just out of reach. I race a long way, eased along by the heavy wind on my back. My dim headlamp beam bounces around my target, trying to zero in. Each time I am about to dive on the bucket, I think, *No, better get one step closer or I will lose it forever.*

Then suddenly I freeze, recalling stories of men who perished just yards from their camp. The bucket disappears into the polar night. Very slowly I turn around into a blank wall of white wind. I try to look up for the boat, but the smoking wind buffets my body and lashes my face. My nose and cheeks grow instantly wooden with frostbite. I drop to the ground and rub the brittle skin back to life. With my anorak hood pulled over my head, I crawl on hands and knees through my fast-disappearing tracks. Looking straight down, using my hands to feel for the next depression, I crawl upwind—the wind being my only point of reference in the white abyss.

I try to calm myself, to think of nothing except finding the next hole in the snow and keeping the wind pressure even on both sides of my hood. But my mind races, and I am distracted by absurd thoughts. *At least have the good grace to freeze in a position that will let them get you into a body bag. You don't want arms and legs sticking out all over the sled, tempting the dogs.* I remember a proverb: Be careful what you wish for, because it might come true. The truth is, I asked for this. No, I demanded it. I handcrafted this "authentic adventure." I wanted solitude, deprivation, and danger. Well, here then, have a second helping; how about a third?

As the snow hurls horizontally, my tracks fill and begin to fade. It is a race now, for even a slight deviation from my outward course will take me past the salvation of the boat and on into an eternal emptiness.

My hands probe frantically. I think, *Surely I have gone too far,* and the dread of death fills my stomach.

Then my head slams against something hard, and through my heavy gloves I feel the aft rail of the boat. I cling to it for a minute as if it were a life buoy; then I crawl into the cockpit and tumble below. With a shaky hand I take an off-budget gulp of Dr. Daniel's and remind myself for the hundredth time that out here, stupidity is a deadly disease.

I find a plastic container among the food supplies—a poor substitute for my waste bucket, but it will do. I drink a quart of melted water, shut off the stove, undress, and slide back into the sleeping bag. I am very cold, but I suspect that's not why I'm shaking. Once again the Arctic has brought me to my knees, and once again I have evaded its icy embrace. So far I have been lucky, but the game is not over, the final results not yet in.

My destiny may be to survive this and go on; or perhaps I will die up here, alone, under drifting snows or the crushing paw of the great ice bear. What matters most is that, even with my life ebbing away, I will still be able to answer in the marrow of my bones the simple question, "Why am I here?"

And so I tell myself again: I am here because in the landscape of each and every human imagination lies one special place. Our inner compass keeps pointing us toward this spot, which is magnetic, mysterious, exotic, and alluring but, alas, always fringed by a frontier of our fears. Still, it is to this specific place that we are compelled to travel in order to know ourselves and, in so doing, call our lives complete.

I am here in search of wholeness, for in my breast, hiding just beneath each breath, lies a hollow, and always it has cried out to be filled.

ONE

Straits of Florida

APRIL 1992

12 HOURS DAYLIGHT

It costs so much to be a full human being. . . . One has to abandon altogether the search for security, and reach out to the risk of living with both arms. One has to embrace the world like a lover, and yet demand no easy return of love. One has to accept pain as a condition of existence. One has to court doubt and darkness as the cost of knowing. One needs a will stubborn in conflict, but apt always to total acceptance of every consequence of living and dying.

—Morris West, *The Shoes of the Fisherman*

WHILE MOST ACCOUNTS of adventure begin at the mountain base or the jungle wall, the adventure itself usually begins as an idea. This idea, if well watered with imagination, will grow into a dream. Such dreams are powerful and, if allowed to grow unchecked, may even become dangerous obsessions, which threaten to take possession of our lives. My Arctic dreams began innocently enough, with an old photograph I encountered one day long ago. Gaunt men in worn clothing stood out on the barren sea-ice, staring the camera and probable death in the eye. Trapped in the Antarctic ice pack, they faced unimaginable deprivation and cruel hardships, but together, the men of the doomed ship *Endurance* would endure, would be narrowly rescued by their brave Anglo-Irish captain, Ernest Shackleton, and at long last would return home from their polar ordeal! My heart soared in celebration, while my stomach sank in envy.

Soon after, hungering for more images, I felt short of breath when I saw a shot of the Danish explorers Knud Rasmussen and Peter Freuchen, men of wild courage yet keen intellect, huddled beneath the Greenland ice cap. We call them explorers, but I knew that look in their eyes. They were seekers, and that is a different thing. They sought that spot from which in every direction lay one of the essentials of self-knowledge—uncertainty. When Rasmussen found that spot he christened it *Ultima Thule,* "the Last Unknown," and that name echoed in my psyche. I could not know it then, but somehow I sensed that in those pictures of the past I was glimpsing my future.

From earliest memory, my life was shaped by two distinct yet converging forces: a compulsive, even obsessive need to test myself, and a profound love of the natural world. The reasons are as open and direct as was my father, a battle-hardened Marine who had very defined notions of manly behavior, notions easier for him, at six-foot-three and 230 pounds, than for me, far short of that. When I was ten a brute of a thirteen-year-old, thick fisted and stupid, chased one of my sisters home. My father said matter-of-factly, "Alvah, go defend your sister." My scrawny body quaked in fear as I shuffled out there like a lamb to slaughter, but I never considered falling short in his eyes. The beating I took was nothing compared to that.

Fortunately, my father imposed upon me other adventures in which preparation, not poundage, won the day. Dropping me off at the edge of the woods one Friday night, he said, "I'll meet you here at exactly one o'clock on Sunday." He knew I had no way to tell time other than by the sun. He knew I had only a knife on my belt and anything I had been able to fit into an empty pack of cigarettes, nothing more. I had never thought so hard about what really matters as when I packed that pitiful little box—waterproof matches, ultrathin dry-cleaning plastic as shelter, aluminum foil to make a boiling pot, fishhooks and line wrapped around the outside to save precious interior space, and kernels of corn to fashion a Native American bird snare. He had taught me to tie birch bark into a loose cone shape, lay it in the grass with a trail of corn leading to the wide end, and place a single kernel visible through the funnel. The pheasant pecks its way toward the cone, slips its head through for the last morsel, and tries to pull back, but because of its flared feathers it cannot shake the collar. Confused, it simply sits down and waits. To me this was a natural wonder and a good thing to know.

As I grew, I never mastered my fears, yet I began to crave the extreme situations that provoked them. Skydiving wasn't enough; I had to be last to pull the ripcord. And when even that paled, I escaped the terrifying prospect of responsible adulthood through the back door of America, Key West, on a leaky little wooden sloop, accompanied by my youngest brother and dearest friend, Jonathan.

Through the next thirteen long and lingering years I followed the winds to the farthest reaches of the planet and my imagination, with no thought of date or deadline other than a vague awareness of season. A sail well stitched and a sack full of rice were all I needed, for those granted freedom, and freedom was everything. Jonathan sailed with me for the first two of those thirteen years, but although we shared the same boat among the same islands, he was searching for something different than I. When he found it with an American woman, without hesitation they jumped ship, returned home to Key West, and happily began building a life together. They had a son and looked forward to a shared future. I wished them well and carried on in search of raw, glorious adventures. Each one well handled led to a greater challenge. I would be momentarily exhilarated, then inevitably dissatisfied, plagued with self-doubt: *I should have gone higher up the mountain, deeper into the ocean, or farther into the desert. Next time. Next time I will walk that final mile on swollen feet and I will find something wonderful.*

I assumed no woman could ever share my life. Then in 1982 I met Diana White behind the Great Barrier Reef of Australia, at a party where cheap wine and hollow talk flowed freely. I told her I was heading off for the crocodile-infested Fly River of Papua New Guinea in search of lost tribes. Jokingly, I asked her if she wanted to come along.

In her lovely New Zealand accent, she replied, "Actually, that depends. I have just returned from New Guinea and did not have time to investigate the weaving and pottery traditions of the Sepik tribe. Do you plan to swing by there?"

Swing by? We were talking about one of the wildest and most primitive places on earth! After an embarrassingly long moment, I closed my mouth. While other men hovered, vying for her attention, I coaxed out the exciting details of her life.

Diana had just come back to Australia with plans to set up a pottery cooperative and settle down after ten years of global travel. She had sailed through Melanesia, trekked in Nepal, hitchhiked through Iran, skirted firefights in Afghanistan, lived on an Israeli kibbutz, worked in England and South Africa. She was independent, adaptive, and—increasingly difficult for me to ignore—very attractive. We spent Christmas together on the Daintree River searching for crocodiles, New Years in the Atherton Tablelands looking for the duck-billed platypus. In gradual increments she moved aboard my thirty-one-foot sloop, the *Zenie P. II.* Soon there was less and less talk of a settled life on land and more longing looks at the distant horizon.

Before we set sail together for that horizon, I walked the dewy lushness of her family's New Zealand dairy farm and found the origins of her gentleness in those wholesome hills. But early in our relationship I learned not to confuse gentle with soft. As months floated into years, this woman stood beside me under attack in the bone-in-the-nose highlands of Papua New Guinea, drifted in the pirate-plagued waters of the Sulu Sea, rafted down swollen Bornean rivers. Diana dragged me, delirious with cerebral malaria, out of African swamps. She sailed Cape Horn, our small boat blasted to its beam ends by ferocious winds. She sat awaiting my return from solo jungle explorations with simple instructions: "If no word, set sail, remarry." She wept over the bodies of dead comrades, drowned or shot in far outposts of a dangerous world. She rose to every challenge and remained a steadfast companion at the front lines of adventure and experience. She was driven by her own deep love of life and, I hoped, in part by love for me.

But the years exacted their toll, and her dream of a home, a garden, and a community began to resurface. For a decade she had given me what I viscerally needed. In fairness, if such a thing exists, she expected that, someday, I would do the same for her. For too long I clung to that *someday,* like the sensuous Saint Augustine in his heartfelt prayer, "Oh Lord, give me chastity and continence, but not just yet."

At long last, I promised her we would settle down once the circumnavigation Jonathan and I had begun so many years before in Key West was completed. I even thought I had reconciled myself to that, until the day I looked again at those old polar photographs only to find that their allure was stronger than ever.

Surely Diana suspected my change of heart when I began to stumble conversationally around the Arctic's edges. My tactics were timeworn and transparent. I had too often used temporary truths to lure her into adventures, thinking she would thank me in the end, but on this subject she would not engage. Perhaps she hoped that if she remained quiet the dream would die a natural death. Most do. This one would not. It lived and grew. I felt as if my life had been but preparation for this, my unknown, my Ultima Thule. It became the symbol of my ability to still rise, reach, and risk. I had to go.

This was no defense to offer Diana, for she would view it as nothing more than the final spasms of a middle-aged machismo. In spite of her many adventures, Diana saw no romance in unnecessary risk and had no tolerance for bravado. She had become the conservative balance to my cowboy ways.

But there was, in addition, a promise of intellectual discovery, and with this I might yet lure her. After sifting much of the earth through my hands, I felt a hint of pattern had begun to emerge, a fascinating interplay between terrain, people, and wildlife, one influencing the others in powerful ways. I began to grasp why it might be that the world's tallest people, the Watusi, live on the open savannas where stride and speed mean water and meat, while in the jungles just adjacent, the slight Pygmies glide through dense growth that would ensnare and overwhelm the great Watusi. I had seen the pale Nordic contrast to the sooty darkness of equatorial people. I could imagine how even the peregrine nose of the Arabians would disappear through natural selection in the frostbit climes of the far North, until it veritably hid behind wide Mongolian cheekbones.

The implications of all this gripped me. If the differing forces of nature can mold a people physically, then how much more easily can these forces also shape their psyches and culture?

Through a diversity of terrains comes a diversity of life experience. I had come to believe that native people tell us something with their lives, something important and relevant to the pressing problems of our age. In the Bushmen of the Kalahari I saw the skills, knowledge, and philosophical structure required for a sustainable harvest of earth's natural bounty. I had been touched by the soft but binding structure of the Tahitian family and encouraged by the racial tolerance of the Mauritians. I suspected that the cures to many of our ills might lie in the botanical knowledge of an Amazonian shaman.

I am no scientist and have no academic authority. Still, was it possible that I, just a kick-about yachtsman, might return from the Arctic with something of genuine value?

Around the world, in the art of boat design I had found elements reflective of local culture. I know of no design taken to such elegant simplicity as that of the kayak of the far North. With some skin and a few bones, early Inuit frugally fashioned a craft that was at once light, fast, silent, and unsinkable. This provided them access to northern life's most precious resource, marine mammals, for there are no amber waves of grain, no sheltering forests, no kindling, and no clothing apart from these scant sources. A craft made of animal in order to hunt animal reflects an environment of very low biodiversity. The links in this chain are few, each impacting the other in exaggerated ways. Might the very leanness of this land serve as a student reader, a "See Jane Run" for my education into the relation of things?

There was one more thing. It is an environment that demands cleverness, as many do. It also demands something of perhaps rarer value—patience—and the patience of the Inuit is legendary. Their minds and bodies move to longer rhythms than those of temperate-zone peoples. Their coming of dawn is measured not in hours but in months. Their days last great portions of a year and so too their nights, not neatly balanced in tropical diurnal convenience. In their storms, to press on is to perish; one must wait, remaining always subservient to the cruel forces of nature, moving when and how allowed. In the Arctic, one must be bold but never brash, a lesson I might yet learn. There one needs endless acceptance of what is, spending little time in a world of what was or what might be. It is the "beginner mind" of Zen teachings. If this land could teach this to the Inuit, might it also teach me? I had no way of knowing how terribly important that question would become.

CUBA SLID BENEATH THE SOUTHERN HORIZON as our sails pulled hard for my homeland, the United States of America. It was April 1992. A Florida skyline of artificial angles loomed large before us. Ahead was the global center stage, the cutting edge of modernity, humming with such pace and commotion as to be daunting to a couple who had too long known warm sands beneath bare feet, balmy days, and native ways.

The bow of the *Zenie P. II* sliced through the imaginary line of Jon's and my outbound track, officially tying the knot on my circumnavigation. But my pride was laced with bitter regret, for the surrounding waters were all too familiar. I was last here in 1986, having left Diana with *Zenie P. II* in Borneo to meet my family in Key West. Four brothers and four sisters, we gathered with our mother to mourn Jonathan, who had died close to the spot where Diana and I now sailed. He had been skimming along in his speedboat when the steering cable snapped. The engine slammed over, and he was thrown out and probably beaten to death by the wildly spinning boat. We don't know for sure because we never found his body. The family laid a wreath on the spot, letting it drift off in search of his soul.

I looked across the cockpit at Diana. Her long blonde hair was flecked with gray, testimony to the years and miles. She sipped Earl Grey tea, no doubt mentally decorating the front room of our future. The log ticked off one more mile to our approaching landfall, making my stomach tighten. The poorly trimmed headsail shuddered, but I did nothing about it. Diana looked up at me in surprise. Normally, I would have leapt to the sheets to nurse the last iota of speed from our creaky little craft, but in truth I was in no hurry to get where we were going. Yes, I longed to see family and old friends, but as a passing wanderer, not a resident. I shuddered like the sail, imagining that once the novelty of our return had worn off, I would be greeted with the obligatory, "What's new?" and I would lift my shoulders in resignation and say, "Nothing."

Along the shoreline I could see gray air clinging to a ribbon of traffic crawling down Coastal Highway Number One. But I couldn't see myself there in some meaningful guise, challenged but content. The first distant glance confirmed that this was no longer my land or my life. After sending me on a fluctuating course across the world's oceans, my compass now pointed north and it would not waver. What I saw ahead were the thousands of miles between me and my real dream, my forbidden dream—for after all, a promise is a promise.

The log ticked again. This, I judged, was the precise square mile of ocean that had claimed Jonathan's life. How could I pass through it and not be reminded how tenuous life is, how unknown its course and length? And knowing that, how could I also not know that a dream deferred may be a dream denied?

Before I knew it was me speaking, I said, "I just can't do it."

So there they were, little wings for those words until now unspoken. Diana looked at me sharply, then shook her head and sighed, understanding immediately that one more time I would choose the road less traveled, and that road would now turn toward Arctic ice. And knowing me, she also knew the hard truth of it: I was going to do this no matter the cost.

Just as the Gulf Stream waters forked to their different destinies, we too came to a junction. As we neared the port, I searched desperately for a way to explain myself to her, but words are just words and, as the Inuit say, "they fade away like hills in the fog."

The channel into Key West was well marked and the message clear: Stay between the lines. We left behind the wild anarchy of the high seas and entered the land of law.

Diana took the helm while I doused and bagged the headsail. As I dropped the mainsail, she sheeted in the boom to keep it from flailing dangerously across the deck. We rolled the mainsail, and she made her three ties aft, I my three ties forward. I switched to the helm while she flaked the docking lines with precision, every knot specific to that task and agreed upon long ago. On a moonless midnight we could fly to any line aboard and flick it free. She slipped the tie line on the anchor in case of engine failure, when seconds may count. I tied soft fenders to the rails and flipped them overboard to protect the topsides.

We did all this without a word, as if we were a single will and purpose. I wondered, *Am I obsessed, possessed? What else could make a man risk the love and loyalty of this fine woman?* Would I, could I go north without her?

As we neared the docks of Key West, Diana said, "Alvah, finish your circumnavigation and take pleasure and pride in that. Then we will talk."

We tied *Zenie P. II* to the customs jetty and for the next several hours waded through the bureaucratic necessities of legal entry. I tried to follow her wise counsel. Indeed, I was elated to have completed the circumnavigation officially. But my heart was already well north, buffeted by cold clean winds, and my mind could not rest until I knew where Diana stood with my dream—on the deck or the dock.

T W O

Key West, Florida

APRIL 1992

13 HOURS DAYLIGHT

Until one is committed, there is hesitancy,
the chance to draw back, always ineffectiveness.
Concerning all acts of initiative and creation there is
one elementary truth, the ignorance of which kills
countless ideas and splendid plans:

That the moment one definitely commits oneself,
then Providence moves too.
All sorts of things occur to help one
that would never otherwise have occurred.
A whole stream of events issue from the decision,
raising in one's favour all manner of unforeseen incidents
and meetings and material assistance,
which no man could have dreamed would have come his way.
Whatever you can do or dream you can, begin it.
Boldness has genius, power and magic in it.

—Goethe's *Faust*

OVER THE DAYS THAT FOLLOWED I talked of the Inuit's land, wide and wild, their culture, their clever arts and crafts. But my enthusiasm alone could never sway Diana, for she knows her own mind and cannot be told otherwise. In the end, I believe she acceded and signed on because her desire to settle down once again could not withstand her own unsatiated curiosity and wanderlust. She said, "I am afraid in two ways—one, that I will go and terrible things will happen; the other, that I will not go and miss what is wonderful."

Being for the moment uncharacteristically wise, I kept my mouth shut. I could almost hear the scale tip as her imagination created a lonely yet lovely northern landscape. When I saw that telltale spark in her eyes, I did a celebration jig on the foredeck.

Tied up to the southernmost docks of the nation's southernmost city, we talked, bargained, and bartered, struggling to shape a plan from the formless clay of private longing. Only when the adventure was at least roughly defined would I dare venture farther into America, for it is a large and tempting land, in many ways uncharted. One should not pass through without a vision.

Slowly a plan emerged. We would sail north, far north. There we would listen to the lives of the Inuit. But through our years of travel it had become axiomatic that to truly understand a people, we must first understand the land in which they live—that is, get a hands-on feel for the demands it places on them and the rewards it bestows. We could not rush in, shake a few hands, take a few snapshots, and then retreat south with the sun, full of ourselves and cocktail chatter: "When I was in the Arctic . . ." No, "When the Arctic was in me . . ." might better define our success. This required that we stay through the full cycle of seasons, however harsh, and that we do so alone and unaided.

Initially, we thought we might attempt to sail through the historic Northwest Passage. We were dissuaded after reading several books by people who had tried. All these attempts, successful or not, were feats of derring-do, but no one seemed to be having a good time, and none celebrated the Arctic itself. In fact, their goal was always to pass through the Arctic as *quickly* as possible, and their success was measured in miles, not memories. One protagonist met a single Inuk in his travels, and thought he might have seen one caribou on a distant beach, but he did not take time to investigate further. After dismissing the Northwest Passage, the farthest northerly point achieved by a small yacht, and several other media-magnetic events, we concluded with certainty that we were looking for a study, not a stunt.

To privately fund a serious expedition requires either great wealth or great patience. In spite of our eagerness, we dismissed the idea of soliciting sponsorship. We wanted to move to natural rhythms, not to a commercial date and deadline. Sponsorship also requires that an expedition be dipped in a thin veneer of some scientific or social significance. The truth is that this was just a deeply personal adventure.

With all this in mind, we finally settled on attempting a winter in the Thule (pronounced tü-lē) district on the far northwest coast of Greenland. Historically this area was the last penetrated by Western exploration, and it still sustains some of the most traditional of the Inuit people, has ample wildlife, and semiannually basks in perpetual day, then cloaks itself in a frightfully cold and seemingly endless night.

This would be more easily said than done, for Thule lay many thousand gale-tossed, ice-strewn miles poleward. It is further protected by an amazingly short navigational season. In a good year we might expect four weeks of open water to push toward our winter haven; then the door would suddenly slam shut and we would be trapped behind a continent-sized shelf of impenetrable sea-ice, waiting, hoping the ice would open enough to allow our escape the next year. Faced with the capriciousness of northern nature, there can be no neat timetables, no guarantees. This required that we be well prepared and get north in time, waiting just behind the retreating ice for even a chance of penetrating deep into the landscape of our desires.

A naval superior wrote of the young Robert Falcon Scott, "He appears to trust to luck what ought to be a matter of precise calculation." Years later, woefully ill trained and ill equipped, Scott marched off toward the South Pole and his infamous death. Scott's last journal entry read, "Had we lived, I should have had a tale to tell of the hardihood, endurance, and courage of my companions which would have stirred the heart of every Englishman. These rough notes and our dead bodies must tell that tale."

Diana preferred to return and tell our tale in person, and so she laid down the law. "We will be entering an environment that demands our total respect. We must plan meticulously, know where to go, when to go, and exactly what we will need to survive there. I will not go north in the *Zenie P. II*. We need a stronger boat. And not some stripped-down steel cave, but a home I can be happy in. I want modern safety equipment—no make-do's. That means radio and radar, no matter their cost. I cannot live for an entire year of my life with my heart in my throat."

In May we set sail for St. Petersburg, Florida, to establish our base of operations near my older brother, Raoul. In our youth, he had a big fist, I had a big mouth. The two were well acquainted. I hoped that while preparing for our voyage I might also bury old hatchets and bask in a familial closeness, something I had increasingly longed for through many years adrift.

Raoul met us at the St. Petersburg Municipal Marina. From his home I called my mother in Illinois to tell her we were finally home. She asked hopefully, "To stay, Son?" I wanted to say, "Yes, Mother, of course to stay," but I remained silent.

The best time to take action toward a dream is yesterday; the worst is tomorrow; the best compromise is today. We rented a liveaboard slip in the marina and immediately began our project. The *Zenie P. II* had been a simple but loyal workhorse through those many years and miles, but Diana was right—her thin plywood sides would not last a day in the Arctic ice. Wooden boats are demanding and at times frustrating, but now I ran through every maintenance task with a nostalgic pleasure. Each boat part acted as a page of our atlas or a day in our diary. This yacht had become more than a toy; it had become my primary tool with which to dig through this world in search of life's lessons.

As pelicans glided past the rigging in tight formation, my mind came back to the present and the task at hand. For one month we scoured, scraped, painted, and varnished from stem to stern. It was with an aching sadness that I hung the For Sale sign in the rigging.

We sought gainful employment and began the search for an ice-resistant boat. Diana took a job selling tickets for a dolphin-sighting tour boat, patiently answering questions like "What time does the twelve o'clock tour leave?" as if indeed it took some figuring.

I found odd jobs in the forest of surrounding masts and launched a slide presentation of our travels for schools and clubs. After one show, a line of well-wishers formed. One elderly gentleman grabbed my hand in a two-fisted, pumping shake and looked me excitedly in the eye. "By God, son," he gasped, "if I was twenty years younger, I'd be out there with you!"

A voice behind him said, "Mort, if you were twenty years younger, you'd be seventy."

I laughed, but I was stunned by the thought that our dreams had the power to touch the lives of others. Whatever my doubts and fears for the future, that sealed the deal in my heart, then and there.

The Florida boating world is mostly space-age and sparkle, and the *Zenie P. II* was stripped-down simple. The few serious inquiries dried up quickly with the discovery that we had no refrigeration system or hot-water pressure pumps. But one man kept returning to our boat. He was intensely serious and seemed undeterred by an honest list of what I considered existing problems.

One day he said, "I want to buy your boat and I don't want to argue your asking price." (I held my breath. Too good to be true is just that.) "But," he continued, "there is one problem . . ." He hesitated, then gushed, "I don't have any money, and I've already checked—I can't get a loan on a wooden boat over ten years old. But I *need* this boat. God told me to buy this very boat."

Who was I to question a divine commandment? We devised a plan of lengthy monthly payments and mutual assurances, most of which were unnecessary because there was no question of goodwill. In the end, the agreement did not run its full course. Hurricane Andrew devastated southern Florida. The buyer's work was the disposal of toxic waste, of which there was much in the storm's aftermath. He was in such demand that, after just eight weeks, he asked if he might not pay us in full and move aboard before New Year's Day.

I said, "You are a lucky man."

"It's not a matter of luck," he answered quietly.

Of course, he was right. This was the first in a series of unlikely events that propelled us through this adventure, but I wasn't paying attention to such things then.

We moved into a studio apartment. I could not sleep at night in the still bed, wondering from which direction the wind blew. Diana took a long, hot bubblebath, got out, dried off, then took another. She baked gooey treats in an actual oven, perched flowing plants on the acreage of counterspace, and left her delicate teacup on the table with reasonable expectation that it would remain there until her return. She cheerfully cautioned me that it might take an additional year to find and afford a suitable craft.

We sandwiched visits with family and friends around never-ceasing efforts to earn money and find our new boat, but buying a good boat proved even more difficult than selling one. Stout timber vessels sheathed in bulletproof ironwood, greenheart, or purpleheart were relics of a glorious but faded past. Wood is a sympathetic material, easy to work and easy to love, but we were faced with the unromantic reality of Arctic ice. Wood-epoxy composites, fiberglass, or the less-dense woods now available were unsuitable, for they would quickly be ground to pulp. The remaining choices were aluminum and steel. Aluminum stock is very expensive and usually worked by professionals;

thus, aluminum boats cost twice as much as backyard steel projects—
most of which are testimony to the triumph of hope over experience.

It was soon apparent that there were startlingly few of either type
available. I saw an ad in an East Coast paper with a California telephone number I recognized as already called and culled from our list.
In a big nation, that is slim pickings. Time passed, and our savings
from the sale of the *Zenie P. II* dwindled.

From our apartment balcony, I could see the waters of Tampa Bay. I
am a sailor; I understood that those waters are molecularly connected
without interruption to the Gulf, to the Atlantic, to Davis Strait, even
to Baffin Bay. Those many miles were not my problem. My problem
was the distance between me and the shoreline, a distance that seemed
to grow with each passing day.

AT TWO O'CLOCK one March morning, my mother received a call
from Cartagena, Colombia.

"I am Jean, Frenchman, friend to Alvah. Heez boat eez 'ere! C'est
magnifique."

The seed of that call had been planted a full year before on the Isth-
mus of Panama, where in the off-lying islands we met Jean on his small
sloop. Jean is French but of Spanish Gypsy descent, dark and stocky.
Travel and trade are in his blood, and his eyes lit up when I asked him
to join me on an upriver expedition to a jungle village. Reportedly, the
villagers had unearthed pre-Columbian stone tools and pottery while
searching for gold artifacts. Once there, Jean took charge and bartered
hard in fluent Spanish for a particularly ugly stone carving. He howled
in delight on the downriver dinghy ride. This carving would fetch a fortune in Germany, another of the arenas in which he traded. Jean wandered the world with one keen eye always aimed ahead for opportunity
and the other prudently over his shoulder—not because he considers
himself a conman, oh no, but because some might have misunderstood
the terms of his deals. In any case, he had an impish humor and a con-
tagious joe de vivre.

That night, in the island village of Bahia Honda, we swung in ham-
mocks under an open cabana, drinking too much of a dreadfully raw
chicha (a corn mash left to ferment in old fishing buoys). As bosom as

only drunken new buddies can be, Jean let me in on his latest scheme. A newly liberated Eastern European nation was auctioning off their fishing fleet to raise hard currency. If you knew the right people and were willing to, "let uz say . . . express your gratitude," higher bids could be lost in the shuffle. Their resale value would be manyfold. He insisted that this was so secret he dare not mention which nation—but as a trusted friend, I should invest in him. My money troubles would be over!

I put it delicately: "Jean, if you touch my wife or my wallet, I will shoot you." That got his attention. "Look, if you have to have some of my money, keep your eyes open for an affordable vessel, one capable of high-latitude work. For such a service, I might . . . let uz say . . . express my gratitude."

In spite of a year's passing, he had remembered well. On seeing the little steel cutter *La Busse* sail into Cartagena's harbor with a *Se Vende* sign on it, he tore his boat apart looking for the scrap of paper bearing my mother's telephone number. Nothing ventured, nothing gained; besides, the call was collect.

By then, caged in that Florida apartment, I was depressed and desperate. Still, it costs the price of a mainsail to jump a jet to Colombia, and I knew Jean, so I questioned him carefully on the phone.

"Jean, you know I need forty feet or more on deck. Is it forty?"

"Oh! Eet eez wonderfool."

"Is it forty?"

"And fast? Mon Dieu!"

"Jean! Is it forty?"

He screamed, "You Americans, *beeg! beeg!* You think only for *beeg!* Okay, eet eez forty!"

The boat did not start losing length until I had purchased a non-refundable ticket. By the time I reached Colombia, it had shrunk to four inches shy of a modest thirty-six feet. I glared at Jean.

He just shrugged, "You would not 'ave come. Doan worray, you will zank me in zee end."

Jean proved to have an eye not only for opportunity but also for boats. He had listened carefully and understood my criteria perfectly. He maneuvered me and the young French owners with aplomb.

When it was a done deal, I teased, "Jean, how can I ever thank you enough?"

He smiled and rubbed his forefinger against his thumb.

I called Diana. "Quit your job, notify the landlord, arrange your air-fare. We are landlubbers no more!"

Usually, compromise is a formula ensuring the misery of all parties involved, but there are the occasional exceptions. Arriving in Colombia, Diana found the interior much to her discerning taste, while I found the steel thick where it should be, thin where it could be. Thus, at only nine tons, we had the marriage of strength and speed. Either might tip the balance in our favor in the Arctic icefields.

French naval architect Jean-François Andre designed this fourth in the series of bluewater vessels called Damiens. The French do not visualize yachting as sipping gin-and-tonics on the aft deck at sundown. They see it as a proactive and dangerous sport and thus lead the world in what might be called "adventure designs."

Each deadlight, porthole, hatch, and vent was watertight and bullet-proof strong. Seawater valves were minimal, stout, and accessible. The engine well was central and low, with walkaround working access. Three inches of insulation had been laid in from the flooring up. The bilge was neat and dry, crisscrossed with closely spaced frames and stringers. The cutter rig, with only one mast but two headsails, provided a simple and safe sail plan for extreme conditions. Footsteps led up a thick-walled mast to high lookout positions. The mast was stayed with thumb-thick wires, heavy enough to survive a roll and perhaps even the dreaded pitchpole, an end-for-end somersault slam of fatal force. A see-through Plexiglas bubble, the poor sailor's pilothouse, provided some shelter from the expected frigid winds. The deck was beamy (wide), flush (no high cabin structure), and heavily cambered (curved) for strength. The low-slung hull was constructed in chines, or angles at which the longitudinal plates are welded. This is a less expensive method than rolled plating and is unpleasing to some eyes, but given the sailing accomplishments of similarly styled boats, this look speaks of utility and adventure. Even so, normally the first chine is cosmetically hidden beneath the waterline. On the Damien IV it lay unashamedly six inches above, presenting a lifting surface to ice pressure from below. Jean-François was speaking my language.

Diana and I had discussed taking additional crew for safety. Traditionally, Arctic expeditions are heavily staffed, for it is assumed that much muscle is needed to kedge out huge anchors and fend off ice. Watch rotation must be shortened because of the cold, and there is expected loss of functioning crew due to injury and general decline. We decided the advantages of larger crews were offset by the inevitable clashes of personalities when already stressed people are crowded into dark and dangerous spaces. In isolation the mind becomes obsessive, and fancied slights fester into mortal challenges. Many an expedition has been doomed by discord. Although the petite size of the Damien IV proved a problem in stowing aboard two years of autonomy, it made the boat manageable for the two of us. And two would do, for I know a lot of tough men, not one of whom I'd sooner travel north with than Diana.

Before we left the fortressed old city of Cartagena for the open sea, there was another detail to attend to. The naming of a vessel is a serious matter. Our houses, no matter their expense and importance, are ignobly numbered, but not the loosest affiliation of planks afloat is left unchristened. Faced with the unfathomable forces of the sea, this is totemic. Our new boat had been named *La Busse,* after a small French province. Superstitions warn that renaming a vessel brings ill winds, but we wanted a more personally meaningful connection and decided to break the taboo.

Both my father, Roger Henry, and my brother Jonathan died young and in action. When my father's small airplane failed, he fell to the land; when my brother's boat failed, he fell into the sea. My life had been linked so inexorably to theirs that either might have taken my next breath for me, but I could carry only one name north. In the end we chose my father's name because I felt my life had been shaped most by his credo: "Fortune favors the brave." While to some my father's and brother's ends might indicate otherwise, I look at it differently. Death is only one of many ways to lose your life.

After a short test sail, we set straight out to sea. With only two seabags and a few charts below, the boat echoed in emptiness as we pulled nonstop for Florida.

A ripsnorting blow against the Gulf Stream, over the shallow Yucatán Channel, is not something most prudent sailors wish for.

However, we happily put our new vessel through rugged paces in those warm waters and in winds that could not freeze flesh on contact. We were elated with the speed, safety, and comfort with which the *Roger Henry* charged into St. Petersburg through steep seas on April 30, 1993, after only twelve days. To the day, we had sailed those very Caribbean waters one year before. The year had been difficult but well invested.

IT'S A DREAM until you write it down; then it's a goal. On the calendar we marked June 1, 1994, thirteen months hence, as our target date of departure. From that moment on, the clock started ticking.

With every job completed, the long work list seemed to grow in a biblical fishes-and-loaves fashion. But any sinking discouragement we felt was buoyed up by the reaction to our plans in the sailing community around us.

Old Ed, a local sailor, owned a sharp little "pocket cruiser." Every day he lavished it with attention, then set sail into Tampa Bay with a contented grin. Out and back, he never tired of this or of helping people get their dreams onto the water. One day he handed me a set of miniature screwdrivers. "I know space is important," he said. "You'll need things that are small but useful." I assumed he meant the screwdrivers. Later I found a one-hundred-dollar bill hidden in the lining.

The steel sloop *Tin Man* lay next to the seawall. Its quality of construction caught my eye, so I asked around. Someone said it belonged to David Jackobson, a Canadian engineer who built it after he got fed up with working on oil rigs in the Arctic. Tracking down that enticing lead, that night in the marina lounge I heard the telltale Canadian accent: "oot" for out, eh?

The speaker was friendly but somehow no-nonsense, so I said it straight. "Look, back on my boat I've got a cooler full of beer and a long list of problems. Where do you want to start?"

He grinned. "The beer."

David donated endless hours. He was patient with me unless I suggested some form of payment for his help. He had no concern whatsoever for cosmetic image but would not cut a single corner of sound electrical, mechanical, or structural engineering. He set high standards for material and workmanship to which I was forced to rise. He had been up there; he *knew*. He recommended the model of new engine I would need. I felt faint when I heard the price. He told me that in the ice I needed power, not speed. That meant I had to swing a large-diameter propeller, which required an appallingly expensive gearbox.

"Damn it, Dave, I can't afford to!"

"You can't afford *not* to. And what about that radar, eh? I told you—you have no idea—there's icebergs, fog, rocks. And remember, never *ever* underestimate the polar bear. They will hunt you. Hunt you and kill you. Took our cook right off the rig, they did."

Up in the Arctic I would learn much about myself. In getting there I was learning much about others. Encouragement and advice poured down our dock daily.

We found that the devil was in the details. I divided the expedition into two parts: sailing in and freezing in. The first was familiar water, but the second carved in harsh relief the inexperience with which we approached our overly ambitious first Arctic venture.

Through the searing summer months, we woke early and worked late, all thoughts and efforts shaped to one end: going north. The cabin was papered with lists and reminders.

Alternators: Two, interchangeable.

Batteries: Two gelcells, 180- and 90-amp capacity.

Charging: Main engine; wind generator; hand-starting air-cooled diesel; solar panels? Is the sun strong enough at low declinations?

Charts: American, Canadian, Danish—50 at $15 each!; photocopies?

Mechanical: Wrench set; socket sets; Allen set; drill; bits; files; hacksaw; Vise-Grips; pliers; sledge hammer . . .

Medical: Bandages; sutures; I.V. solutions and setup; injectable adrenaline; antiseptic; antibiotics; catheter; eyes, ears, nose, and throat medicines . . . Note: remove snakebite kit.

Permits: Yacht importation exemption certificate; registration; radio license; Diana's alien registration card . . .

Publications: Light List; Radio List; Tide Tables (three nations); Ice Atlas . . .

Repair Materials: Extra steel, aluminum, copper; tubing; fiberglass; epoxy resin; rubber; glues . . .

Survival Equipment: Sleds; harness; skis; poles; backpacks; ice axes;
    crampons; shotgun; rifle; ammunition; flares; sleeping bags; face-
    masks; parkas; pants; gloves; goggles; ice chisel; snowknife; camp
    stove; signal mirror . . .
And on and on, into dizzying detail.

We were outfitting for two years of autonomy, and weight was a
pressing concern. We looked for pounds, then ounces. Each and every
little choice we made, when aligned with many other little things, might
spell the difference between life and death. I drew upon our years of
sailing memories. Austrian sailors were usually preemptively meticu-
lous, while Australian sailors had a casual and cheerful "aw, she'll be
right, Mate" approach. The first were efficient but rigid; the second
were ill prepared but adaptive. The Arctic demanded that we combine
the experiences of the Alps and the Outback.

While I watched the August heat rise off the bubbling asphalt of a
Florida parking lot, I tried to imagine the inert coldness of a polar winter. What should our source of heat be? Our research revealed that
diesel oil has 18,000 British Thermal Units (Btu's) per pound compared
to coal's 12,000. Carrying diesel would save weight *and* bulk. In addition, we needed multiplicity of purpose. We changed the generator,
heater, stove, and oven to diesel. If only I could have learned to drink
the stuff at happy hour, it would have been a clean sweep.

To determine how much diesel per day we'd require, I placed the
heater feed pipe into a plastic jug, adjusted the drip rate to the manu-
facturer's recommendation, and measured the fluid after twenty-four
hours at two liters. By multiplying that times 365, I established our
minimum requirement. I was by now so immersed in the Arctic that it
never occurred to me to wonder whether the author of the instruction
manual had ever been north of the Mason-Dixon line. Later I would
pay dearly for that mistake.

Arctic extremes demanded of us a new way of thinking—or perhaps
it is a very old way. The igloo (*ik-lu*) is a marvel of thermal engineering.
With an intuitive grasp of thermoclines and draft, the Inuit of old
heated the snowdome with a single blubber lamp, yet ventilated it
safely. We installed an air-intake system, much like a snorkel, in case

the *Roger Henry* should be covered by snowdrifts. The arctic musk ox produces no more body heat than its more temperate cousins, but it retains that heat with underhairs eight times more efficient than sheep's wool. We scoured the boat for heat leaks and plugged them with foam. Could we emulate the successes of northern human and beast? To know that with confidence, we first had to sail to a higher latitude in search of a winter testing ground. We did not want to enter the Arctic cold, so to speak.

I had made a lifestyle out of leaving, but on our mid-September day of departure I had an unusually hard time saying good-bye. My brother Raoul is a big man who likes to talk of caliber and muzzle velocity. Still, he had to turn and walk away to mask his tears. We slipped our lines, and the *Roger Henry* headed out to sea.

FIFTEEN HUNDRED MILES and one month to the north, autumn gales pushed us into Maine's Penobscot Bay. I located our position in the atlas and was shocked to discover that, in spite of the many miles already traveled, we were closer to our starting point in Colombia than our proposed destination in the Arctic.

In the Camden office of Wayfarer Marine, the young supervisor, Wilson Darwin, pulled on his long moustache. "I don't understand. Why would you want to winter on board? People don't even leave their boats in the water here. It's cold—wicked cold!"

"Exactly."

He shook his head. "Okay. We'll settle you in the corner of the harbor. But get yourself a good snow shovel," he warned.

Every detail of our preparation was critical because of our commitment to live on our own resources. That meant we would sink or swim with whatever skills, tools, and foods were contained within the gunwales of the *Roger Henry*. We would not hunt for meat. Yes, I wanted to share experience with the Inuit, live as they live, eat as they eat, but I had to tailor this to our modern context. We did not want to arrive uninvited in another's land and immediately be perceived as competitors for their scant resources. Instead, we laid up 300 pounds (160 pounds dry weight) of smoked pork shoulder, bacon, beef soup stock, and jerky, all prepared at a backwoods Maine smokehouse.

The quiet of the first snowfall was broken only by the haunting cry of Canada geese heading sensibly south. Our cozy cabin was in chaos as we competed for space on the salon table. Diana had the medical kit spread out among the vegetables, fruits, herbs, meats, poultry, and fish she was dehydrating and vacuum sealing. Under there somewhere lay my blocking diodes for the wind generator.

Moving down her alphabetical list, Diana said, "I'm provisioning for our planned year in the ice, plus a six-month contingency supply. That's over five hundred days at four thousand calories per day each to compensate for the cold. I must test our rate of consumption for everything. We have five gallons of alcohol for preheating the stove, eighty pounds of beans, nine gallons of cooking oil . . . two hundred fifty pounds of flour . . . seventy-five pounds of rice, fifty pounds of sugar . . . (She was approaching a subject I would rather not have discussed. Between teabags and toothpaste lay thin ice.) "Toilet paper: fifty rolls . . . hmmm . . . but wait, if there is no water when the boat is iced in, then how . . . ?" Her voice rose, "Will we even *have* a toilet?"

When cornered, try vagueness. I said, "You modern women expect all the luxuries, don't you?" Not amused, her hard look silently said, "Sort it out, Buster." The next day I bought a plastic bucket with a toilet seat and sealing lid. By adding a powdered biodegradable enzyme we would render our waste environmentally harmless and easily disposable.

Through this period of frantic preparation, there was no manual we could refer to, but in a sense we still planned by the book, or rather *books,* which formed the bedrock of our geographical knowledge of currents, winds, fog, gales, ice movements, and seasonal limits. These books laid a foundation of practical detail and built historical and cultural perspective. Some provided the big picture, some the fascinating minutiae; others bridged our periods of doubt and despair.

We sailed through this sea of words, immersing ourselves in Arctic lore. I shared exciting accounts from historic journals; Diana read aloud conflicting theories on the best treatment for frostbite and hypothermia. She read that to this day there are those who will erroneously advise you to rub snow over areas of frostbite.

It was sadly relevant to what I was reading. The first Europeans, through the ignorance and arrogance particular to the times, straggled in to suffer and starve in nightmarish tragedy. Their ways did not work, but they were slow to learn. Many felt nothing but disdain for the indigenous "savages," finding them difficult and dirty, their foods and customs disgusting. That thinking generally proved fatal as even large and well-provisioned expeditions ground to a halt, floundered, and then perished piecemeal.

The most famous example was the two-ship, 129-man Franklin Expedition of 1845. They were in search of the elusive Northwest Passage, a shortcut to the rich trading waters of the Pacific. Amid much fanfare, British naval officer Sir John Franklin and his crew confidently disappeared into the fog and ice of Lancaster Sound, in what is now known as the Eastern Canadian Arctic. Then there was silence. A season passed, and then another, and another. They neither emerged in the Pacific nor reappeared in the Atlantic. Prodded by Franklin's concerned wife, the indomitable Lady Franklin, both England and America belatedly launched the largest search-and-rescue mission in history. It became a cause célèbre involving the pride and agendas of nations, military bureaucracies, Arctic theorists, privateers, and scoundrels; in other words, a real zoo. Knowing gold and glory awaited the party that first lifted the veil of silence, teams fanned out in every direction except the correct one. Some of these parties themselves became lost, spawning yet more search parties.

This was Franklin's second Arctic command, and he bungled both badly. Nevertheless, his final contribution was inadvertently significant in that the search for him vastly expanded our knowledge of the Arctic, even as it failed to turn up a shred of evidence as to his fate. Years later, a trail of vague clues appeared: a button decorating an Inuit snowhouse, a silver spoon fashioned into a native fish lure. British naval officer Leopold McClintock followed this trail to its appalling conclusion. It is now known that Franklin died in June 1847 aboard his flagship, H.M.S. *Erebus,* while irrevocably beset in ice in Peel Sound. His men depleted the supplies and eventually set off to the south, manhauling sleds, hoping to reach the mainland shores of the American continent and relief. On that savage trail they found only death. McClintock uncovered a 650-pound navy sledge, further loaded with a twenty-eight-foot-long, 700-pound boat lashed on top. In the boat, beneath the freeze-dried blackened corpses, lay a heap of heavy loot: silver dinner plates, cigar cases, soap, even sheet lead. They had weighed themselves down with both the materials and the mentality of a misplaced culture.

Diana and I huddled below as winter gales blew in moist air off Penobscot Bay. The *Roger Henry* was soon buried beneath heavy snows, and still our reading continued. Although I was often torn as to how best to spend our time, ultimately nothing we did proved more vital to our success than that research.

The Arctic challenged the expansionist impulse of the British unlike any environment they had encountered. Navigation was expectedly difficult because of ice movement and frozen sails and rigging, and it was also uniquely perplexing due to the proximity of the magnetic pole and the presence of thermocline-generated optical illusions. Low pans of ice appeared in the distance as towering walls, mountains appeared where there were none, and those that were indeed there rose into the air upside down, dumbfounding the practical-minded and sending ominous shudders down the spines of the superstitious.

Western foods proved unsuitable for climatic demands. Men grew weak, petulant, and befuddled, not understanding the erosions of scurvy. Woven clothing, worn too tight, was porous and always wet and cold. Deep-bodied, heavily hulled boats were too easily icebound. Once ships were beset in ice, at sea no longer, the strict chain of nautical command collapsed. Anarchy overcame communal effort. Mutiny, murder, and even cannibalism followed.

But huddled among these shocked and shivering men were the few more enlightened who watched the natives closely. The Inuit's quiet admirers were amazed by the cheerful confidence with which these people dashed about their enormous landscape. Close observation revealed that every detail of Inuit life was a cunning adaptation to this stark yet living ecosystem. The observers realized that their path to adaptation was imitation. Considering the rigidity of Victorian thinking and pride, this was a philosophical leap difficult for us to appreciate.

This handful of enlightened Europeans wondered: Could that ghastly raw meat and putrid blubber hold the elusive antidote for our terrible disease? Are those furs carefully selected to be light, durable, and warm? Are they worn one layer hair-in and one hair-out because they shed ice easily due to natural oils and texture? While Europeans fell to temperatures in which the Inuit frolicked, some asked, Could those ludicrously peaked parka hoods collect and recycle the body's highest area of heat loss? For that matter, was the very "slovenly laziness" of the "savage" a carefully crafted rhythm of inaction and exercise, burning bodily fuels exactly when and how best effective, without the deadly buildup of perspiration?

Especially within military expeditions, underlings were not encouraged to share these new insights. Thus their fate lay in the hands of leaders who simply could not understand that the human body is the best furnace, fatty foods the best fuel. They chopped up their boats for firewood, piled it high, then stood back, their backs still frozen as their frontsides burned.

Diana and I discussed all this in detail. While the stories frightened her, they thrilled me—the more harrowing and gruesome they were, the better. I pointed out that these journals included those who learned from the Inuit, and we could learn from them as well. For example, in 1853 American Elisha Kent Kane could have safely wintered his ship *Advance* in the small bay of Etah on the far northwestern coast of Greenland. Ambitious and determined to set the record for the farthest point north, he instead chose to push on. He made meager miles farther to a less suitable winter site, where he was trapped for two years. His ship was eventually crushed and his crew torn apart in the standard cycle of starvation, attempted murder, and mutiny. The lesson for us was that, even today, the limits of prudence and foolhardiness lie within sight of each other in the Arctic.

Through the Maine winter, we became almost insular while preparing for long separation. The "Mainiacs" never noticed, for they are notoriously insular themselves. Camden is too quaint for its own good. Its snug little harbor, gabled bed-and-breakfasts, fleet of old gargantuan schooners, and autumn gush of color draw a choking crowd of tourists. If your accent betrays that you are "from away," you are considered a part of the occupying army. A local bumper sticker says, "If you can't take winter, you don't deserve summer." We well understood the concept of first lasting a cycle of seasons before earning the local's nod of recognition. A haunch of moosemeat in your pickup truck might accelerate the process slightly.

When the temperature dropped to twenty-five below zero—rare for Maine but mild compared to what we might expect—paint leapt off the contracting deck, foolproof systems failed, and through a process of natural selection, the less-than-hearty equipment rolled over and died. I learned to work above deck in furious bursts to warm my body. I also learned, the hard way of course, never to let bare skin touch cold metal and to first carefully plan every motion of even the simplest tasks. As we had hoped, it was a good time for training and tuning. We plowed through the still-long work list with a will.

Although we had no sponsorship, we lacked nothing in support. Geoff Somers, an English friend, had once accompanied me on a difficult journey through the center of Borneo. His jungle skills were exceptional, but his real forté was Antarctica. Because no person alive has logged more nights down there huddled in a tent, he understood that, at our proposed latitudes, the quality of life might well parallel the quality of our equipment. He sent us a huge box jammed full of thick sleeping bags, parkas, facemasks, gloves, mukluks, and a tent. Hearing of our plans from my mother, a young doctor sent a box of medical supplies. My mother donated a laptop computer, hoping to encourage my aspirations as a writer. It did double duty as an ice map receiver when connected to the single sideband radio.

Just as we adjusted to the idea of perpetual winter, ghost white birches sprouted the first hints of green against now softer blueing skies. Our preparations quickly outpaced our finances, and the checkbook raced the calendar toward D-Day—debt and departure. When the ship's coffers again echoed in emptiness, we rented a hall and advertised a slide show. During the show I quipped that on land man's best friend may be a dog, but at sea it is a handy piece of line. The next morning a man knocked on our boat. He had an uncontrolled grin spread across such an open, boyish face that I could only stand there grinning back. Some faces celebrate life. He handed me a ball of twine with no explanation, but I knew he must have seen the show. George Jennings is a marine illustrator, inventor, trader, a bit of this and that. Mostly, he is a man committed to the history of northern seafaring. He placed himself at our service and introduced us to the local boatmen and -women.

George and I pulled onto a tree-lined dirt road that ended in an open barn workshop with anvils and furnaces, masts, rigging, blocks, and huge anchors lying about. He introduced me to Havilah Hawkins, who had grown up on his family's graceful schooner the *Mary Day.* A friend described him best by using the sandpaper scale: "Haddie, now he's yer sixty-grit kind of guy."

George said, "Now, Haddie, where this man's goin' he needs a special ice chisel."

Havilah was a big man—fully two of me—at ease with hard work. He talked continuously about schooners, shoals, old captains, and named storms. He pulled an old caulking iron off the wall and welded it into a pipe. He threaded the ends to make it expandable, asking how much ice I expected.

I said, "About two meters."

He frowned, "Ayuh, you mean one fath'm then?"

He ticked off my list of needed metalwork, accepting no pay.

Back at the docks, once again Diana and I heard the high honking of geese, this time urging their leader northward. In the mud banks above the boat, woodchucks emerged from their holes while baby raccoons were patiently taught the art of banditry. The sun climbed higher in the sky, making the breezy days of spring longer, but never long enough. No matter our efforts, a mountain of preparation remained. The ship's calendar no longer recorded the date because I had written over it with large red numbers, counting down the days until our proposed June 1 departure. Delays in shipping of essential equipment disrupted their order of installation. The outboard was declared unfixable; the camera lens was lost in the process of repair; the compass still had to be swung.

At the end of a particularly unproductive, discouraging day, Diana said, "I don't feel that we are ready. Perhaps it would be best to wait for next year."

I overreacted. "No one is ever perfectly ready, Diana. You do your best, then you go! Half the world is waiting for some perfect time to start living their lives. No; we said it, we do it. And I don't care a good goddamn what happens after that!"

I am very good at saying incredibly stupid things. I was worn thin with work and worry and shocked that at this late date she would suggest a cancellation. More likely though, I was angry with Diana for saying exactly what I silently felt. She stomped her foot in frustration. "Damn it, Alvah. I'm afraid, and I have every right to be. I am not like you. I lie awake at night thinking about polar bears, ice crushing the boat, how I'll handle the dark. I need to feel ready." She was giving back my anger in spades. "What do you want from me?" she demanded. "When other wives feel insecure they ask, 'If I died, would you remarry?' I have to ask you, 'If I died, would you eat me?'"

I took a long breath, and then said, "Well, I can't tell you what to do, Diana. But I can tell you this—waiting until next year will not change the elemental forces up there. It will only exponentially increase the risk that our wills will fail and our plans founder. I promise as captain I will be prudent and protect you and our home. And if you tell me your specific concerns, I'll redouble my efforts and try to correct them."

She did not speak a word to me until the next day, when she said, "What are we waiting for? Let's go."

When George dropped by I was on the dock staring at our dinghy. It had been built in Florida for a water clown's stunt show. With its perfectly flat bottom, I had hoped it would double as a sled in the event of abandoning ship in the crushing ice. But I now noticed how low it lay in the water—that cold, killing water. It was a warm day, but I felt a chill, a small sense of dread. I told George about my concern.

He said, "Why don't we just go get another?"

"Too late," I explained. "We leave in the morning, hell or high water. Anyway, I'd need to sell this one before I could afford another."

Just then a worker from Wayfarer Marine shouted, "Hey, I know that model of dinghy. I probably built that very dinghy when I worked in Florida! They're rare. Say, it wouldn't be for sale, would it?"

He bought it where I stood. I knew the timing was too tight to be coincidence, but at that point in the adventure and in my life I was still not able to call it anything more. We jumped into George's jeep. He recalled an ad in the local paper for an affordable dinghy.

We homed in by knocking on farmhouse doors. Behind a shed we found it and immediately understood its affordability.

George asked the owner, "My goodness, what happened to this dinghy?"

She said matter-of-factly, "A building fell on it."

I believed that. George was undeterred, assuring me that a quick little fiberglass patch here and a bit of wood there would do wonders. Back at the dock, I was thanking George as Havilah came by with an old axle, cut sharp as a piton to hold to an ice floe in the lee of an Arctic gale. The dock filled with well-wishers. In Maine, they may be slow to it, but they make fast friends.

On the last day of May, two years and two thousand miles from our Key West decision, we found ourselves out of time, money, and energy. Our passion for history had helped fuel us this far, and historically, we kept good company. Norwegian Roald Amundsen was the first to crack the Northwest Passage and the first to the reach the South Pole. Both were such hotly contested prizes that it is nearly impossible to believe one man could snatch both. He was arguably the finest sailor, explorer, and leader of his age. Yet even he had been reduced to sneaking out of harbor in the dead of night to avoid his many creditors.

Broke but without debt, we could at least wait for first light to cast off our lines. On the morning of June 1, 1994, the *Roger Henry* slipped out as quietly and unnoticed as Amundsen's *Fram*, but unlike the crew of that fine vessel, we were not in search of glory, only the glorious.

THREE

Camden, Maine

JUNE 1994

15 HOURS DAYLIGHT

Once a journey is designed, equipped, and put in process, a new factor enters and takes over. A trip, a safari, an exploration, is an entity, different from all other journeys. It has personality, temperament, individuality, uniqueness. A journey is a person in itself; no two are alike. And all plans, safeguards, policing, and coercion are fruitless. We find after years of struggle that we do not take a trip; a trip takes us.

—John Steinbeck, *Travels with Charley*

A S CAMDEN'S STACKS AND STEEPLES slid beneath the horizon, so did the stresses of two years of intense preparation. We had made a thousand decisions, many based on the firm foundations of ignorance. We had many hopes, and not a few fears.

With a fresh wind and a widening Penobscot Bay, the *Roger Henry* pulled hard for the northlands. Still, we fell back on our old sailing custom and found the first safe anchorage. There we slept for twenty-four hours with breaks only for mounds of simple food. This pause before rolling up our sailing sleeves recharged our bodies' batteries, refocused our minds on the task at hand, and deposited precious sleep in the bank for when conditions would inevitably worsen. I awoke to the sound of chanting as the crew of the charter schooner *Roseway,* tacking powerfully into the bay, tamed a cloud of sail. It is old music, played on taut rope and muscle.

For our first two days under sail we were finding our sea legs, losing our stomachs, and locating hard spots with our heads. It would be better called a "shake-up" than a "shakedown" cruise. Eventually, order prevailed. "Shipshape and Bristol fashion" it is called, after that orderly English sea town. We established watches of four hours on and four off. These shortened as the temperature dropped with each mile north.

The on-watch was either at the helm steering, adjusting the wind-driven self-steering vane, trimming and reefing sails, navigating, or keeping up the logbook. The off-watch had chores before falling gratefully into a seaberth: assisting in sail changes, galley work, bilge checks, handing up the last steaming mug as the lonely night-watch began. At the change of watch, a compass course was called up, the new helmsperson repeating it aloud in confirmation. The newly off-watch checked the drowsy oncomer for harness, lanyard, and strobe light and relayed any pertinent information: "I sighted a ship four points off the port bow and closing." A cadence developed, miming the weather from tranquil to frenzied. We had serious duties, among them to sleep whenever possible, so we spent little time together. Still, we shared a strong sense of closeness, team effort, and trust.

The yankee headsail curved like a wing in flight and pulled the *Roger Henry* to windward. The boat heeled, then hardened up as it found its groove. The unreefed and tightly sheeted mainsail filled. Then the wind began.

Off the coast of Nova Scotia, with the *Roger Henry* bucking steep, cold seas, I took the captain's timeless tour with my hands and eyes. I looked up the stout rigging cables for signs of slack or fray, checked the play in the rudder's pintles and gudgeons, and inspected the sheets and halyards for chafe.

As seasoned sailors we thrive on the fluid uncertainty of the sea because we carry with us a comforting familiarity: this deck beneath our feet, heeling, pitching, and yawing. This humble lump of Dacron and steel was the vessel into which Diana and I had poured our hopes for a meaningful life. To the last, in our hearts and, ultimately, with our hands, we would cling to this. On land we would be blind to her faults, sing her graces, defend her honor. At the docks we would scrub and scrape, paint and polish. At sea we would constantly caress her, whispering encouragement. She was our ship; we were her crew. We had a bond of faith. The basics were sound: The plan set, the ship stout, and the crew steady.

Now that the lines were cast, the fuzzy edges of the dream were hardening into reality. The system of designating one and only one person to command a vessel at sea has endured through the entire history of humankind afloat. It is a time-tested method of assuring that, in an unforgiving environment where conferences cannot be held and second guesses are inevitably too late, one person (usually the one with the strongest skills and greatest experience) will make quick, confident, competent decisions. Where the navigation and operation of the *Roger Henry* were concerned, Diana approved of my command without reservation. Command, however, is not about authority, it is about responsibility. I recalled the haunted faces of Shackleton's men in that faded photograph. They had not started like that. No, they left their homes cheerful and confident that they were many, skilled, and hearty, that theirs was the ship capable of withstanding the crushing force of ice. Don't we all? And yet the Arctic shores are littered with the beams and bones of failure.

I crawled up to the bow and turned my face toward the blustery northern sky. Far over the horizon was an appointment to be kept. I thought of Diana and threw my arms open. With the halting embarrassment of a foxhole convert, I did something I had not done since childhood—I prayed. I prayed for the safety and survival of the woman huddled below with her fears and misgivings. I prayed for the wisdom to know when to be willful and when to acquiesce to the immutable forces of northern nature. And I prayed that, whatever came, I would keep my courage and do my best.

WE PRESSED ON into America's neighboring nation. Canada is captivating, in no small part due to Canadians. In cobblestoned downtown Halifax, the Maritime Museum offered us free dockage. A yachtsman lent us a car for the day. An Air Force major introduced himself from the dock and took us on a tour of the waterfront. He explained that the city felt so new and orderly due to a tragic incident in 1917. Two munitions ships collided in the harbor, caught fire, and burned beautifully as thousands of the city's residents watched the spectacle through their windows. The shrapnel from those windows exacerbated the injuries when the ships vaporized into the largest explosion of the pre-atomic era. The devastation, casualties, and deaths were unimaginable—and then it got worse. A blizzard beset the town before the survivors could crawl out of the rubble. An SOS was sent out and help poured in from around the Allied world, but most forthcoming were contributions and volunteers from Boston, Massachusetts. To this day, the city of Halifax annually sends a giant Christmas tree to the city of Boston as an expression of continuing gratitude.

We'd stopped in Halifax to relax and relish our final days of hot water, films, and fine meals. We would be forgoing these luxuries for a year at least, and if severely trapped in the ice . . . well, we weren't talking about that. Never give your worst fears the breath of life.

We went to a flea market early on Sunday morning in search of the odd bits of this and that. I saw Diana looking into a cardboard box, and her serene smile left no doubt as to the contents. I looked in the box; one kitten was beautiful, mewing contentedly, a precious little peach. The other, a little female, was motley and mean. She spat, hissed, and tried to tear great hunks out of any hand offered. Diana could not decide, so I told the woman to give us the wild one. On the long walk back to the boat, with scratched and bleeding hands, we settled on the name Halifax. Due to limited space on a yacht, every piece of equipment must serve at least two functions: she would be our bed warmer and polar bear detector. Months later, when I needed one like at no other time in my life, she was also my friend.

Having said that, we got off to a rocky start. Halifax took to shredding my charts, scrambling across my computer keyboard precisely when critical weather facsimiles were being received, and most infuriating, peeing on my pillow. She took an obvious delight in tormenting me, waiting until I was watching and then letting fly. She might have walked the plank had she not quickly learned that only she could slip under the inverted dinghy on the foredeck.

We followed the pastoral Nova Scotian coast east, then north around Cape Canso, cutting the forty-fifth parallel. The St. Peter's Bay canal locks lifted us up and through to Bras d'Or Lake. This rolling, wooded terrain pulled us forward around new points, down deep arms, and into hidden coves. The great northern woods swept down directly into the mighty north sea, the frontiers of two ecosystems smelling of sap, smoke, salt, and seaweed. We were spat out spinning into Cabot Strait by a fast-running tide through the narrows of Cape Breton. The wind held favorably, and we quickly crossed the Gulf of St. Lawrence to close with the west coast of Newfoundland.

Newfoundland is, I suppose, the Ozarks of our experience—a rugged people reflecting a rugged terrain, doing the best they can with little more than family, friends, and good music. Okay, a little moonshine, too. The groundfisheries had been shut down, and the economy was devastated. They've seen hard times before and will see them again. This has never diminished their love of The Rock. To understand this love, simply sail into Gros Morne, halfway up the western shores. Nothing subtle here: It is thrust-up, chopped-off, in-your-face scenery.

We will go back, but when faced with the decision to press on or linger, we had already lingered too often. The window of opportunity in the far North is predictable only in its brevity; to be a week late is to be a year late. It was already late June, giving us less than six weeks to arrive at the sea-ice's eroding edge, fifteen hundred grueling miles north. I decided to sail nonstop for St. Anthony at the island's northern tip.

Given the chance, prudent captains should learn from their mistakes. Based on annual averages, I mistakenly theorized that there should be no icebergs in the Strait of Belle Isle. Sail on, fool. Too impatient to slow down for the few hours until daybreak, I pressed ahead at seven knots through fog and darkness, leaving the fiftieth degree of latitude astern. To my starboard beam inshore, I saw the navigational lights of two larger vessels paralleling our course and assumed that, under power, they would soon pass us. When they fell behind, subliminal alarms went off. At sea, there is message and meaning in everything. I eavesdropped on their VHF radio conversation.

"Did you see *that* one?" (*That one what?* I wondered.)

"Yeah, but I'm only twenty feet above the water, I almost didn't." (I was six.)

"Roger that. I only got six millimeters of steel; four knots is too fast." (I had four millimeters. What evil lurked?)

A chill and then a shape appeared out of the fog—a wall of ice, granite-hard, bow-crushing, bone-breaking ice. I slammed the helm over, ran up to the bow, dropped the yankee, and reefed the main. When the boat and my heart slowed, I thought about the promise of prudence I had made to Diana. I had nearly turned our beginning into our ending. At the dock in St. Anthony, I had to purge myself of it. I spit the whole story out to the first person I met, a rather simple-looking fellow.

When I finished, he said, "He who knows nothing, fears nothing."

He pointed to a slight, roughly dressed man on the dock and said that was Selby Weisman. His tone meant *the* Selby Weisman. I confessed ignorance. It seemed to be in season for me. Selby is an experienced ice pilot. He has pushed all shapes and sizes of boats through the Strait of Belle Isle, through Frobisher Bay, through the Northwest Passage. He has had successes and failures, and he told me that you cannot sail in the Arctic and not expect both. I described my plans and my experience.

He asked me, "Are you lucky?"

"I'm here," I said.

"Good. First, if you do not know exactly what you are doing, do nothing. Don't enter the pack ice until you understand the dynamics. Ice cover is described in tenths. Ten-tenths is solid cover; one–tenth is widely scattered. Limit yourself to three-tenths at first, but don't confuse cover with density. Six-tenths of rotted old brash ice is not the same as six-tenths of high, hard pans. Remember, it's tomorrow's not today's winds that count. The ice will flow thirty degrees to the right of the true wind direction due to the rotation of the earth. It's called the *Coriolis effect.* Black ice is frozen fresh water; it's colorless, low in the water, and as hard as stone. If you see a piece, it means you just sailed by some you didn't see. Slow down. If you get in trouble, look for a big berg. It's deep and will move with the currents, not the wind, usually against the smaller ice. Get behind it and it will have a clear pool in its lee . . ."

I have a mouth and I have ears. I knew which to use during my short time with Selby. Boiled down, the lesson was: Assume nothing, anticipate everything. This talk made Diana nervous. She counted the canned goods . . . again.

The laptop computer linked to the single sideband marine radio churned out ice and weather information. On July 5, we set sail in spite of reports showing dangerous ice remaining in the Labrador Sea, Davis Strait, and both north and south of Greenland's capital, Nuuk (previously known as Godthaab.) The season was simply too short to wait for ideal conditions at our destination. We had to anticipate a change in the ice status upon our estimated time of arrival, ten days hence.

Our sail to Greenland was uneventful because we carefully avoided event. One of us remained dressed and on deck at all times, despite the increasing cold. We hove-to in gales. We slowed down in the dark and fog to a speed at which we would be willing to collide with the million-ton icebergs hidden within. The standing rule in the cockpit was that the helmsperson must be tethered to the ship at all times, to eliminate any possibility of being pitched into the freezing sea. Below, the person off-watch slept with feet to the bow. This way, in the not-so-unlikely event of collision, we might break our legs, but not our necks. On the nautical chart, dead reckoning plots ticked off the fifty-fifth and then the sixtieth degree of northern latitude.

I had originally balked at the concept and cost of radar, but Diana's sense of caution prevailed. After the Belle Isle incident, I was determined that in the ordeal to come I would not defeat myself. The Arctic would be enemy enough. When I learned to tune and interpret the radar properly, it became a useful tool, but not foolproof, for high waves and hard ice often appeared the same on its screen.

Heavy fog hid the coast of the world's largest island and, at 3.7 billion years, the oldest known land on earth. On July 13, a humpback whale, its basalt flukes blending into the background of stark slate towers, led us through the mountainous leads into clear air and the safe haven of a long fjord. Since leaving Maine we had sailed 1,840 miles, but we were still many hundreds of miles from our goal, and the remaining miles would be harder.

The shoreline was shocking. What wasn't rock was glacier—unusable inclines and inescapable ice. Diana gasped in dismay at the initial impact of this rugged, lifeless landscape. Once on shore, however, she was surprised and thrilled to find delicate poppies and rosebay willows clinging to the lee of every rock, hiding from the frigid winds. However tenuous, life prevailed after all. I was not as pleased to see, even from a distance, that the town of Nuuk ("the Headlands") was surprisingly modern. It seemed that at least some of the nation's fifty-five thousand Inuit had neglected to wait in quaint antiquity for my entertainment.

It was here that I had to face my weakest link in planning. We hoped to reach the northernmost and remotest spot possible in Greenland for our winter shelter. According to law, what we planned to do required written government approval based on specific geographic locations and dates, a captain's résumé, evacuation insurance, special radio license, firearm permits, medical histories, physicals signed by approved physicians ... the list went on. Three months prior to our departure, we had received a brochure from the Danish embassy suggesting we begin the paper process at least one full year in advance.

Because the law demands that only the captain of a vessel report ashore for entry procedures, I sat alone in the office of Eric Moller, the Danish port captain. I was sick with dread, but I was not going to lie. I wanted to look over forward horizons, not over my shoulder. The fate of the entire expedition pivoted on a bureaucratic reprieve of unknown probability. Even a delay was effectively a cancellation, for it was mid-July and each day was critical. Eric listened patiently to my plans and smiled at my obvious turmoil. Then he said, "Relax; you can do what you want. That's what Greenland is for."

He suspected in me a kindred spirit and excitedly pulled out photos and plans of the motorsailer *Kivioq,* built for the Danish explorer Knud Rasmussen. In Greenland, the words *Rasmussen* and *God* are almost interchangeable, for no one knew the Inuit and their ways better than the Dane. Rasmussen once said, "Give me winter, give me dogs, keep the rest," but he learned that one cannot ignore the rest. Albeit short, a summer of sorts does come, and the highway of sea-ice splinters. The Inuit resorted to large walrus-hide boats called *umiaqs,* which are well adapted to icy conditions, being easily hauled out of harm's way. But their range is limited, and Knud wanted to explore the northeast coast of Greenland above Ammassalik. This required a huge hold and a thick hull, for nowhere in Greenland is the ice more dangerous. After Knud's passing, his boat changed hands, fell into disrepair, and eventually foundered. Eric beamed as he told of finding it sunken in the harbor, raising it, and meticulously resurrecting it. When it was restored in all its glory, rather than pampering it as a museum piece, he and his wife set off to the north, retracing the many adventures of Rasmussen.

It may be a stretch to call Nuuk itself the front line of Arctic adventure. But if I was the nervous new soldier approaching the distant thunder of battle, Eric was the hardened veteran who had been to the front, beyond, and back. I listened in excited awe, marking both his words and the charts of Greenland and Canada that soon covered his office floor.

I asked, "What about wintering in Parker Snow Bay?"

"No, no, too shallow. We went aground there, almost lost the boat."

"Where would you winter on board?"

He smiled and said, "I wouldn't."

"Okay, then where was your favorite spot?"

"Well, remember, we were there in the summer, so I can't say it's right for you, but nothing compared to Dundas Harbor on Devon Island. Mountains, rivers, lakes, musk ox grazing on the shores like pigs in a pen." Four hours were not sufficient to exhaust my curiosity. He invited Diana and me to his modern home for an evening of unexpectedly elegant dining and more sound advice.

Verbecca, Eric's effervescent young wife, traveled about Greenland's remote regions as a nursing supervisor. She had come to love its craggy emptiness as deeply as Eric, and neither longed for their native Denmark. They had found ways to accommodate their European tastes by building a greenhouse where they lovingly nurtured vegetables. She plucked a ripe tomato and sliced it with ceremony befitting a cherished delicacy.

Over a fresh salmon dinner, we discussed the unique historic relationship between the Danes and Greenlandic Inuit. During the early 1700s, Europe had little knowledge of Greenland and even less interest in it. It was Terra Incognita, even though it had once been colonized by the exiled murderer, Erik the Red. Despite estimates that six thousand Norsemen had lived in southern Greenland and even carried on a brisk trade with Europe, all traces of that colony had disappeared. In later years the island was considered useless to all but a few whalers who ventured up its western shores. Their eyes were focused on the steamy waters for the telltale spout or the arced fin of the right whale (so named because it contained the greatest yield of precious oil and baleen, making it the "right" whale to take). Rarely did they venture ashore to cache supplies or to shoot caribou and musk ox. That changed quickly when they discovered something they felt well worth trading for: the uninhibited sexual favors of giggling young Inuit women.

This was a treeless land starved for good building materials. If a simple plank to form a sled runner was a coveted treasure, imagine the value of a nail or sharp iron blade. A rate of exchange was soon established. The Inuit husbands laughed at the unfathomable Kabloonah (white man). "Before, he has knife, I have wife. After, I have knife, I have wife. Ha!" They would rock back and slap their fur-clad knees.

Back in Nordic Europe, listening to the bawdy stories of returning sailors, a pious young preacher took interest in this barren land and its people. He prayed, and his calling became clear. Hans Egede campaigned for many years to obtain the endorsement of a missionary society and the financial support of the Danish king. He then packed up his wife and three children and in 1719 was dropped off on Greenland's western shore, at the site of present-day Nuuk.

His original goal of colonizing and Christianizing the so-called savages soon gave way to the more pressing task of staying alive. Only with the kind help of the native people did that happen. The Egede children rapidly adapted to this harsh land, learned the language, and formed fast friendships with the Inuit children. They in turn tutored their father, who carefully recorded the language. He too came to know and love the ways of the Inuit, and he dedicated his life to protecting them from lawless whalers and championing their cause in the courts of Europe. Anchored by Gertrude, a stalwart wife and mother, this family almost singlehandedly blunted the typically tragic outcome of European expansion into primitive areas.

Although it has known cultural suppression (such as the missionaries' banning of the Inuit's spiritual Drum Dance, replacing it with Christian rituals) and some economic exploitation, this nation has never known invasion or occupying armies. However uneven, the relationship has been viewed by both parties as something of a partnership. Home Rule Autonomy was granted from Denmark in 1979. Recently, modern Inuit youth have clamored for complete independence. Not all think that is a good idea; next door to Eric lives an old Inuk who is very upset that the name of the nation has been changed to Kalaallit Nunaat and that the Danish flag has been replaced. He calls the new design the "terrorist flag," and he fears the movement is infiltrated with Communists. The irony is that no culture on earth is better known for its communal structures.

Over the last drinks of a long and educational evening, Eric told us a story that attests to how difficult it can be to understand the nuances of another culture. In the mid-1970s, a wealthy Italian count proclaimed that he wanted to dogsled to the North Pole. Actually, he wanted an army of paid help to get him and his sled to the North Pole. Eric signed on as navigator. Before they departed, Eric mentioned to the count that the Inuit respect a man who possesses much meat. Say no more; the count immediately ordered in a cargo plane full of meat, which was then piled sky-high for all to see. The count was surprised when this did not seem to impress the locals. He had missed the point. In a hunting culture it is the ability to amass that mountain of meat, not the meat itself, that elicits respect. Truth was, the count was a lousy shot and a pitiful hunter. To the Inuit mind, nothing except perhaps impotence could bring more shame to a man.

Nuuk harbor is a slash in a rock wall surrounded by storage sheds and cranes. It services the twelve thousand residents of Nuuk and acts as the central distribution point of virtually every item imported. We were tied up alongside a black hulk of a motorsailer. The next morning an Inuk in paint-splattered overalls was working on an ancient, open-geared winch on the foredeck. I pantomimed the question, "Me, help you?"

He answered in a refined English accent, "That's very kind of you, but my energy has fallen short of my ambition. I think I will call it a day." Ingmar Egede was tall, thin, and handsome. Though graying with age, he remained fit and active. He invited us to his orderly home, decorated with spiraled narwhal tusks, bear skins, walrus skulls, harpoons, tools, soapstone carvings, native art, and a wall covered with books. Over coffee and pastries, he introduced us to his girlfriend, an attractive Danish woman half his age. He teased her openly, telling us that he had met her at a museum conference in Copenhagen. She was a lauded expert on Inuit art and culture, although she had never been to the Arctic nor met a real "Eskimo." She smiled and said, "Now I have met one, and he can't get rid of me."

We talked about the West's fascination with Inuit culture. I asked if they found all our probing intrusive. He answered wryly with the question, "How large is the average Inuit family?" I shrugged. "A father, a mother, two children, and an anthropologist."

As he talked of his youth, I realized we had stumbled into yet another storehouse of information. No more book learning; here was a man who was born in the far North, ran wild as a child up there, and even though selected to be educated overseas, returned there to share his new knowledge.

Ingmar has Greenland's past in his blood and its future on his razor-sharp mind. As chairman of the Inuit Circumpolar Conference, he travels the world representing his nation and his people. He was softspoken but intense when explaining his work. The international association was formed to identify and promote common issues among the polar people of Sweden, Norway, Finland, Russia, Alaska, and Canada. These tribes share similar languages and lifestyles. Although their situation is much like that of the Kurds, this is not a movement of independence. For that matter, Greenland's Inuit are already independent. Rather, it is a need for their collective ethnic voice to be heard at the global table. Many feel micromanaged by capitals that are technically within their borders but are so far to the south and share so little common experience that they are nothing less than foreign. Ingmar used the heated issue of native whaling as an example.

He said, "When I was in your country, I often watched your public television. One show would encourage you to understand and respect the different cultures of the world, and the next program would demand a complete moratorium on whaling worldwide. It is not my people who hunted this animal to near extinction. It is not my people who hover off these shores with factory ships. It is not my people who waste whalemeat as feed for fur farms, as the Russians still do. And for what? Profit! We do not hunt for profit, we hunt for food." He pointed out the window to the barren peaks. "Did you see any cattle grazing as you sailed in? It is too cold. At my last conference, one of your activists suggested that we import beef instead. Oh, that is good for your economy, but what of ours? That means that we must generate much hard currency. The value of our currency will be determined by your banks.

We know what that means. We will have to sell off our other resources undervalued in order to buy your expensive beef. We do not like beef. We do not like being told how to live. There has been a recovery, and scientific studies prove that we can hunt certain species on a sustainable basis. But at every conference, your scientists try to hide or discredit their own numbers. They veto any motion to raise our quotas. Why? Because it is not a scientific issue. It is an emotional issue. It is true that whales are a beautiful animal. But so are moose, elk, and deer. You have a multibillion-dollar hunting industry in a country that does not even need the meat, but you tell us to stop hunting." Ingmar shook his head sadly. "Your journalists always show the blood, but do they show the pride an Inuk feels when he provides for his family in this traditional way? Do they show him sharing that meat with the elderly and the sick? Do they explain that this system of distribution is the single thread that binds our communities?"

When he finished, all I could say was, "Ingmar, if ever I get the chance, I will tell your story."

Back on board we fed up, fueled up, and headed up the jagged coast. Vertical headlands marked narrow entrances to a succession of fjords, which cut inland for up to one hundred miles. The increasingly smaller towns to the north were modern in a rough, mining camp way. Most everything was available, although very expensive. A shriveled imported cucumber cost us six dollars. Shrimping, halibut fishing, and sealing are the main industries. Because of the growing trend toward eco-travel, tourism may soon explode. Although there is no mining at present, commercial eyes are focusing on the graphite, lead, coal, and zinc found beneath Greenland's frozen cover. Work is abundant; the minimum wage is ten dollars per hour; social services are available. Boom times. Greenlanders, however, cannot be defined out of context with their land, for like everywhere else it forms the national character. It is a big, open land, wild and unregulated. The New North is like the Old West in its code of heavily armed, rugged individualism.

We watched as Inuit signed off the shrimping trawlers with cold cash in hand. They rushed into the co-op store and reappeared on the street with a crate of beer costing the equivalent of seventy-five U.S. dollars. It went down fast, and the drunken dance began. They swaggered, then staggered, then shattered glass on the streets. Another crate and they crumpled unconscious in the shrapnel. Later, in the Greenland equivalent of the morning, wives and girlfriends who were not indoors hiding their black eyes and swollen lips rifled the fallen's pockets for food money. The more forgiving dragged the bodies home. There are, of course, many upstanding men, sober and serious. But the problem is clearly a rent in the social fabric, one so serious that the *Inughuit* (the "Polar Eskimo" first named by Knud Rasmussen), a northerly subgroup of Inuit with the purest blood and oldest ways, view alcohol as the greatest threat to their culture. They have voted in a coupon rationing system to control its flow.

When Diana and I had rounded Cape Horn, we felt we were at the bottom of the earth. We were now already six hundred miles farther north than that is south, and just beginning. We pushed on behind the retreating ice, ceremoniously crossing "The Circle" at sixty-six degrees, thirty-three minutes north. In trying to define the frontiers of adventure, this can safely be called the edge. The Arctic Circle is the theoretical point at which, depending on the season, the sun either does not set or does not rise at all. It was an important milestone in our journey, because it shattered time as we know it. The Arctic is technically defined as all lands and seas north of this, but a better test is all permafrosted land and adjacent waters above the treeline. That is an erratic line that lies far to the north of the circle on the slopes of Alaska, dropping far to the south as it passes through Quebec and Labrador, then north again above Europe and skirting Siberia.

Along the Arctic Circle, at any point of longitude one thing remains the same: A compass becomes useless for navigation. The flow lines of magnetic force emanate from the earth at a point called the *magnetic north pole*. Near this the pull is more downward, toward the center of the earth, and weaker. This phenomenon is called dip, and its effect was the sluggish spin of our compass card as we twisted through islands of rock and ice. Added to that was the distance between the *geographic north pole* and the always moving magnetic north pole, which today lies four hundred miles from where the first explorers plotted it, and was then a thousand miles from the real pole. From our position it lay due west, and as we sailed north it would lie to the south of west. This is unsettling to a sailor, for what can you hold to when north is south, when dawn is dusk, when the sea is solid?

The central ice pack almost entirely filled Baffin Bay. A narrow lead of water opened from the coast outward. Nervously, we clung close inshore, fearing a wind or current shift could close this ice vise. We hoped the fractured coast would provide a quick retreat behind a hook or island that would deflect incoming ice. When possible, we used inland passages, mistakenly assuming them safer. In fact, as we approached Disko Bay, one of earth's most prolific iceberg factories, we ran afoul of that perpetual miracle in the making.

Above us, the Greenland ice cap stretched 1,500 miles from north to south and 450 east to west. At up to eleven thousand feet thick, it is so ponderously heavy that the continent's interior actually sags a thousand feet below sea level. Locked up in it is ten percent of the earth's freshwater supply, a volume so enormous that the world's oceans would rise twenty feet if it thawed. Trapped in that ice cap, exploding loose in monstrous chunks, thundering into the sea, was the earth at its most essential: water, hundreds of thousands of years old, pure, pre-atomic, pre-industrial, primordial. It is the same cycle that tropical rain takes into rivers and back into the ocean to begin again; but here the flow hesitates, frozen for millennia.

Down the long fjords, these moving mountains jammed through hourglass narrows in their relentless push to the sea. Watercolor monoliths, reaching hundreds of feet above the sea's surface and plumbing the dark depths below, paraded by us. They allowed little rest, for we had to ask ourselves what would happen when the irresistible force met the immovable object and we lay in between. As they hit land and shallows, they crashed and crumbled, screeched and split. The resulting wake could completely overwhelm our small craft, yet we had no choice but to slide silently by. A particularly unpleasant surprise was the sudden surfacing of many-ton ice shards that had broken off the bergs' bottoms. Silent behemoths rose from beneath, smashing everything in their paths. Neither skill nor caution could avert disaster. It was simply hit or miss.

Perhaps here lie the roots of the North's fatalistic philosophies, all tightly packaged into the word *ajaqnak* (the only close equivalent in

English being "shit happens"). Ancient Inuit carvings, called *tupilaks,* depict god spirits as gargoyle-ugly and vicious, not a sweet baby Jesus or comforting Madonna. In their myths, as in their lives, death often is sudden and without meaning. They share with the South the same fear of claw and fang, but because of the cold, here starvation occurs within days; here they die of thirst, surrounded by water. Even the air they breathe, the very gift of life, may be the agent of death should it penetrate their inner sanctums of warmth.

There was now no night, for the muted sun skidded in continuous circles low on the horizon. Only fog, wind, or fatigue halted our progress— or ice, for increasingly all decisions were ice oriented as we entered the thick of it. In a dynamic process, currents sweep down the east coast of Greenland, collecting the "field ice" that forms in the Arctic Ocean and continually breaks off at that ocean's revolving fringes. This five- to seven-year-old pack ice can be one hundred feet thick and can break off into islands fifty miles long. First marching them south, the current then sweeps them under Cape Farewell and pivots them up the west coast. Here the current adds to its flow four- to eight-foot-thick "fast ice," which is annual sea-ice formed in fjords, bays, and coastal waters above sixty degrees north. When used as a nautical term, the word *fast* is not a description of speed. It describes a line or object being tightly fixed or *fastened* to another object.

As it sweeps by Disko Island, Melville Bay, and the Kane Basin, the current grabs the crowned beauties of the parade: the freshwater icebergs. Snow continually falls on the ice cap, compacts into ice, and adds to the downward push, forcing the taffylike glaciers to flow outward. When this ice river meets the sea, it sheers, giving birth to icebergs sculpted by wind and water. The world's most active glacier, at Ilulissat, moves eighty to one hundred feet per day and calves bergs across its six-mile front. Like snowflakes, no two icebergs are alike. In fact, none is even like itself when viewed from different angles. As we passed or as they slowly spun, landscapes, buildings, animals, and faces appeared. A frog turned into a prince, kissed by the magic hues of Arctic light. The waters turn west and south, scouring the length of Baffin Island and eventually sending their cargo to the ice graves off Newfoundland, as the great ship *Titanic* discovered.

As we crossed the seventieth parallel, these thickening formations dwarfed us in their majesty, threatened us with their power. The Inuit use the word *ilira,* a word whose meaning combines the English words *fear* and *awe.* Perhaps it means deadly beauty, but to our minds the word increasingly incorporated the concept of respect.

Only when a secure nook or cranny protected the boat could we escape to shore to wander through tundra fields, fly fish the braided streams, or watch an eider hatchling struggle through its egg wall. Arctic foxes, still their mottled summer blue, yelped signals back to their pups in the den. This land was treeless, steep, and seemingly stark, yet somehow satisfying, perhaps because of the sheer joy of its size. Arctic beech, willow, cotton grass, day-glow mosses, lichens, and even orchids grew into a spongy ground thatch. Stunted berry bushes swelled briefly—we knew, in truth, all too briefly.

In trying to recruit reluctant colonists, Erik the Red perpetrated one of history's most famous cases of fraudulent advertising. The green land to the east was called Iceland, and the iced land to the west he called Greenland—green as in growing, checkered with pasture and paddock, a lush land of milk and honey. Read the fine print. Perhaps the open land in southern Greenland had in those days been more extensive, but the living could never have been easy. The looming ice cap is a weather factory. As the air above the frozen dome cools, it becomes heavy, flows outward, and falls off the escarpments at paint-stripping speeds of up to 160 miles per hour. Cold air's density gives these winds more force than warmer winds of the same velocity. Whole villages have been blown out to sea. The terror of these katabatic killers, called *Piteraq,* is etched in the Inuit psyche.

Always feeling the pressure of a short season, we sailed hard, ticking off widely spaced towns anchored to rocky outcrops with railroad spikes and guy wires. The gingerbread houses are wooden, with steep roofs and carved eaves, creative trim and clapboard combinations. In a land otherwise devoid of color, no part of the spectrum is unrepresented, from electric purple to distress orange. The streets were blasted from the steep cliffs in cutbacks. All piping runs above the rocky ground and is either heavily wrapped or useless much of the year. Mostly, locals hand-haul water daily in five-gallon jugs. Each village has an insulated waterhouse with an external filling station. At first we were confused because there was no valve, but we learned to press and hold a button that releases water from the inside, which prevents the valve from freezing and assures it cannot be left running accidentally. I missed and would later pay for an important lesson hiding here: Despite massive amounts of surrounding ice, during the ten months of winter you have only as much water as you have fuel to thaw it. Waste not.

Because there is no inland, every town is a port with a public jetty and warehousing facility. As our latitude increased, the shipping season decreased. Food, parts, hardware, and heating fuel for the coming winter were hurriedly offloaded. The ice-rumpled ships turned around, hoping to squeeze in one more run. Always near the wharf are the Commune Offices, the Poste, and the Policia.

The center of action is the Braettet (the Plank) for the Danes, or Kalaaliaraq (the Little Greenlander) for the Inuit. Here fresh seal meat, *mataq* (narwhal skin and fat), whalemeat, wildfowl, caribou, musk ox, trout, salmon, halibut, and cod are sold in the open. It is an important place to be and be seen, for an empty stall means one has not hunted well of late, and tongues begin to wag. Blood by the bucketful runs to the stone floor and is tracked outward as a welcoming red carpet. Men carving crimson meat wipe the blood from their mouths and the dripping blades on their pants. There is no aversion to blood. It is the symbol of the cycle of life into which this hunting culture is locked.

Much as the buffalo was the foundation of American Plains Indian life, the marine mammal is the building block of the Inuit culture. Nothing is wasted. The fur makes soft clothing. The skin, cut thin and stretched, makes strong rope that does not stiffen in the cold. The bones make tools and toys. The rest is eaten.

On a plank, hunters line up headshot seals, skinned to the nose but with head, eyes, and long lashes intact. The carcasses look hauntingly human and are vaguely upsetting. I tried the raw meats and chunks of gooey fat. The flavor varied depending on species and age of the animal, but on the whole it was palatable, even good. The Inuit gobble the blubber first, then lick their fingers and shiny lips with gusto. Only when that is gone do they boil up some meat in a pot of purple blood.

Cardiovascular disease is almost unknown among the Inuit, because the oils of marine mammals and cold-water fish are full of unsaturated omega-3 fatty acids. But the true miracle is that the same vitamins normally derived from direct sunlight are transformed and stored in the blubber's oil. It is this liquid sunshine, first and foremost, that has allowed *Homo sapiens* to bridge the seasons of light. In our pastoral lands we beseech, "Our Father ... give us this day our daily bread," while the Inuit pray, "Nuliakjuk, great god of mankind, send us seals, send us bears, send us walrus, so that we may have food, and fat, and clothing. Beasts of the sea, come offer yourself, in the cold, clear light of the morning."

In each town we found a Seaman's Mission, run by a Dane, offering satellite television, European newspapers, and hot meals at the relatively affordable price of fifty krona, then ten U.S. dollars. They also provided clean beds and, to Diana's delight, hot showers. They were bleach-scrubbed havens of order and hygiene. "Cleanliness is next to Godliness" has been preached here for many years by Europeans—frustrated Europeans, for the missions stood in stark contrast to the scene just outside their doors. Dust devils picked up the accumulated litter of a Westernizing culture. Piles of seal gut, shimmering with blowflies and mixed with plastic and Styrofoam, covered the broken sleds, dead puppies, ropes, household garbage, and derelict machinery. And, of course, piled high, skated on, and smeared everywhere, was the perennial dog scat. It was at first disgusting. I wanted to shout, "Why don't you pick it up? Why do you live with this filth?" The reason, of course, is that we were seeing the town during the brief period it lies unfrozen and not covered by snow. The foul smell and scenery would soon fade beneath winter's mantle.

The Greenlandic customs brochure warned in large red letters that cheese and chocolate were restricted imports, considered contraband. We had thirty pounds of cheese because of its high fat content and trail handiness. We carried forty pounds of chocolate because . . . well, Diana. We must not have looked the type to push it to school children and luckily had been exempted by customs in Nuuk.

It is also against the law to take any nonnative dog north of the Arctic Circle. Any foreign dog that isn't rendered into bloodmud by the fierce Greenlandic sled dogs might interbreed—an apparent abomination, for the Inuit feel theirs is the finest breed on earth.

Here is a relationship best understood when compared to others. The horse extended the range, speed, and cargo capacity at which Europeans, Asians, and much later the Native Americans traveled. But horses require much water. Thus, in the deserts of Africa and the Middle East, the camel was indispensable. At the high altitudes of the Andes, llamas and alpacas shouldered the loads. Each environment demanded that its people tame a beast before taming their surroundings.

In the case of the sled dog, the word *tame* is only marginally useful, for they are fierce, and their wildness cannot be beaten out of them. They often fight to the death in establishing their working order. The Inuit stand back, having always understood the process of natural selection. They admire and encourage this *ningaq* (fighting spirit), knowing that this spirit, once harnessed, finds outlet in the dog's will to pull beyond natural limits. *Ningaq* has its risks, too. Every so often an infant wanders within the range of a chained dog pack and is torn to pieces.

A man is judged by the dogs he drives. The processes of breeding and training have become cultural rites of passage into manhood. I watched a woman pulling a miniature sled. A boy, no more than three years old, slid behind, cracking his whip on the ground, authoritatively shouting "Ili, ili, [right], iu, iu, [left]." When she stopped acting the dog and tried to act the mother by wiping his nose, he gave her a stern tongue lashing. She smiled, satisfied that neither dog nor woman would ever dominate *her* son.

Cats are a rarity, for they would be torn into tufts before you could say Halifax of the North. As we pushed quickly up the coast, in spite of our best efforts, at each port Halifax made her escape onto the town dock where dog packs roamed freely. I was a nervous wreck, having grown inordinately fond of the little beast, but she seemed to enjoy the titillation of narrow escape. That training was to come in handy later. In one port, we invited a man and his daughter on board. The little girl was fascinated, and even after holding and petting Halifax for some time, she had to ask, "Papa, is it real?"

We sailed cautiously beneath the massif, passing Mantisoq (The Uneven), Sisimiut (The People at the Foxholes), Aasiaat (The Spiders), Ilulissat (The Icebergs), and then snaked behind the glacier-capped, turreted island of Disko. Playing cat and mouse with ice through shifting fog, winds, and currents required continuous decision making of a very serious nature, but it stirred action, exciting and engaging. On the Nuussauq Peninsula fifty-knot winds kept us pinned down in a keyhole-shaped anchorage for three long days. The time to catch up on maintenance and sleep should have been refreshing, and indeed Diana relished our short respite from ice, but I began to wear myself down with worry. The days may have been endless, but the season was not. It was clearly a heavy ice year, and I worried about what we would do if Melville Bay did not open. Then I worried about what we would do if it did.

Upernavik is the northernmost town before Melville Bay. We rafted alongside the forty-foot, flame-red sailing trawler *Sila*. The stout, double-ended vessel was planked with two-inch-thick hardwoods and sheathed to a foot above the waterline with copper. The stem was an iron I-beam, designed for serious ice work. A phone-booth–like pilothouse jutted up out of the central deck under heavy rigging. Two Danish men were booming on board hunks of drifting saltwater ice and packing them into perforated crates. When I asked why, they explained that, if it is left to melt, the salt will leach out in two to three days, leaving the water potable. They introduced themselves. Jens, the owner and charter captain, was the bantam rooster type, small, fit, and cocky. Christian was Nordic-blond, stately tall, and reserved. They were awaiting a scientific team that they would guide deep into the glacier-rimmed bight of Melville Bay to count and tag narwhals.

Jens asked what on earth we were doing way up there. I confided that we hoped, in fact, to carry on much farther, and I explained our plans. Christian frowned. A serious conversation in Danish followed between them. They turned to resume our talk, but I felt something was astir. They asked to see the boat and checked the deck carefully. Once below, they took unusual interest in the details of our equipment and experience.

I invited them to dinner. As purser, Diana wisely exempted the evening from our usual rationing of luxuries, and we fed them thick slices of smoked salami, dried tomatoes, mashed potatoes, and, of course, good cheese and chocolate. This far north, whiskey costs the equivalent of one hundred U.S. dollars a bottle. I opened one anyway, and Jens helped himself heartily. We talked pleasantly and at length. He was married to an Inuk and made his living as a sailor, carpenter, and judge. In Greenland, one who sits in judgment of others must live much as they do. Nice idea.

I asked Christian what his work was. He hesitated. He and Jens conferred in Danish, and then he confessed that he was a policeman. He explained that we put him in a bit of a dilemma. The small police force is in charge of virtually everything. In his position, he had been forced to question if, indeed, Eric had the authority to approve our plans. He also questioned the very wisdom of them. The rules are written for a reason: Rescue missions are expensive and dangerous. The evening had, in fact, been an inspection and interview.

"I do not think that you should do this," he said. "I might even have tried to stop you, but I am being rotated back to Denmark. Officially I am off duty and on vacation. So, my friend, you have slipped through the cracks."

The scientific team arrived by helicopter the next day. The head professor was not as approving, and when we were introduced, he was curt to the point of rudeness. He turned to Christian, and I did not need to understand their Danish to understand the problem. Through years of wilderness travel, I have often encountered an unmistakable resentment from scientists. From large institutions like the National Science Foundation, to universities, and downward, they do what they can to discourage, even obstruct privateers from entering their fields of study. This is often less for the sake of science than for the sake of scientists. The use of dwindling wilderness laboratories is hotly contested among the growing number of Ph.D. programs.

Wilderness, however, is about more than serving your time, punching your ticket, and returning to the Halls of Ivy. Yes, knowledge of the wilderness may be the salvation of it. There is much to learn, and many do an admirable job of amassing this knowledge. But knowledge is not in itself wisdom. In *Arctic Dreams,* Barry Lopez recounts entering a research cabin that had bunks assigned to a biologist, a geologist, an ornithologist, a paleontologist, and an ichthyologist. He wondered why none had been set aside for a poet or a painter. I wonder and worry about this too. Access needs to be assured not just for those who seek to measure the wild, but also for those who seek to be measured by it.

In the morning, after tending to last-minute details, I fired up the engine and we said our good-byes. Jens nimbly tossed off our bow line, while Christian held the stern. Handing me the line, Christian said, "I can see that in your heart you must do this, but honestly, I will worry about you. Do not underestimate the dangers from here north." He put his hand on my shoulder. "Please, winter near a village. Just being that far north is more than enough adventure. A little help would not hurt."

FOUR

Melville Bay

AUGUST 1994

20 HOURS DAYLIGHT

And now there came both mist and snow,
And it grew wondrous cold:
And ice, mast-high, came floating by,
As green as emerald.

—Samuel Taylor Coleridge, *Rime of the Ancient Mariner*

I N 3 5 0 B C the Greek explorer Pytheas discovered a land far north of the British Isles, probably Norway, which he named Thule (Greek for "the unknown"). He told an unbelieving audience that "no night exists in summer, and neither Earth, Water, or Air exist separately."

Two millennia later, in 1853, ostensibly searching for John Franklin but actually angling to reach the farthest recorded point north, Elisha Kent Kane pushed his small ship *Advance* through dreaded Melville Bay. He understandably described it as "a mysterious region of terror," for it had already bested many a stout vessel. In 1830 alone, nineteen whaling ships were sunk and twelve more seriously damaged while trying to pass through this foggy cauldron of ice pushed by contrary winds and confused currents. Time has changed nothing; Melville Bay remains the crucible of the North.

We had no whaling grounds to rush to and no commercial commitment hurrying our pace. Wintering north of Melville Bay would offer us the historically unusual advantage of not having to retrace our track in the same season. Thus, the cornerstone of our strategy was to pass as late as possible to the open-water *polynyas* (pronounced po-lin-yahs) lying north and west. Due to localized confluences of upwellings and currents, these pockets of water remain open even through the winter, and we might use them to our advantage in pushing our small craft to an extreme northerly point. However, it was late August. Freeze-up was only weeks, if not days, away. This timing was a double-edged sword—we might more easily dodge the remaining ice, but at these high latitudes a snap freeze could occur at any time, leaving us beset in the open ocean. History tells many a gruesome story about the consequences of that mistake.

We tentatively probed north out of Upernavik toward the Devil's
Thumb, a rocky promontory that juts into the bay. From there we
could evaluate the ice situation. As the *Roger Henry* rumbled through
the brash ice at three knots, I kept an eye over my shoulder for possible
havens of retreat. Before a dog will lie down, it may circle an area many
times, looking for exact alignments, guided by criteria unknown to us.
So too, I scrutinized bays and fjords for a certain look to the lay of the
land; a rocky hook that might deflect ice pressure; good depth just outside the tidal fracture zone; a bay plentiful with drinking water ice but
without active glaciers, closed enough for protection, open enough for
assured breakout the following year. In short, I was looking for that
one spot on earth where all my senses said we belonged. I could not
find it, and the pages fell from our calendar like leaves from a tree.

As we passed the mouth of Melville Bay, we tucked in behind a small
island and anchored for some much needed sleep. I tossed and turned
in my berth, knowing there would be no real rest until we made the big
decision: go or no go. At low tide the icebergs in the bay grounded, so
they posed no immediate threat to the boat and wouldn't pin down the
anchor. I asked Diana to go ashore with me for a climb up a high hill
where we could assess the ice conditions in the bay. We rowed toward
a black stone beach with Halifax sitting in the bow, quivering in anticipation. In an impressive but ill-timed leap, she fell just short of land.
Very hot and very cold feel much the same; she shot out of the sea as if
scalded. We dried her off with clothes from the emergency shore box,
and then the three of us bounded uphill over the rocky tundra.

We reveled in the stillness, safety, and certainty of dry land. The
knowledge that no ice could threaten us made me feel I was free of a
long-held burden. But I later learned that even on land, the Arctic ice
can be a killer. The Inuit have long talked about a rare phenomenon
called *ivu*. They claim the shore-ice pressure builds until, suddenly,
great sheets of ice slash far up the beach, shearing or crushing everything in their path. Westerners dismissed these stories as quaint
melodrama until 1982 when archaeologists discovered the ruins of the
devastated village Utriagvik, near Barrow, Alaska. The inhabitants appeared to have been caught so off-guard that they died in their sleep
under the rush of ice.

At the crest of a ridge we sat on the soft mossy tundra, all huddled close for warmth. Before us lay a breathtaking expanse of white icebergs, green sea, black rock, and purple heaven. At exactly midnight, hues of pulsing pastels hung low on the northern sky. This was the kind of beauty that demands sharing. Through the harried months of preparation, departure, and hard travel, Diana and I had passed few warm moments together.

I pulled her close to me. "Are you all right? Are you ready?"

"To be honest, I'm afraid," she said. "I never imagined the Arctic could be this beautiful. But now there's more ice, and we keep going north. That means the winter will be sooner, and longer, and colder. Everyone keeps warning us that things get very difficult and dangerous past here." She turned to look directly at me. "Couldn't you be happy with a winter haven near here? It's really awfully wild and we could . . ."

I put my finger on her lips. "Just listen. What do you hear?"

"Icebergs, exploding like thunder. And some birds."

"What else?"

"Hmm . . . dogs?"

"Exactly," I nodded. "That means a village, and that means that in the back of our minds, if anything goes wrong, we will not turn to ourselves first to solve it. We'll think in terms of rescue, not survival. It changes everything." I pulled her closer. "We've come this far. We've learned much about ice, and currents, and wind. The ice out there looks difficult, but not impossible. We're working well together, and the boat is proving itself every day. Let's keep faith and keep pushing north."

"How far? The edge of the earth? At precisely what latitude are you going to be happy?"

"I don't know. We'll get somewhere and I'll mark the spot on the chart, and I'll sit back and say, 'We did it!' It has to be like that, Di— the feeling that we really did something."

Diana withdrew into herself, wrestling with her fears. When the chilly late-August winds pierced our clothing, we hiked back down the hill. Halifax understood perfectly that to get in the dinghy meant going back to a boat void of nice stinky scat and carcasses. She backed into a small cave created by two lichen-stained boulders. Two adult humans could not outsmart her with the lure of fluffy feathers on a string, but the mocking twitter of a black-and-white snow bunting was simply too much. She charged and was shanghaied, and we rowed back to the boat.

In the galley, Diana sliced off thick slabs of smoked pork shoulder and threw them into the pressure cooker with assorted beans, dehydrated vegetables, spices, and water. There would be little time to cook in the days to come. The pressure cooker rendered the toughest of foods edible and saved time and fuel. Most importantly, it had a lid that sealed tight. In the event of knockdown winds or an ice collision, the pot might still become a dangerous missile, but the scalding contents could not spray across the cabin.

Diana filled the lanterns and stove, laid out facemasks, thick gloves, and layers of wool socks. I siphoned fuel from the jerry cans on deck into the main tank, pumped full the day tank, which gravity-feeds the engine, and checked the engine oil, water, and transmission fluid levels. Next I changed a broken impeller on the saltwater pump that feeds cooling water to the engine. An impeller normally lasts a year at least, yet this six-bladed rubber wheel was already the third of the four extra we'd stocked. I thought the cold water might be making the rubber brittle, or that ice slush was being sucked up through the raw-water strainer and chafing the thin blades. With each mile we traveled north into thickening ice, the engine became more critical. Even if winds happened to be perfect for winding our way through narrow ice leads, we would have little control over our speed, and no reverse under sail. There would be plenty of wrong turns and box canyons ahead. *Damn!* I thought. *I planned every last detail. I have backups for my backups. Even when the money was almost gone, I bought twice the number of spares I thought we could ever need. Now, it comes down to this—the entire expedition spins around a little rubber starfish.*

That led me to another gnawing concern: the nature of the coastline north of Melville Bay. Until this point a tortured tumble of rock splintered into many fjords, bays, and islands, all offering protection. But from Cape York at Melville's northern end onward, the coast swept this way and that in long, smooth arcs. Moving across the nautical chart, I penciled question marks over even the slightest indentations.

The barometer remained high and steady. Winds were light, the air dry and fog-free. We could hardly ask for more, except a little sleep. With all sail set, the *Roger Henry* entered the wide lead curving from southeast to northwest. I scrambled up the mast to make long-range navigational decisions, peering forward of the bow and calling out quick evasions around ice that looked large enough to hurt. Diana dashed back and forth from the helm to the sheets for a quick tack. Neither of us saw much of our warm berth below.

In spite of all the action, when the endemic fog set in, staying warm required a constant flow of hot broths and teas. The effects were predictable, and the call of nature was insistent. I chose a stretch of open water, dashed to the rail, stripped the safety harness to slip the foul weather jacket over my head, to get at the bib overall zipper, to get through puzzling layers of clothing with frozen fingers toward a recalcitrant digit wisely retreating from the cold. As if it were an immutable law of nature, halfway through my relief mission the yacht swung toward an implacable ice pan. I stretched my foot backward, trying to reach the tiller without losing my balance. Woahhh! No good. I turned back to the rail, calculating speed and distance to impact. There's time. No! Collision minus five seconds! At this point, you do what you have to do, humiliation aside. But after a couple of these Keystone Kop routines, I screwed an eyebolt into the long boathook and fastened it to the tiller. This allowed me to stand up and outboard, using this extension to simultaneously control the course and the flow of events, so to speak.

The rapidly decreasing temperature shortened effective watchkeeping. In warmer waters, if we both were too exhausted to sail on safely we would simply heave-to, which means to reduce sail size, tie the headsail off to one side, and fly a reduced mainsail on the other. This stops the boat's forward progress but steadies its motion. Here in the ice, this tactic was actually dangerous, for it made us a sitting target for the always moving ice. Eighty percent of any iceberg we saw lay beneath the water's surface; thus, it moved more to the forces of current than wind. The three-hundred-foot-high iceberg to our port was affected by currents running much deeper than those affecting the two-hundred-foot iceberg to our starboard; the two ice mountains might move toward each other with titanic force, capable of pulverizing anything in their path. This required a constant eye and occasional hurried evasion.

We became battle fatigued to a point where only sleep, sweet sleep, mattered. We took turns slipping gratefully into a thick, warm sleeping bag, each trusting life itself to the judgment of the other. Still, it took discipline on top of that deep fatigue to sleep while ice banged off the hull and the yacht shuddered in protest. With the sun now dipping below the horizon again, we crossed the seventy-fifth parallel doing four knots on a north-northwest heading, as all the while I tried to answer Diana's eminently reasonable question: "How far is far enough?"

Dangerous fog rolled in, yet strangely, the wind increased. From the cockpit I could not see past the bow rails. The radar probed the mist with its high-frequency signals, which bounced back off a maze of icebergs ahead. I shortened sail and fired up the engine. Within minutes, the temperature gauge climbed into the red. I shut it down and woke Diana. She crawled out of the aft cabin dutifully, but tired and worried. She took the helm while I shut off the raw-water intake, drained the system, and opened the pump to see bits of black rubber dribbling out. I installed the last impeller but did not restart the engine. I could not expect it to last any longer than the others, so we had to proceed as if engineless, saving the last impeller for a real emergency. Something had to be done.

Our marine engine was cooled by internal fresh water much like an automobile engine is, but because the yacht does not move through the air at rapid speeds, this water must pass through a heat-exchanger where circulating cold seawater absorbs the heat and is then pumped overboard. It was this saltwater pump that now malfunctioned. There was no parts store to dash to, no expert to call in. This required the innovative mix of mechanics and mojo called jury-rigging, which asks only the basic question: What needs doing here? Answer: Remove heat from this engine.

While Diana wrestled with phantoms in the fog, my mind raced. *Maybe I could tap into the engine's internal fresh water, run that through the motorcycle radiator I have stashed in the bilge, wire up a twelve-volt fan behind the radiator, and dissipate the heat that way. No, stupid! The exhaust gasses would not be water cooled and would melt their rubber hosing in minutes. Well, then, I could plumb up the manual bilge pump to the head water-intake line and then hand-pump water continuously through the engine. Great, how many hours of that are you good for? Think! Turn the problem inside out, stand it on its head. The electric bilge pump works only if the batteries are charged, which happens only if the engine runs well and often, a Catch-22. It's a sump-type that draws water up from a perforated base. I could plumb its output into the engine, create an intentional leak to fill the bilges at a rate close to that at which the intake draws, dangerous but . . . Wait—I've got it! I can drop that pump into a paint bucket, cut holes into the side to run the intake and output hoses through, then silicone them watertight. That way, if I place the bucket below the waterline, I have a watertight chamber with a positive water pressure.* Neither of us slept much until the red algae–stained snow on the Crimson Cliffs of Cape York appeared through the mist two days later.

At the change of watch, Diana said, "We have to go into Thule Air Base for help."

"I don't want help," I snapped back. "If this is an exercise in self-sufficiency, then we can't go running to Big Brother at the first sign of trouble. Anyway, it's a security zone, off-limits."

"They must have a radio. Just call them and see. They might have the part or someone who can give you good advice."

When Diana finally decides to dig in her heels, they are more like crampon spikes. At ocher-colored Cape Atholl we turned east into the long fjord that leads to the base. From twenty miles out I tried the marine single sideband emergency frequency 2182 kHz, which is monitored by most ships and ports.

"U.S. Air Force Base Thule, U.S. Air Force Base Thule, this is Whiskey Charlie Gulf 4377, yacht *Roger Henry* on 2182." Nothing.

With the fog lifting, from five miles out we could see the bristle of antennae and a cluster of buildings. I called on the short-range VHF channel 16, also universally monitored. Nothing. A mile out, I hove-to for an hour thinking that surely some vigilant sentry would notice our presence and contact us. Nothing. I motored into the bay fronting the base and sat, blowing the foghorn. Nothing. Finally, frustrated, I motored back and forth along the jetty right in front of the harbormaster's office window. Then it hit the fan. People started running around and waving their arms. We anchored the yacht, launched the dinghy, and rowed to shore. Two agitated United States Air Force armed guards met us.

"What are you doing here?" they demanded. "This is a high-security area. You can't be here. No boats ever come here. You can't be here."

"I tried to contact you," I explained. "I have a problem. It's only mechanical, but up here that can be serious. I need an impeller blade for a Jabsco water pump. They're very common. It's a big base, lots of machinery. Is it possible that you could sell me a spare, or even another model I could carve down to size?"

They took us by truck to the port captain's office and explained that the docking facility was Danish Territory, serving the base but technically not part of it. The port captain was a big Dane, full of muscle and good cheer. I told him our problem, and he was sympathetic. He said that, up here, people had to help each other. The guards were not so sure and first wanted to "interview" (read, *interrogate*) me. They met my explanation of our plans with blank, uncomprehending stares. They copied all the details of the ship's registration and crew list, stepped into the next room, and contacted the base commander by radio.

After a long wait, one guard returned and said in a style not his own, "All spare parts are property of the United States Government. We cannot sell machinery or parts for any purpose."

"Can you give it away?" I asked.

"No. Number One says that we cannot help you and that you must leave. We don't want an international incident."

"A what?" I asked incredulously.

"International incident. Those were Number One's exact words."

I tried to control my tone. "Well, we don't want one of those, do we? Thank you anyway. We'll be on our way."

The big Dane jumped in. "Boys, boys. Look, we provide the bus service on the base. That's all Danish property. Why don't you swing past the bus depot and ask Hendrick to dig around the parts room."

The guard said, "I dunno. I don't need no trouble with Number One."

The Dane kept cajoling. "Come on, boys—the Cold War's over. Look out there. There's tourists running around this damn base! There's a hotel, a restaurant. C'mon, just swing by the depot."

The two guards gave in but wanted to double-team me, so we dropped Diana off at the dinghy. At the depot, dusty-blond young Hendrick was helpful and imaginative as we talked over the problem. While he didn't have an impeller, he did have a used twelve-volt circulation pump from a bus heater. It had hard plastic blades and might be useful. I thanked him and left, in as much hurry to get back on board as the guards were to be rid of me.

At the dinghy, I told them we were utterly exhausted and asked if we could sleep before setting sail, promising to remain on board. They called Number One. He ordered them to first inspect the boat and only then approved a maximum three-hour stay. I spent two of those installing the pump—which, incidentally, is still in there and working fine.

As we sailed away, I sadly looked over my shoulder at the exact spot that Knud Rasmussen and Peter Freuchen first called *Ultima Thule*. The Last Unknown is no longer. With radars and radios and airplanes and rockets, they were defending freedom as they understand it. By pushing on north and out of this region entirely, I was defending freedom as I understand it.

Our original plan called for sticking close to the coast. At the first sign of a cold snap we could duck in anywhere, and anywhere would be better than being caught out. Perhaps tiredness eroded sound judgment, or maybe I overreacted to the "incident at Thule," but I somehow talked myself right out of that good thinking. Much to Diana's dismay, we set a course offshore, direct for the Kane Basin, 150 difficult miles to the north. This long body of water lying between Ellesmere Island and Greenland is constricted like an hourglass at the entrance. To the north, in the ever-rotating Arctic Ocean, ice floes break off in epic scale and drift down the Kane Basin toward these narrows, where they compress into a grinding congestion. But just fifteen meager miles beyond that danger lies Etah.

On world maps and globes, cartographers have room to list only the world's great centers: Paris, New York, Moscow . . . and Etah. Etah? It is a lot of nothing in the middle of nowhere, yet it warrants bold print in every atlas. Not a living human soul is there, yet this spot, where English officers Ross and Parry contacted the first "Polar Eskimo" in 1818, remains inexplicably etched into Western memory, the scene forever captured by an Inuk artist named John Sacheuse from southern Greenland. He stood between the two races, interpreting as best his distant dialect of Inuktitut allowed, and skillfully sketched the strange scene. Until Ross and Parry's ship, with its giant white wings, had appeared from over the horizon, the secluded Inughuit, two-hundred-strong, had thought themselves the only human beings on earth—a philosophical perspective almost too profound to imagine today. The English officers presented a ludicrous sight, standing in full dress regalia with polished and pointed shoes punching through the soft snow. Dandy feather plumes swept back from pointed hats that would neither stay on in a wind nor warm heads and ears. The mystified Inughuit asked, "Are you from the Sun or the Moon?"

The closer we crept through the thickening floes, the more excited I became, knowing we had achieved the same latitude that William Baffin had in 1616, a record not bettered for another 236 years. I imagined a powerful magnet somewhere in the ice ahead, pulling the *Roger Henry* forward through any barrier toward this mysterious place. I tested it out loud, "Etah." It sounded like the word *destiny* in an ancient tongue.

"We're only thirty miles away," I excitedly told Diana. "I can almost see it. It may be abandoned now, but Dr. Cook, Robert Peary, and Donald MacMillan used it to winter over. Why, Elisha Kent Kane intentionally beset himself even north of there!"

Diana had read all the books and remembered the details too well. "Our intention was never to set a record for the farthest point north," she argued. "We used too much fuel getting here. These people you mention had enormous boats and huge crews, and there are only the two of us. Kane's boat was trapped for two years, then crushed. Peary's was violently pushed ashore. MacMillan was dropped off and told he would be relieved the next season. It was *four years* before a ship could break through!"

"Oh . . . Yes, that's right."

I climbed the mast as much to escape from logic as to see ahead. I did not want to hear another word. *Why can't this woman understand?* I thought, denial tasting particularly good for the moment. The last thing I wanted was to be confused with the facts. I looked out on a heady view of that which so few have dared—true wilderness. Ellesmere Island lay large on the western horizon. That name rings synonymous with adventure, and I ached to walk its shores. The horizon was solid white; we could make no straight progress. Between the old floes, new ice was forming like congealing fat. The prognosis from the Danish Navy indicated bad weather approaching, but at best these forecasts were general and often overridden by local factors. I tried to dismiss the reports in spite of a fast-falling barometer. Cape Alexander, the sentinel to the Kane Basin, was disappearing in dense fog. We might round it, but if the wind strengthened before we reached the protection of Etah, the grinding polar pack ice would trap us. I looked back at the miles of dense ice through which we had wound our way. A wind shift would compress it quickly, blocking any retreat. *Should we make for the village of Qaanaaq, refuel, and wait?* I had to decide. Ahead, only half a day's travel after half a lifetime's dreaming, there at my fingertips was all the history, all the glory of the North, but that too is the story of the North. You cannot be too timid, nor too bold. You must simply be *right*, exactly and every time. I tried to make all the factors add up to what I wanted them to say: *Press on!*

My head was spinning. I clung to the mast. *Think! What have you learned? Remember the lesson of Kane's unchecked ambition: "Prudence and foolhardiness lie within sight of each other up here." But what about "Fortune favors the brave"? If you hesitate out of fear, then you must move directly toward that fear.*

That thought was based on the silly notion that all fear is unfounded. Still, I might have made the mistake of rushing headlong forward had I not looked down just then from the high masthead. We were butted up against an ice wall. The boat was lost in the brash of ice chips and dwarfed into insignificance by giant floes. Diana stood on the bow. I looked up and out on this tumbled ice and terrible land, and then down again. She looked so small, so vulnerable. I had dreamed just the night before of our home being crushed, Diana thrown into the

black waters, trying to scream but only managing a feeble whisper:
"Help me, Alvah, help me." And then it hit me—hard. I realized how
possible, perhaps probable, that dream was, and I thought my heart
might break. *My God, what am I doing? I've pushed myself this far
north, but I have pulled that poor woman. I'm up here blathering
about the virtues of bravery. What about trust? What about responsibility? No, we are not just at the edge of the ice—we are at the edge of
our experience and endurance.*

I shouted down to Diana, "Please enter in the log 77 degrees, 45 minutes, our farthest point north. You're right; we cannot go farther safely."

She exhaled a long-held breath and rolled her eyes skyward as if a
prayer had been answered. That she wasn't already in open mutiny was
a testament to her toughness. We turned to the southeast and steamed
for Qaanaaq. Diana had seen the accumulating signs of approaching
trouble, and she knew that nature always speaks the truth. An hour
after we altered course the *Piteraq* struck.

Sixty-knot winds howled off the ice cap. The sea boiled. Ice boulders
heaved and rolled on its surface. It is that rumbling noise, as if the ice is
calling out your name, that is most terrifying. We made a run for Herbert Island, looking for protection in its lee, but there was no lee. The
wind blasted us from port, then starboard, then astern, then from
above. Currents rammed the ice in behind the island. Waves pounded
the shores. Clouds hurtled across the sky in confusion. Tying off to
floes that were fifty to five hundred feet long, we trailed along behind,
letting them clear out the smaller brash in their path, but then they
would spin and press us toward another danger. At one point, caught
in the fork of a Y closing with the point of a wedge, we frantically cast
off. We pulled clear just as the ice vise slammed shut. We tucked in behind another. I jumped onto the slippery floes and, one after another,
frantically pounded ice screws into each one's hard surface, shouting
above the din for Diana to throw me a line so I could pull the boat up
tight to its edge. For a while we would remain safe; then the pan would
rotate and we'd be squeezed out. Onto another, then another, always
being pushed down toward Qaanaaq.

After twenty-four hours of this, we passed into the real maelstrom.
The winds rolled off the smooth ice cap, then funneled into steep val-

leys that turbocharged them into screeching williwaws seemingly bent on our destruction. In the open roadstead in front of the village of Qaanaaq, we hove-to, laid ahull, and ran before it. The wind shrieked in the rigging, wearing on our nerves.

Two more days of battle left us exhausted. Too spiritless to fight it any longer, we moved in closer to shore and tried to anchor. We dragged anchor and reanchored a dozen times. My arms ached. I did not think I could haul on the heavy chain again when, finally, the anchor held. But then, to windward, three building-sized blocks of ice pressed down on us. I did not want to weigh anchor again—anything but that. I considered risking that the shallow icebergs would narrowly miss us. These are the dangerous moments, when body and will weaken, when one is tempted to do something less than the right thing.

I hauled away until my arms screamed in protest. I grabbed the handle of the windlass and, with furious strokes, started to ratchet-in the rope attached to the long anchor chain. Just as I threw all my weight into it, the windlass jammed. I heard a snap in my back and fell down in white-light pain. The berg bore down on us steadily. I screamed to Diana at the helm for help. Hand over hand, with me on my knees sweating in pain, we pulled the rope until we could run it aft to a halyard winch on the mast. We ground away, our bodies aching and hearts thumping. The anchor clanged into its rollers just as an ice wall towered over the *Roger Henry*. There was a shudder, then the protest of twisting steel. I watched in horror as a steel stanchion collapsed in slow motion. I rammed the boathook into the berg, planted my feet, and spun us off, paying dearly for that exertion.

Diana ran back to the helm, slapped the gear lever forward, and swung away to avoid the next threat. The engine screeched and belched black smoke. Above the roar of the engine and the howl of those winds, we shouted to each other the location of approaching dangers like a bomber under fighter attack: "Two o'clock, two o'clock!" When the wind stripped the words out of our mouths we resorted to a series of hand signals developed over our years together. And when we said to each other that it simply could not blow much longer, it did, with even more fury.

After three days the storm vented its rage, and conditions abated a little. Relieved, I thought our ordeal would soon be over. By chance I looked back and, heading out over the last ice pan, skipped a happy Halifax. Our thoughts were of survival, hers of freedom. Philosophically, she outranked us, but I was plenty mad just the same. We raced back. I scrambled over the treacherous ice while Diana fought to control the vessel. The more frantic I became, the louder I shouted, the farther Halifax fled. Finally, I sat on the ice as if it was a quiet day in the park. Halifax ran back to me, enticing me back into the chase. I pounced on her and pressed her back into onboard service.

I lay on the bow, trying to relax the torn muscles in my lower back and sneak some sleep between intermittent dramas. The cold wind searched for entrances into my foul weather gear, but if I huddled just right I could husband a modicum of dryness and warmth. In spite of the pain, fatigue, wind, waves, and ice, I realized I was thoroughly enjoying myself. This was true adventure, life in the North, as it was, as it still can be. We were privileged to be able to share in its harsh reality. That privilege, however, lasted four full days, stretching us to our limits.

When the storm was over, Diana tended the boat while I managed to get ashore at Qaanaaq (the Far North), a ramshackle town of five hundred Inuit scattered across an open slope. There is no natural harbor and no apparent reason for placing a town in that forlorn wind tunnel. The entire hamlet was resituated there from Thule when the United States Air Force leased that land from the Danish government. A condition of the lease was that no habitation be allowed near the air base. Even a people this remote became pawns in a Cold War that contested every inch of the sky, earth, and sea. While the Soviets and Americans were the combatants, neither was the loser. Fortunately, the Inuit are accustomed to shifting fortunes.

The presence of that base with its jumbo landing strip broke the seal that held the far North in impenetrable remoteness. Change crept in like water on a floodplain, its tendrils probing in different directions. Their lives now span the Stone Age to the space age. High antennae and satellite dishes make useful landmarks for homebound kayaking harpoonists. Grocery stores, with frozen-food sections full of fish caught in Greenland, shipped to Denmark, and re-imported to Greenland, do a brisk trade in expensive colas and chips. Racks at the checkout counter conveniently display last-minute necessities—bread, milk, matches, pornographic movies.

A people whose minds conceive in circles now live in square, modern houses. Modern but inferior, for the rough wooden shacks refuse to hold their heat, and immense diesel tanks flank the town. Now there need not be darkness, for when the sun goes off the generators go on. Those generators power the VCRs that fill their heads with images of the Rambo culture to the south and the feeling that their lives pale in comparison.

But from those lit doorways still emerge thick-chested men with flat, wise faces framed in bangs of straight, ebony hair. They walk with the shuffling gate of slick-surface dwellers into a world they know well. They are clad in sealskin boots, polar bear–fur pants, and long parkas fringed in wolf or wolverine, and they carry draped over their shoulders rifles, nets, and spears. Always near at hand are their razor-sharp steel blades—blades that were like a gift from God to ease their lives. Robert Peary was that god. But the blades were not gifts, they were payment for dogs, meat, and hard service. After an unsuccessful attempt on the North Pole, Peary hauled back and sold at great profit to an American museum the two meteorites that were the Inughuit's only traditional source of tool-making material. The steel blades he left in their stead were clearly superior, but they created a dependency. Peary would need the Inuit's loyalty for another attempt on the Pole. He was a brilliant man; it is safe to assume he understood this.

The Inuit remain a hunting people, highly skilled and proud. All the modern paraphernalia has not changed their elemental connection with the land. To this day, in these frigid waters, men paddle kayaks of stretched skin or fabric over wooden frames. Lashed on their foredecks are seal-stomach air sacks tethered onto whalebone-tipped harpoons. Like their fathers and forefathers before them, they sit in trancelike patience, slowing the passage of time to the cadence of the drips falling from their double-bladed paddles. Silently they wait for the rise of their quarry from beneath. When a greasy swell lifts the surface, they slash forward with quick strokes, pouncing on their prey of walrus, narwhal, or whale. With a mighty and well-aimed heave, a hunter plunges his crescent-tipped lance deep into the animal's vitals. The beast explodes in pain and fury. The hunter pulls the shaft free from the embedded tip and flakes out the hissing, bearded-seal–hide rope until the prey pulls the connected float clear of the kayak deck. This requires exceptional skill and timing to avoid becoming entangled, capsized, gored, or crushed. Another hunter darts in and strikes, then another. Each must leave his marker in the animal to share in its parts. The battle continues, small men in frail boats working in unison against the giant creatures of the deep. Gushing buckets of blood and exhausted by its efforts to dive with floats and lines in tow, the animal finally succumbs.

If the animal taken is a narwhal, first the savory *mataq* (the outer skin with an inch-thick layer of fat) is ceremoniously flensed off. With its delicate hickory nut flavor, this is the real prize. Then the men carve the meat without finesse into massive chunks and place it in more or less equal piles. One village elder faces the line of hunters, with his back to the meat piles. Another elder, unseen by the first, points a spear toward a pile while the first calls out a name. It is a random and fair way to divide the animal. The meat is then further distributed by complicated personal social contracts.

Because the Inuit believe all living things have souls, and they do not separate themselves from the animal world, the very concept of hunting is inverted. They believe their quarry *chooses* to be killed. That is, if a hunter is particularly respectful and always remembers to pour water into the mouth of a dead seal to relieve its thirst, then the spirit of that seal will reincarnate as another seal and spread the word. Seals will flock to his spear.

A traditional song of the Spring Fjord Eskimos reveals the softer side of these hunters' hearts and their sense that they share this world with others:

> I was out in my kayak
> And the seal came gently to me
> Why didn't I harpoon him?
> Was I sorry for him?
> Was it the day, the spring day
> The seal playing in the sun like me?

No outboard engines are allowed in the rich hunting waters of the Inglefield Fjord. The Inughuit do not want to frighten away or offend the animals. The quaint notion that an animal might be *offended* by the behavior of humans still persists. As snowmobile hunting is also strictly forbidden, sleds and kayaks remain the Inuit's basic survival tools, both physically and culturally.

I bought fuel from the co-op and dragged it down to the dinghy in five-gallon jerry cans. I lifted one into the dinghy and then collapsed in pain. A man stood on the beach, staring at me impassively. He was perhaps forty, well dressed, and not as robust as many of the Inughuit. When I tried again with the same result, he offered to help.

He introduced himself in passable English. "I am Oscar the Eskimo."

I caught my breath. "Nice to meet you, Oscar the Eskimo. I am Alvah the American."

"Oh, American." He frowned.

"Why aren't you out hunting with the rest?"

"I am businessman now," he said proudly. He pointed up the hill. "That building up there: Qaanaaq's first hotel for tourists." His tone became somber. "Maybe last."

"Why? I read that Denmark and Greenland were spending lots of money advertising. They say tourism is going to explode up here."

"It is. Well, it was. See, the airplanes land at American Air Base in Thule and the people change to the big helicopters to come here. If you are not from Qaanaaq, you need letter from native inviting you here. I had group, thirty German tourists coming this week for dogsled trips and watching whales. First big group ever. They want to pay the hunters plenty of money and rent all my rooms. And they like plenty souvenirs. Our boats and sleds were ready. Our women were making the food. The season is short here, this was our whole year. Did you meet the base commander?"

"Well, indirectly."

"I thought a reservation for tour group was better than letter. They had faxes, tickets, tour guide. They flew all the way from Germany. Other people he let through, but he would not let them pass through the base. No letter. They are sitting in a Quonset hut on the base for five days now. They are wait for a plane to take them back to Germany. They are very mad."

"What about you?"

"We are Inughuit. We do not like to be mad, but . . ." He shrugged.

We talked about the storm. He told me that in living memory his people had not seen such a thing. Kayaks and heavy boats had cart-wheeled down the beach. The thought that we were nearly caught in the Kane Basin during such a blow made me shudder. Oscar showed no surprise or undue concern when I explained our plans. After all, winter-ing in the Arctic was not exactly a new concept to these people. I asked him if he knew what conditions were now in the Kane Basin. He said the northerly wind would certainly have closed it off completely. That eliminated both Etah and Otto Sverdrup's 1898 wintering site of Fram Haven on Ellesmere Island.

We talked about other possibilities. The coast leading down toward Qaanaaq was impenetrable, and the area immediately around Qaanaaq was flat, unbroken coastline, offering no hint of protection. Oscar cau-tioned that we must choose quickly. It had been a cold summer, and he expected an early winter. Time was ticking. Options were fading. We still could choose to winter in Bowdoin Bay in the Inglefield Fjord. Admiral Donald MacMillan had wintered there in his sturdy little schooner *Bowdoin* in 1923. It had history; it was protected. I asked Oscar if bears would be much of a problem.

He said, "Bears? No, not many bears here now. Too many people. All the bears are at the big glacier [Humboldt]. Caribou and musk ox gone too."

A blind-side rabbit punch could not have stunned me more. Our mission, which to date had required enormous energy and commit-ment, was not simply to seek out a cold place. You can find that in Fargo, North Dakota. Rather, we had been in search of a timeless Arc-tic experience, an experience upon which we might build a deep under-standing of the land and then the people, and through that, ourselves. Had I overromanticized—and underestimated—the forces of change even at this, the northernmost outpost in the world?

I rowed back to the *Roger Henry*. Diana was waiting expectantly on the deck, anxious to end our long search, to settle somewhere, anywhere, and now.

I reported, "Seems our only option locally is Bowdoin Bay. It's only twenty miles from a village and has very little wildlife." I hesitated. "I know that, up here, twenty miles in winter is a very long way—but is it long enough?"

"Long enough for what?" she demanded.

How do you explain, Long enough to find *Ultima Thule?* "Well, to authenticate the adventure," I said.

"Whatever *that* means," she huffed. "Anyway, if it's the only bay left open, then we'll just have to make do."

"Maybe it's not all we have. Diana, I want to cross Baffin Bay into Canadian waters."

Her jaw dropped. I rushed ahead. "I want to attempt Dundas Harbor on Devon Island in Lancaster Sound. Our charts show no spot in the Arctic more remote—a massive island and not a single human. [I did not stop to wonder why.] There will be musk ox, bear, Peary caribou, even arctic wolf. There are old buildings still standing from the abandoned police station. If we had to abandon the *Roger Henry*, Eric said there may even be old drums of fuel still full and just lying out on the tundra."

Diana shook her head. "And two weeks ago it may have been a safe option. Do I have to go get the calendar for you? It's open sea. It's September. We are above seventy-five degrees."

"I know all that."

"What about your back? You can hardly walk."

"It'll be all right with time."

"Look, I have sailed around the world with you. I know that a boat can have only one captain, and you've been a good one. I've trusted you. I have to keep trusting you, but you are obsessed with this one. *No one* knows what's right or what's wrong up here. I know you have to follow your gut feeling, but you have to use your head too." She looked right through me. "You can be stubborn to the point of stupidity, but you're honest. I'll do it if you can look me in the eye and tell me it's best."

If faith and goodwill were currency, I'd have spent my last. I said, "It's best." She had said it exactly right: It was a contest between my head, heart, and gut. The majority voted to go.

She turned, went below, and started filling the pressure cooker with fatty foods for the cold ordeal ahead. With all sails set and the engine pounding, we sailed by Cape Parry and back out into Baffin Bay. This was a lottery, and the longer we were in it, the worse were our chances. By the next day we were already off the scattered slate hummocks called the Carey Oer Islands. Forlorn and lonely, few places on earth have known less human interference. I wondered if, being in a known polynya area, the islands might remain in open water through the winter. I didn't want to risk the time required to scout out possible anchorages, but I did what I could with the charts and binoculars to familiarize myself in the event we were forced back by a flash freeze.

On the second day we ran into the grinding river of ice flowing south out of the Kane Basin, propelled by the storm. The ice butted up against the southern coast of Ellesmere and blockaded Jones Sound. We turned south and skirted the pack just a hundred yards to our starboard.

As we rounded under Devon Island, my heart sank. The entire Lancaster was fenced off. The ice cover was heavy, but the ice was broken and brashy. We might still be able to ram our way through. It would be a high-stakes bet that the barrier was a thin one. How far in would I venture before turning around? Ten miles? What if it was more compressed in its interior, as might be expected? Did we have the power and weight to ram through? Even if we did, how much fuel would it take? How much time? When would winter fall?

I shut down the engine, and the *Roger Henry* drifted silently. I put my face into my cupped hands. I was done in. I thought, *We are plodding along, mile after mile, day after day, fueled on my vague faith that the waters will remain open. What is this faith based on? I'm a lucky man, but luck is not a substitute for skill and preparation, nor is it a license for recklessness.*

I jumped below and again looked up the average freeze-up dates in the Ice Atlas. At our latitude, we had scant days left. But an average is the divided sum of freeze-ups after *and* before that date. I turned to the pages of worst-case scenarios, which showed years so bleak that the ice snapped shut in late August or early September. Oscar said that this was a bad year. The watch calendar blinked September 4, September 4, September 4, and my stomach churned.

There were many factors to consider. Battering through thick ice sucks up diesel, which is to the modern Arctic traveler what marine-mammal fat was to the old Inuit: a lifeline substance. We had at least one year through which we must drive the boat to its final destination. We must heat it, melt water, cook, burn lanterns, and have enough diesel remaining to safely return to the nearest possible fueling station.

Another problem was one of officialdom. Having never intended to winter in Canada, we had no entry permit nor customs exemption for the vessel. This far north, formalities are traditionally more lax, but presenting the authorities with a radioed *fait accompli* was pushing the limits of courtesy and legality.

We paralleled the ice south toward Bylot Island, which forms the southern shore of Lancaster Sound. The barricade ended too near that coast. If we entered the thin lead and the wind went north, we would be caught between the proverbial rock and a hard place: the granite cliffs of Bylot and sixty miles of pack pressure. We could turn back for Greenland, push through into Lancaster Sound, or pass under Bylot Island into Eclipse Sound and attempt Dundas Harbor from Navy Board Inlet. In this baffling mix of wind, current, ice, and stone there was no logic to lead me. I wavered.

With the strength of certainty, Diana said, "Alvah, you are injured, stressed, tired, and indecisive at a time we can ill afford delay. You are in no condition now to do battle with that ice pack. We *must* turn under Bylot Island."

She chose a critical moment to get tough with me. My hand pushed the helm over to starboard. We swung out to port and down around the east coast of the mountainous island, named after the mutinous Robert Bylot. In 1610, as Henry Hudson's first mate, Bylot participated in the mutiny that set Hudson, his young son, and loyalist crew adrift in a small boat in a huge bay far to the south. Hudson pleaded for a fowling gun—anything that would give them at least a fighting chance—but his requests were denied and his small group was never heard from again. The events leading to this were typical of most Arctic mutinies: The captain wanted to push on into the misty abyss, the crew wanted to be done with this horrid nightmare and turn for home. Bylot should have been hung at the dock upon his return, but the Admiralty

showed its true colors and real priorities. Not only did his feat of seamanship in returning the valuable ship intact win his reprieve; he was
immediately awarded command of the vessel. He captained two more
voyages of exploration to the Arctic. No doubt he governed with a
heightened sensitivity toward his crew. His gifted pilot, William Baffin,
who carefully charted and noted details of the voyages, eclipsed Bylot's
historical recognition, as the immense Baffin Island and Baffin Bay took
his name.

At Bylot Island's southeastern tip, we swung west into narrow Eclipse
Sound. More miles required more time, time we might not have, but
Diana was right—there would be a Royal Canadian Mounted Police Station in Pond Inlet, where we could do the right thing as guests in this
great nation. We might also get fuel and local advice.

Soon after we altered course, strong winds shifted to the north and
the first snows of the year began to fall. To be in Lancaster Sound now
would have meant serious jeopardy. Instead, Bylot Island blocked the
ice and we sailed through clear and calm waters past Albert Harbor,
hidden behind Beloeil Island. The diary of an old-time whaler trapped
here read, "A more desolate, bleak, and forbidding spot than Albert
Harbor can hardly be imagined."

Had I agreed with that assessment, we would have stopped and wintered right then and there. Also in disagreement was the unsung hero of
Canadian exploration, Captain J.E. Bernier, who intentionally wintered
his ship there in 1906. Bernier did have his problems, though. The
breakup left his icebound ship a heartbreaking one mile from open
water, and it appeared they would remain trapped for a second year, an
eventuality he feared his crew was not up to. Bernier was both clever
and determined. He had his men shovel soot from the steam furnace
onto the ice in a long line leading out into clear water. The black dust
sucked up solar radiation and, as if cut by a laser, the ice underneath
melted into a trench. With that chink in the ice's armor and a nudge
from a little dynamite, they opened a lead and escaped. We had already
collected a full bag of soot and stashed it below, along with a handful
of small explosives.

We anchored in the roadstead off Pond Inlet, a hunting community
of eight hundred Inuit. It sits on a high spot on the rolling tundra on

Baffin Island's northern shoreline, facing across the ten-mile-wide Eclipse Sound toward Bylot's southern shore. We were stunned into silence by what we saw, for not the Alps nor the Andes could outshine that shoreline in dramatic beauty.

Although parts of Baffin Island lie below the Arctic Circle, it has always been known to the Inuit as *Auyuittuq,* the land that never melts. It is the world's fifth largest island, covering more land than Sweden and, if possible, even steeper and starker than Greenland.

It is likely that the Vikings, under Erik the Red, were the first non-natives to view its shore from the high mountains across Davis Strait. Nordic sagas indicated, and archeological digs confirmed, that Vikings had landed as far north as Ellesmere Island; from there they pushed their way south to Bylot, Baffin, Labrador, and finally to known settlements such as Lance Aux Meadows in northern Newfoundland and beyond. The details are vague, but it is clear that this was an astonishing feat of seamanship and discovery, considering the state of navigation and shipbuilding in that era.

In the late 1500s, the peppery Martin Frobisher made a series of voyages to Baffin Island, then called Meta Incognita, in search of a passage to Cathay and its riches of silk, gold, and spices. To solicit interest and funding for his second and third voyages, he returned to England with lumps of iron pyrite (fool's gold) and claimed that "any man of our country that will give the attempt, may with small danger passe to Cataia." If only it were so, for even in this day of nuclear icebreakers, no commercially viable passage exists.

Pond Inlet is rough without the Greenlandic architectural charm. Square, prefabricated houses line up along muddy, littered roads. It is tacky and, on the surface, perhaps a little pitiful. On the other hand, its very good airstrip provides the regular freight and passenger service that fuel growth and modernization. There is a power station, a water plant, two stores full of varied foods, a hunting and fishing cooperative, a ramshackle hotel, a good school, a health clinic, and a charming little library. Not bad, considering its remoteness.

When Father Guy Mary-Rousseliere, known to all as Father Mary, came here in the early 1940s, he found twenty-two native people. The rest were scattered across the land in their seminomadic search for game. Father Mary devoted the next thirty years to helping and understanding these people. Few foreigners have ever grown more intimate with the Inuit. He was a sensitive man who deeply appreciated the native culture and spirit. He did not miss the irony in his efforts to better their lives when he wrote, "In Eskimo country, the bitterness of the struggle for life has always heightened the sweetness of living."

We anchored the *Roger Henry* in the open roadstead fronting Pond Inlet, then rowed to the pebble beach fringing the village. We headed for the tallest pole with the largest flag flapping, knowing officialdom would lie just beneath. The stiff-spined RCMP officer was mostly concerned with the nature of our cargo. He told me that they have a rationing system for alcohol, but some nefarious outsiders see quick profits in smuggling contraband in by boat, much like the Old West. We filled out an entry card designed for more typical travel situations. I found the incongruities amusing and had to bite my cheek to keep from smiling. Check one. Are you here primarily for business or pleasure? Well, it's not business, but I doubt it's going to be very pleasurable. Did you arrive by plane, automobile, or ship? At 36 feet, I hesitate to call it a ship. Will you be staying at a hotel? Only if Diana has her way. Do you have in your possession firearms or explosives? Lots.

I was sure it would turn some heads in Ottawa, but I was not sure the officer fully understood what I told him. I did explain our purpose, but I did so in a carefully casual tone, knowing that our ears hear only the expected. He stamped our papers, smiled, and told us in a practiced voice, "Enjoy your stay in Canada." When I stepped back into the cold, I realized I had been sweating. I had no contingency plan had he denied us permission.

We rowed back to the boat to sleep, together. Before I could lure Diana below, an open-decked workboat with a pilothouse pulled into the roadstead and anchored. I was surprised to see a boat of its size, given the shortness of the navigational season and lack of hauling facilities. Then I saw on the beach a massive old-fashioned manual capstan. A big rope and the collective muscle of the village could yank any vessel clear of harm's way. An Inuk man and a boy jumped into a rough dinghy, and I waved them over. As they approached the boat, I motioned to them to come up. They looked at each other shyly and shook their heads as if to say, no really, they couldn't. Insistent, I took their dinghy line and tied it off to the rail. They grinned and jumped up. The man was of medium height, with thick arms and an amazing barrel chest. His face was Mongolian flat, nose pressed close and wide, his eyes just slits from years of burning-bright snow. His skin was muddy brown and his smile was like a sunrise.

The Greenlandic Inuit had been somewhat aloof, hard to connect with. Here, the first hard hand I shook grabbed mine with enthusiasm. I looked into his intelligent eyes, and he stared back calmly for a long moment. We had not spoken a word, but we had already communicated. The concept of not judging a book by its cover may not apply to the human face, for by fifty, everyone has the face they deserve. I liked this man, instantly and intuitively.

I asked, "Do you speak English?"

"Yes."

"What is your name?"

"I am Charlie Inoraaq."

"Charlie, please, would you go get your family and bring them back to have lunch with us?"

He lit up and smiled that smile. In spite of his bulk, he nimbly jumped in the dinghy. An hour later he rowed out with a boat dangerously crammed full of laughing people. They scrambled on board, and Charlie headed back to the beach for the many others waiting for him. Lunch was a crowded but pleasant affair. As quartermaster, Diana worried about the amount of supplies consumed, but I felt they could not be put to better use.

I let the raven-haired children play games on the laptop computer. They were old hands on the track ball. Taking turns politely, they zapped Nazi soldiers at a record-setting pace. I took my animal books off the shelf and turned to the Arctic species. The cabin exploded into Inuktitut when the page turned to reveal the polar bear. "Nanook, Nanook!" they cried. Men jumped up, aimed imaginary rifles, mimed great hunts, poked fun at one another, and laughed with abandon. The teenage boys turned and listened attentively to every detail. We turned through the pages of bearded seals, ring seals, hooded seals, beluga, narwhal, orca, caribou, fox, musk ox, geese, ducks, ptarmigan. Their heads bobbed and grinned. They pointed this way and that. If I understood them, there was not a species that was not plentiful and near at hand. My heart started to race.

Their language was music. A background chant of agreement urged on the speaker's voice. He speaks; they hum: hmmm, ahhh, ayyyy, eeeyyy. Each sharp intake of breath means "Oh, how true."

Our cabin was packed full of Inukwarmth, laughter, and the faint smell of seal meat. I watched the smooth, dark faces, the sparkling almond eyes and small noses, their round strength that conserves body heat. I watched them cradle their young, lean against each other, always touching, always connected, and I knew I was witnessing what all my reading had only hinted at.

Although a young race of people, the Inukhave had millennia enough to absorb the tundra that absorbed them on their push across the Bering Ice Bridge, then east and north. Historically the nuances of their culture—rumors of setting the elderly adrift on ice, or euthanizing the young during famine—have seemed harsh to us. But that is because we did not put them in context with their land—*always the land.* They can be a people as cold and stark as their land. But they can be gentle and loving, laughing and light, just as their land so fleetingly is.

The Inuit have never invented a radio or a rocket ship, but they do know what the glue is that holds a community together. They have a legendary love and leniency toward their children. A child behaves as it does because it is too young to understand a better way. Hitting the child cannot change that. I had told Charlie to bring his family, and he brought the village. That is because he thinks of the village as his family and believes that every member of the community holds some responsibility for the welfare of the others.

Charlie shared a timely gift: his extensive knowledge of the surrounding land, coupled with a boater's knowledge that dealt specifically with nautical considerations. After hearing our plans, he said, "Don't do it."

"Charlie, I have to."

He nodded his head. "Then please, do not go to Dundas. I was there once. We lost a boat. Big winds, too much ice . . . and fog. Always fog."

He was telling me not to go while smiling wistfully at the memory of his own adventure. "We could not see through the fog." He squinted and swung his head back and forth, acting out the drama. "But we know from old people's story there is a rock in the middle of the mouth. Yes, the walrus like this rock very much. So we listened for their sound." He cupped his ears and swung his head searchingly. "Hhaarrrumfff, aaar-rrr, haaarruumfff." He lifted his buttock and made a long farting sound. The children exploded into laughter. "We go slow, and we smell the air. Snfffff, snfffff. No, go there," he pointed. "The smell is strong there. Then . . ." he rocked back, startled, "there is the rock! There are the fat walrus." He put his index fingers to his mouth like tusks. His voice rose in delight, "And we are in the bay!"

Charlie was boasting, but not about himself. An Inuk with any pride would never do that. It was the intricacies of nature that he was proud of. Nature provides all he needs to know. Perhaps Charlie cannot write, but he can read. The tides are written on the rocks, tomorrow's winds in the clouds, the lives of the animals in their tracks and trails, the turn of season in the flight of the birds, the depth of the coming winter in the thickness of the middle band of the woolly bear caterpillar. If it matters, it is written there. This natural literacy is the language of the earth, of pattern, relationship, and connection. It is a language nearly lost to our Western world. It is a language I long to learn.

Charlie told us there were only two alternatives to Dundas Harbor. The first was Hatt Bay, forty-five miles west in Milne Sound. He said it was a good choice—protected and maybe just close enough to Pond Inlet that we could walk out when we had an emergency. (He said "when," not "if" we had an emergency. Charlie's English was not perfect, but I did not think it was a mistake.) The second spot, Tay Bay, was little known. On the northwest coast of Bylot Island, just inside Navy Board Inlet, it was one hundred miles from Pond Inlet. Charlie shook his head and said, "In the winter, in the dark, that is too far." Charlie is as tough as they come. When he started the "abandon all hope ye who enter" talk, I knew I should listen. Still, I asked him who might have more information on Tay Bay. He smiled at my stubbornness and said only one old hunter knew it well.

Later that afternoon, I went to Old Man Jacko's wooden house on the cliff's edge over Eclipse Sound. A beautiful girl in her twenties, with long shiny hair and smoky black eyes, answered the door. She stared at me coolly.

I said, "Hello, is Jacko at home?"

"No," she said in a disinterested tone. "He is hunting."

"When will he be back?"

As if she pitied my stupidity, she answered, "When he is done hunting."

"Yes, of course. Well, maybe the hunting will be bad and Jacko will come home soon."

Again I forced her to state the obvious, "If the hunting is bad he will not come home."

"I see. Thank you." I started to turn but then asked, "Does Jacko speak English?"

"No, he is old."

My confidence could take no more. "Right, well . . ." I started to turn.

She finally took pity on me and smiled. "Come back later. I will help you talk to my grandfather."

That evening she led me through an entryway over a mountain of boots, heavy coats, fur hides, and guns and into the living room. The interior of the small house was bare bulbed, bare floored, and empty walled, offering stripped-down, run-down living, but it was warm. The main room acted as kitchen, dining room, and living room. Old Man Jacko was chewing the fat, literally, at the table with another elderly man. He did not look up. He was gray but thick, fit, and energetic. His wife sat on a couch, the only piece of furniture besides the Formica-topped table and chairs. She was shaving pieces of raw meat off a caribou haunch with a large bowie knife and deftly flicking bloody strips from the knife tip to her mouth at a steady pace. Her coal-tar–black hair hung to the floor, framing a perfectly round face on top of a perfectly round body. She was as enormous and regal as a Tongan Queen. With the smugness of a cat, she turned to get a look at me, and her blank eyes never left me for a moment. I stood there awkwardly while Jacko turned and slowly looked me up and down. He was in no hurry to put me at ease. Finally, without being asked, I took a chair between the two at the end of the table.

Jacko questioned his granddaughter. He said something to his friend and they laughed. I turned to the girl. She looked down in embarrassment.

"What did he say?"

"It is not important."

These are a people that think of the tongue as the finest cutting instrument, and the only one that sharpens with use. At public dances in days of old, rivals took turns singing songs that ridiculed each other. The song that cut deepest, using the cleverest insight into the personality and past of the other, won the loudest laughter. If it was exceptional, the loser might even be shamed into exile. This sharp taunting satisfied a need for cruelty without violence.

Jacko spoke again to his granddaughter. She turned to me. "He asks, who are you, and why are you here?"

"I am a sailor. I am here to talk about ice, and animals."

She conferred, then said, "He says, what else is there to talk about?"

"Women?"

They laughed so hard I thought they'd cry. Jacko slapped my back and poured me a cup of coffee, urging the girl to scoop more sugar into it. His wife offered me some of her raw meat, slipping the big blade beneath my nose. I asked Jacko's granddaughter to explain that I wanted to winter on board in this area. I spread my new chart over the table. I have met native people who know the land like the back of their hand but are unable to locate themselves on a map. They simply do not relate to this two-dimensional symbolism. But Jacko immediately put his finger down right on the same two spots Charlie had mentioned.

On the chart I drew two simple pictures. One was a boat sitting flat in the ice, a stick figure standing by it with a happy face. The other showed large ice boulders crushing the boat, the stick figure running away in terror. Jacko pointed to Hatt Bay, then to the happy face. I put my finger down on Tay Bay and raised my eyebrows in question. He leapt up, bared his teeth, raised his hands above his head spread like claws, and teetered toward me. He took a swipe at me with his left hand. (The Inuk swear the bear is left-handed and that you must roll to your left away from the raised paw. Scientists insist it is foolish folk-lore. There is no proof either way.) I was vividly imagining the bear's great paw thudding down upon me when I heard a sickening cracking sound. Bloody bits of meat and bone shrapnel rained down on the chart. I spun around. Jacko's wife was beating her bone with the back of the huge knife, cracking it open and sucking out the sweet raw marrow. She smiled and generously offered me some of the succulent treat.

"Ask your grandfather," I said to the girl, " if I do go to Tay Bay, or as he calls it, Kangilukuluk [little bay], will the bears attack the boat?"

"He says, Yes. They will come for you and open your boat like an egg."

"Tell him my boat is made of steel."

She did. "He says again, like an egg."

"How would he scare the bears away?"

"He says that he does not scare bears, he kills them."

"Yes, but these are not my bears. I am not supposed to kill them. Pretend, if he did want to scare bears away, how would he do it?"

She posed that question to him. He thought about it for a moment and then raised his open hands next to his head, put his thumbs into his ears, stuck his tongue out at me, and wiggled his fingers. That broke them up completely. Kabloonahs! Scare bears! They just howled amid the shower of blood and bone. Perhaps the Inuk allow a few of us in the Arctic for our sheer entertainment value.

Back on the yacht, Diana, Halifax, and I slept until we couldn't; then we sailed for Hatt Bay. Hatt is shaped like a musical note, a long thin arm leading into one edge of a perfectly round bay. It is surrounded by rolling hills rising to steep mountains. Apparently, Charlie and Jacko were right. It offered good protection and met all our criteria. We spent only one night there, during most of which I lay awake. In theory, this bay was perfect. Why, then, did I have this vague but persistent feeling that something was wrong? I dreaded trying to explain this to Diana. I expected argument; she would think the strain was becoming too much for me.

In the morning she said, "I don't like it. Something's wrong."

Based on nothing more tangible than our concurring intuition, we pushed fifty nautical miles farther north through the ice-choked waters of Navy Board Inlet. To the east lay a rocky beach spreading inland as a boulder-strewn plain, then rearing up to immense ice-clad peaks. To the west lay sheer barrier coastal cliffs rising vertically out of the dark waters into brown, layer-cake strata usually associated with desert mesas. The inlet was only five miles wide, with shores running parallel and unbroken. There was not even a hint of bight or bay to hide in.

The darkness was growing rapidly now, and we were forced to stop, looking for pools large enough to drift in safely until the blush of dawn brought relief. With this combination of darkness and ice, we were truly grateful for calm weather.

On Bylot Island's northwest coast, twelve miles south of the perpendicular junction of Navy Board Inlet and Lancaster Sound, lies Tay Bay. This is the only remnant of protection in the region. If it proved unsuitable, we were in serious trouble, because a Canadian Coast Guard facsimile ice chart clearly showed that Lancaster was not navigable and that Dundas Harbor was firmly beset. I was deeply disappointed that I would now be denied my second choice of havens.

On September 12 we encountered a long thumb of steep rock jutting deeply into Navy Board Inlet from the eastern shore. We rounded the lichen-stained, fifty-foot vertical cliffs and followed closely down their backside. This led us into a quarter-mile-wide entrance, which opened into an oval bay, two miles wide and three in length. When the wind or current swept to the south, the splayed entrance funneled small bergs and large, flatter floes into the bay. That would be dangerous unless we could tuck in behind the cliffs south of the opening for protection and into water shallow enough to ground out large ice before it could reach us. A glazing of ice held motionless the ice jumble littering the bay. Before the final freeze is laid down, for a few days or even a week ice will form during the colder night, then thaw by the following midday. It was high noon and we saw ice lying in stubborn thickness throughout the bay. I had taken us right down to the wire. It was no longer a question of *where* we would shelter, but *if* we would shelter.

In the cockpit, I closed the companionway hatch. I did not want to see the tachometer below, because there was no holding back now. I wound the engine up until it whined like a banshee, gave a good guttural yell myself, and crashed through the skim. It was, at first, glorious—man and machine versus nature. The sharp bow sliced through the ice—lifting it up, throwing it aside, and leaving a glistening ribbon of open water behind. But too soon the *Roger Henry* started to slow, then labor. I reversed out of our cut and slammed back in, carving our way just under the cliffs. We needed to get farther in, but during each attempt the boat backed up less and stopped sooner. Finally, the boat stopped dead, the engine belching black smoke. I urged it on like a child whipping a rocking horse—all that commotion standing still. I slammed it in reverse; the *Roger Henry* shuddered but did not move. I shut down the engine in surrender. My nerves were overloaded, my ears were ringing, I was breathing hard. *This is it! Our position in twenty feet of water, fifty yards from shore, one hundred miles from the nearest village, high in the Arctic, will have to do.*

I shouted, "Finally! After three and a half months of hard travel, too little sleep, too many decisions, ice, fog, rocks, and gales; finally, we can *relax!*"

Diana said. "Oh yeah? Turn around."

A giant male polar bear stormed down the gravel beach, crashed through the ice and aimed straight for us. I turned to Diana with my mouth open. Her eyes bore into me with a look that said she dearly wished she had married a farmer. I turned back toward the bear. I never knew. My goodness, he was big, and coming fast!

I spun around once slowly, taking in the mountains, the depths, the trapped freshwater bergs, the inactive glaciers. I saw the protective hook at the entrance; I saw that the bay was small enough to provide protection yet large enough to assure breakout the following year.

I smiled and said, "We're here, honey. Home at last."

FIVE

Tay Bay

SEPTEMBER 1994

14 HOURS DAYLIGHT

The most beautiful thing one can experience is the mysterious. It is the source of all true art and science. He to whom this reaction is a stranger—who no longer can pause to wonder and stand rapt in awe—is as good as dead, his eyes are closed.

—Albert Einstein

B Y NATURE, adventure cannot come in timely, premeasured amounts. The *Roger Henry* was stuck against a high ice island forty feet long, a perfect platform from which the bear could pounce. The boat itself would not be a visual deterrent because, instead of painting it the traditional Arctic red, we had left it white, hoping it would help us approach wildlife closely. From the beach, the massive predator had seen nothing out of the ordinary, just two fat seals on a block of ice.

Although ungainly on land, once under the sea-ice he moved gracefully. A shiny hummock rolled along like a tsunami beneath the milky veneer. The ripple stopped, and the bear poked his head through the ice as if it were paper. He sank silently and, with sweeps of his great forelegs, slinked forward again, and again, each time punching through the crust closer and closer, probing with those keen nostrils. The white shadow beneath the ice angled behind the adjacent floe. For a dreadful moment I could not find him. I spun around—over which rail would he explode? Then I saw a discoloration in a brash pool at the floe's edge. With the stealth of a crocodile, he lifted just his brow out of the slush. When those cold, calculating eyes locked on mine, I heard a lonely wind whistle through my bleached bones.

In the game of predator and prey, events unfold slowly through the exchange of sound and smell and through distance, but eye contact triggers explosive action. He knew we had seen him and that the element of surprise was lost, so he quickly sought his second-best advantage—high ground. He burst out of the water onto the tall pan, looming above us, fully exposed in awful dimension.

I mouthed the same words I heard Diana shout: "Oh, my God!"

He was enormous but thin. Thin means hungry, but I was too fascinated to turn away. My instincts shouted to fall back, run away, yet my muscles drew me forward as if I were caught in some magnetic force field. His brow furrowed. He was thinking, *Yes, they have seen me, but they have not snap-rolled into the water as all seals do. This is different*. He hesitated.

I whispered to Diana, "Remember the story about the two trappers being chased by a bear?" (One yelled, "Do ya think we can outrun this bear?" His partner said, "I don't have to outrun the bear. I only have to outrun *you*.") She slipped strategically between me and the narrow companionway.

I slowly reached back for the camera, thinking, *There are people who would die for this photo*. The bear quivered, flexing that half-ton of taut muscle. He poised to pounce. *Well, forget the photo*. I wished my heart would quit making so much noise, so I could concentrate. I slid my hand into my jacket and pulled out a miniature compressed-air horn. The bear's eyes riveted on my movement, his butt twitched, and his sharp claws curled into the ice, ready for takeoff. The horn's timely shriek shattered the frozen silence. The beast shook his great head at the piercing pitch and indignantly retreated a short distance. Craning his long neck, he poked his head this way and that, rocking side to side in indecisive agitation. He inched forward and lifted a plate-sized paw with a jet black underside, a paw with the power to crush a beluga's skull with a single swipe. I gave another blast, and he jumped back again.

I leapt to the rail and screamed, "Ha! I've got you on the run, Bruno."

Psalms warns that "pride goeth before destruction." I gave a third blast, and the sound of a dying duckling dribbled out. The can was now so cold that the air was no longer compressed. Bruno stepped forward, clearly regaining the edge. My sweat froze. My best hope now was a quick dive down the companionway. *He is so damn big, maybe he can't fit through the hatch*. The thought of being inside the boat with that bear was unimaginable, but I had to imagine it. *We'll hole up in the port cabin—that's where the guns are. Port cabin. Remember, chamber a round, take off the safety. The skull is too thick. Heart shot only! Oh, but I don't want to* hurt *him. Kill him or die, but do not wound this animal!*

Suddenly, the bear spun like a dust devil and slid back into the water. I breathed. He crept around the ice edge just behind the boat and stopped still in the water. With his huge paws, he deftly piled slush on his head until he was buried. He was there, right there, but when his eyes narrowed, he was gone, invisible. Incredible. Of all predators, the polar bear has perhaps the largest repertoire of hunting strategies. He had used this trick before. We would relax. We would forget. He would be ready.

I would not have chosen for our opening experience a heart-stopping encounter with a thousand-pound carnivore. Yet there was no other way to shock me into the heightened awareness and humility required to share space for a year with these wild giants. You can read about the great bear, its size and speed. You can be warned. You say, "Yeah, yeah, I know," but you cannot know until you see with your own eyes. From day one the ground rules were set: Nanook is out there, cunning and concealed. Any piece of ice could hide him; any piece of ice could *be* him. That thought was frightening yet thrilling—*ilira*.

Although legendary in their patience, polar bears know that in their precarious struggle for survival they must use time effectively. Each time the bear opened those calculating eyes, I pointed at him, yelled, and waved my coat in the air. We can't know their range of emotions, but I seriously believe this angered and embarrassed him. When he'd had enough, he turned in disgust and headed for the beach. As he hauled himself out and shook, I saw a beautiful big female with a year-ling cub slink over a tundra rise like a wisp of fog to avoid him. This was no isolated incident. We were deep in the kingdom of the Ice Bear.

As captain, it was my unfortunate duty to enter a poor performance memo into the logbook. Halifax, our bear detector, had slept through the entire episode.

For several days the ice thawed, froze, broke, and shifted. Huge, twisted hunks of multiyear ice and berg ice lay between us and the shoreline. A fierce wind from the head of the bay pressed similar box-car blocks down on us. A stanchion hooked under an ice ledge and slowly, inexorably crumpled toward the deck. We had to escape this box canyon before we were pushed ashore. As one pan bore down, we rafted to it with pitons and ropes and gunned the engine to spin the

entire pan slowly. After 180 degrees of turn, we peeled off into the alley
of clear water it had carved through the new ice, but another pan
waited there. We had to go *now!* I hauled on the anchor rope, grunting
and straining, but I could not gain an inch. The anchor was pinned beneath the ice.

"No time!" I shouted to Diana, "Put it in gear. Go, go!"

I unfastened the line from its cleat. It hissed overboard as I hurriedly
tied an orange buoy to its end. The buoy leapt over the rail just as
Diana maneuvered us clear of the oncoming ice. I rigged a second anchor while Diana threaded her way upwind. I threw it overboard in the
open-water alley less than one hundred yards from where we started. I
could only hope we had not lost the protection the cliffs provided from
the outside pressure. The meager distance we moved would prove more
valuable than we could ever have imagined.

With the second anchor deployed, I began to connect new line and
chain to a third as a deck spare. Because the boat was being buffeted by
strong winds, I planned to lash the forty-five pounder to the rails first.
With one anchor probably gone forever, we could not afford to lose another. The boat lurched, I slipped, and the anchor banged down on the
deck, bounced off a stanchion, and started to fall overboard. Without a
thought, I dove on it and pulled it to my chest. *If it goes, I go!* Then my
already injured lower back came apart. An ionic wind of pain swept up
my spine. I felt faint. The air filled with lace as I slipped toward unconsciousness. When the world refocused, I still clutched the anchor to my
chest. I pulled it onto the deck, literally crawled below, undressed, and
slid into a sleeping bag, waving away Diana's questions. I was in too
much pain to talk.

I awoke in the middle of the night, having to get to the head. I sat up
well enough and, encouraged, took a step toward the bow. I fell to my
knees, crippled with pain. I took ten deep breaths and tried again. The
legs beneath me refused to move. I couldn't retreat, I couldn't carry on.
The pain made me dizzy. I don't know how long I was there.

Diana slipped below after a long anchor watch. From the darkness I
heard her voice: "Alvah, *what* are you doing?"

I was cold and confused. "I don't know. I can't move, Di."

Just her warm touch unlocked me enough to help me back into my bag. She brought me a plastic bottle to relieve myself and prepared a hot-water bottle to rewarm me. For the next seven days I could barely move. Diana was attentive and tender while at the same time single-handedly managing the *Roger Henry* in difficult conditions. I can only imagine her doubts and fears, because she did not share them.

All she said was, "What if you don't recover?"

"No, Di. Don't even say it. I'll be all right. We'll be all right. I promise."

Trying to restore Diana's confidence, I held my face in a smile and twisted my back. I went gray with the pain, but I held that smile. "See, everything's fine, just fine." Then I focused on healing, visualizing myself as agile as an ocelot. I had to beat this, to will it gone. There was so much to do to prepare for winter, and so much of it required our combined knowledge and strength. I did not know then if the injury was muscular or if it involved ligaments, nerves, or bone, so I alternated rest with stretches and managed to reappear on deck for the autumnal equinox of September 23. The sun was now directly above the equator, slipping south toward the Tropic of Capricorn.

We were mostly confined to ship during the transition from sea to solid. The ice was too thick to dinghy to shore and too thin to walk there. Until the *Roger Henry* was held firmly, we'd have to use multiple anchors and lines to keep the bow facing southeast, into the expected prevailing winter winds and fiercest blizzards.

The spongy new ice terrified Diana. She told me she would not go out on it until it was safe for a horse, but I don't know how she planned to test that. I had faith in the Inuit's belief that, even though thin ice could roll in front of you like a wave, it wouldn't matter as long as you kept moving. Freshwater ice is hard but brittle, while sea-ice's strength is in its salty elasticity. Still, it was so thin that the bay waters were visible beneath it, and I had to force myself to move out over it. At first it undulated like a waterbed, and I felt sick with fear. I shuffled around the boat in the skating motion I had read about, keeping one hand on the deck rail. Then I peeled out onto open ice. The cartoon character Wiley Coyote streaks off a cliff in hot pursuit of Roadrunner, then stands still, frozen in midair. It is not until he looks down at his impending doom, and turns to look at us with quizzical chagrin, that he plummets into the canyon. Knowing that both experience and confidence were essential for sea-ice travel, I forced my feet and attention out ahead of myself, refusing to think or look down for fear of punching through. At one hundred yards out, I stopped and turned to looked back on our boat, helplessly trapped and pitifully small against a stark background of spectacular scale. In all my life I had never seen anything so beautiful.

Trying to conserve our fresh water and, indirectly, our fuel, we left the through-hull saltwater valves open as long as possible. Although it's undrinkable, we could use seawater to brush our teeth, wash dishes, or boil an egg. When the thickening ice skim pushed beneath the waterline, we were finally forced to shut off the valves. We slid foam plugs down them until flush with the hull, closed the ball valves, and filled behind each with nontoxic antifreeze that would seep down and fill any voids. In theory, the foam would displace most of the water and absorb the tremendous force of expansion.

I chipped an ice hole next to the boat for seawater. The moment the shaft of sunlight lanced the deep waters, we heard bubbles beneath the ice, and a glistening baby ring seal popped out of the hole. Its soft brown eyes looked at us plaintively. Its lonely little barks saddened us, but we were glad for the company. The kitten and the seal pup stared at each other in wonder.

The real wonder is how a species that is the favorite food of three of the world's most deadly efficient hunters—Inuit, orca, and polar bear—prospers in the millions. The answer is their loneliness, for they are weaned very young and scatter widely into coastal and bay-ice areas. Orca cannot herd them up and swallow them wholesale as they do with some seal species (one orca was found choked to death on a harbor seal, with twenty-four others crammed into its stomach). Polar bears must cover up to one hundred miles per day in search of perfect opportunity, for that is what it requires to capture a quick, intelligent, and attentive prey. The European sealers called the ring seals *ice rats* and dismissed them as unprofitable to hunt due to the enormous time involved. The Inuit, however, have that time and the deep patience required, called *quinuituq*. They will stand over a ring seal *agloo* (blowhole) for hours, waiting motionless for the fluffy feather they place over the breathing tube to pop up in signal of approaching prey. The seal spends most of its forty years of life under the thick ice, using its sharp claws to maintain breathing holes and pupping dens. It dives to three hundred feet, staying submerged for up to twenty minutes in search of crustaceans and small fish.

We turned back to our task at hand. We somehow had to adapt the spare alternator to the three-horsepower, hand-started, air-cooled diesel in the forepeak, making a reliable electrical generation plant. From aluminum scrap I sawed, drilled, and filed mounting brackets and a tensioning bar. The work was slow but satisfying, allowing my mind to inventory the many details we had yet to attend to. I could have bought commercial brackets, but had I not developed a hands-on familiarity with these brackets, the consequences might have been dire during an emergency I would face months later.

The flexible metal exhaust hose from the small engine ran out the hawsehole on the foredeck. I bought that exhaust hose new, thinking it was airtight. Nevertheless, I wrapped it in asbestos wool, cut a Mylar space blanket into strips, wrapped the asbestos with that, and duct-taped the entire affair with plenty of overlap. I assumed that it *had* to be airtight now. Little events, one by one, kept aligning for future outcomes.

To winterize the main engine, we ran it with the saltwater intake hose in a bucket of antifreeze, sucking the cooling fluid through the seawater side of the system. I then drained the freshwater side and filled the radiator with a 100 percent antifreeze solution. I emptied the strainer and intake hose, then slid the foam plug down the hose into the through-hull fitting. After filling the transmission and engine oil pan to overflowing, I removed the injectors, filled the jugs with oil, sprayed the air intake with lubricating oil, and wrapped it in plastic. I tightened the propeller shaft stuffing box until no water dripped in.

We pulled the transducers for the log and depthsounder out of the hull. Freezing water gushed over us with terrible force before we could shove the plugs home and secure them. We hung our wet clothes out to dry. They froze stiff in minutes. (After several days in the wind, they freeze-dried to the point that an hour in front of the heater made them ready to wear.) I wrapped the radar dome in foam and sailcloth and lashed it tight. I climbed to the masthead to remove the navigational light fixtures and the wind direction indicator, then slacked off the tension on all the stainless steel wire rigging, not knowing how much they would contract in the coming cold. We took the heater apart, cleaned and reassembled it, and then took it apart again. Every part had to be familiar, every motion second nature, because when we next did this we might be fighting for our lives, with frozen fingers, in the dark.

Meanwhile, Diana inserted two-inch-thick foam into all the dead-lights, hatches, and vent holes. She cut out sheets of aluminum-backed plastic bubble wrap and taped them to the back of the louvered doors to the forepeak and two aft cabins. By opening or closing them, we could direct the heat efficiently at will. From the same foil she cut a curtain that unrolled from the top of the companionway hatch to the cabin sole, creating a foyer smaller than a phone booth. Climbing into it from either direction felt like entering a decompression chamber, but it helped keep out cold air. She emptied the water tanks into a large, round jerry can with a spigot at the bottom. From out of our lazarette emerged bulky parkas, insulated pants, pack boots, and felt liners.

Diana organized emergency supplies that for now we would store in a sled on deck but later would move to an emergency tent set up well clear of the boat, in the event of fire. The boat could conceivably still be crushed, but the most likely danger would be a flash fire or smoke-out below. If we were forced on deck in the middle of the Arctic night, our life expectancy could be measured in minutes were we not to lay up in the exact order of immediate need the lighting, clothing, food, fuel, extra shotgun, flares, ice ax, crampon . . . in short, every item needed to attempt the hundred-mile trek to safety.

For days Diana was pensive, worrying that we might have over-looked some dreadfully important little detail. I urged her to relax. Then, in the middle of the night she bolted upright out of a fitful sleep.

"Alvah, we made a mistake. Wake up, we made a mistake!"

I groaned, "What mistake?"

"The engine . . . you slid a foam plug down the hose and into the through-hull valve, like the others."

"That's right, Di. Now go to sleep."

"No, don't you see? You said that next year you would just push them out with a long stick. But this one has a filtering screen on the outside. We can't push it out and we have no way to pull it back in now. When we start up in the spring, it will plug our water intake and damage the engine."

It was my turn to bolt upright. She was right. The plug was stuck down a narrow hose and long pipe. She got up and turned the ship's log ahead to June 30, where she marked in large red lettering a reminder to solve this problem before turning the ignition key. She then fell soundly asleep while I lay awake wondering about this woman I had considered going north without. Diana knows little about engines, yet a subliminal detail had lodged itself in her subconscious. Her unresting mind had replayed my every action, detected my mistake, and woke her on the spot.

In the closing days of September, I coaxed Diana out onto the thickening sea-ice. We surveyed the freshwater icebergs in the bay and chose one twenty feet high near the boat, naming it Big Boy. We had begun to create the language of our new terrain. We hauled a sled to its base, Halifax hitching a ride. I laid the shotgun near at hand and climbed to the top. First I pulled out binoculars and swept the area for bears; then with an old army ice ax I hacked off great chunks of hard, translucent ice. They crashed to the base, and Diana loaded them onto the sled. We hooked into the harness and together hauled load after load to the boat. We would need drinking water no matter the weather, and we thought this cache ensured that we would not have to go stumbling around in the bear-infested dark looking for it.

We fashioned a tent over the cockpit by extending a spinnaker pole from the mast to the backstays, stretching a canvas tarp over it and lashing the corners to the outside of the cockpit coamings. This left open vees at each end, but a deflated rubber dinghy, sailbags, and supply boxes filled in the front end of the vee, while at the cockpit end we hung a clear plastic tarp with a stout zipper down the middle, creating an entryway. We hoped the tent would keep snow from drifting over the cockpit and burying our escape hatch. A fabric tent would not stop the bears, but their racket tearing through it would at least sound the alert. Once the snows began to fall in earnest, I planned to continuously flatten the drifts near the boat, leaving the stalking bears nothing to hide behind.

By this time the boat was constantly in the shadow of the mountains to the south. We woke each day to a later sunrise, colder air, and a shorter list of winter preparations. We jumped up and briskly slipped into heavy clothing. Diana sipped her Earl Grey tea as I called out for honey in my first cup of scalding coffee. She looked into the honey jar and asked, "One lump or two?" We talked over the day's work list. Diana separated the food supplies into two eight-month portions and stowed one half in the port aft cabin, leaving the starboard cabin, which was closer to the stove, free for us to sleep in. She divided the other half into monthly rations, labeling each container and keeping a careful inventory, for we did not want to find ourselves halfway through the adventure and all the way out of matches. Taking turns cooking, we practiced using just the head end of the match to light a small pool of alcohol, which preheated the burners, which vaporized the kerosene, allowing it to burn in the stove. With the other match end we would catch the last of the alcohol flame to then light the kerosene gases, effectively doubling our supply.

This was the second valuable level of awareness forced upon us—our resources were so finite that we must not squander them. We had to use them with reverence. In less, we found more—more appreciation, more value. This truism is so simple, yet it evades us on a global scale. In our hearts we know it to be so, but we cannot help ourselves; we rip through our natural bounty with the reckless greed of unchecked children under a Christmas tree.

When we felt ready, we turned our attention outward to the bold beauty of Tay Bay. Tyrolian peaks towered above us on three sides. Razor ridges ran from both port and starboard toward the bow and head of the bay. There the summits rose even higher. Each was isolated by shimmering, deltalike fingers at the terminus of an eighteen-mile-long, three-mile-wide, winding river of ice called Inussualuk Glacier. Each summit was crowned in white. Each mountain waist exposed a belt of black, broken scree. Each foot was skirted with a mint green or aqua blue glacier. They stretched inland as far as the eye could see, forming the western end of the Byam Martin Range. From the north, another glacier ran perpendicularly into the bay, being forced into a final sharp turn by a twisting, rocky canyon. The outer edge of the curving glacier was serrated by hundred-foot, sheer ice walls, each at a slightly different angle to the sun. Like a faceted crystal, these edges spread the soft sunlight through the limits of its color spectrum.

All this granite drama fell steeply onto rolling, rocky coastal plains. Although by then sparse of plant life, these plains somehow sustain a blessed litany of wildlife: lemming, hare, fox, wolverine, caribou, ptarmigan, snowy owl, raven, gyrfalcon, oldsquaws, eider ducks, and snow geese. Near the boat slept fat seals—bearded, ringed, occasionally hooded, and harp. Outside, in Navy Board Inlet, orca, narwhal, beluga, and walrus worked the deep water until freeze-up.

We hiked the burnt-orange hills, stopping to run our hands over wall-sized pallets of rock painted with the flaky lichen. They looked like old Dutch masterpieces. We measured the patches' diameters from thumb to little finger and counted back in time the hundred years required for each inch of lichen growth. As we became familiar with each valley, lookout, peak, pond, bay, hummock, or lone rock, we christened them. Our icebergs became The Chicken and Fat Frog. Notable stones became Fox Rock and The Thinker. A rolling stretch of tundra we dubbed Ptarmigan Hills. We scanned the distant horizons of haunting wilderness, knowing that, on this planet of more than five billion people, as far as the eye could see there were but two. As the sun skidded beneath the southern rims, we lingered on deck to absorb the new hues of amber, crimson, lilac, and lime. Waking, we went out into the lengthening night in the hope of being graced with the real "Greatest Show On Earth": the Northern Lights.

Our language is anorexic when trying to communicate the subtle complexities of ice and snow. So too do I find our tropical-to-temperate adjectives unable to tame this Arctic light. It roams the skies in fluid flux. It will not hold still for our eyes or cameras, much less our pens. Sun dogs race to the four directions of the solar winds, becoming bloody crucifixes ringed in halo. Mountains stand on their heads in the sky. Fireballs of light roll along like tumbleweed. One of us would hurriedly call the other to look, but by the time Diana or I had turned, it would be gone. We carefully explained what we saw. It was important that the other understood.

Diana said, "I am not crazy, Alvah. It was a ball of fire and it rolled off the cliffs on the Borden side and shot across the inlet and over that hill and past the boat, getting bigger and bigger. Then it just disappeared. Say you believe me!"

Through two years of frantic preparation, three months of hard travel, and the hurly-burly of preparing ourselves for the winter, Diana had lived with the constant fear that we *would* find Ultima Thule, I that we *would not*. Perhaps to tax one emotion means to atrophy another, because we had drifted apart into politeness. But now, settled and secure, we shared a warmth as intimate as we had ever known. After I returned from a long solo hike, we laid under a sleeping bag as I described every detail. When I saw that she was truly interested, I felt a deep desire for her. We traded body warmth like a currency. "If you let me put my feet on your stomach, I'll warm your hands under my arms." As to our worry about what we would do with the time, there seemed never enough to just sit there and look out on all this splendor.

In our own private wildlife preserve, we sat on the bow of the boat with steaming mugs of coffee, watching a juvenile bear clumsily sneak up on a ring seal lying next to its hole. I trained the telescope on the bear and could watch even his facial expressions. He slid forward stealthily enough, his stubby tail twitching, but he impatiently broke into his charge too early. The seal, one moment apparently asleep or oblivious, was gone in a nanosecond. The bear sat down and slapped the ice in exasperation. I named him Dufus. The fox that had been following him apparently agreed with me and peeled off in search of a more skillful patron. The bear found another hole and stood in the classic arced pose above it, still as an alabaster statue.

I slid on my stomach out onto the ice toward the bear, pushing the small sled with a white covering before me as a blind. I moved along almost effortlessly, and an eerie feeling came over me; for a moment I did not know if I was pushing or being pulled. I approached perpendicular to the wind, hoping a shift would not bring my sound or scent toward the hole. The bear and I waited for the precursor bubbles of a ring seal's approach. After an hour and a half, I was too cold to remain still, but the bear would see me if I jumped around to warm myself. I was probably the only creature around stupid and slow enough for him to catch. Reluctantly, I slid away backward, leaving Dufus to his vigil.

Back at the boat I felt the same renewal I felt as a boy in church, when the voices of the entire congregation rose up as one in "Ave Maria." The common thread is harmony, the voice of relationship. If I could have chosen a living talent, first I would have sung about how the seal and the bear define each other's life. Next, I would have painted it, opaque and misty. I could only write down some vague impressions:

> Arctic nights, Northern Lights, crystal cascades, frostbit air
> Surfaced seal, silent, scenting, ah, sweet safety of her lair
> But there, ice bear, poised, patient, brute paw to tear
> Crushing blow, life's blood flow. How soul and sinew bind this pair

The average temperature dropped substantially below freezing in early October. The boat stood out too proud and the early winter winds sucked our heat away. For days I shoveled what meager snow I could collect against the topsides for insulation. Shortly thereafter, the real snows came and I reversed my efforts, continuously having to unbury the boat.

Diana's birthday is October 6 and was the first of several holidays we looked forward to as a break from rationing. We went for a long hike on the orange cliffs that faced north toward Lancaster Sound. The view was our favorite, because on some days we could see the ice-capped peaks above Dundas Harbor on Devon Island, a full seventy-five miles away. They lay beyond our borders of the known, deep in the land of fantasy. In the other direction, Navy Board Inlet appeared as a thin alley of ice that drew our attention one hundred miles south to that first trailhead of civilization, the village and airstrip. I looked over the scene methodically, committing landmarks to memory, for soon all this would be cloaked from human sight. Even the Inuit, who have a lifetime of experience with this, say:

> There is fear
> In feeling the cold
> Come to the great world
> And seeing the moon
> Now new moon, now full moon
> Follow its old footprints
> In the winter night.

Yes, I thought, *our two deepest primordial fears are that of darkness and of being alone.* I looked over to Diana—my sweet, patient, enduring Diana—and took deep comfort in the fact that I would have her at my side to face the polar night.

Diana was the ship's quartermaster. She claims a pure English ancestry, but I suspect a Scot in the woodpile, for she has never been called lavish in her spending. I had to smuggle on board sweets for such occasions. I slipped a birthday treat—a stick of her favorite black licorice—on a rock near where she was sitting. When she saw it, she stared at it incredulously for a moment and then pounced on it as if it might slither away. Hand in hand (actually, thick glove in glove), we walked back to the boat. I cooked for three hours, producing a handsome quiche from dehydrated eggs, smoked bacon, dried mushrooms, and sharp cheddar, plus a sprouted salad. A dessert of gooey chocolate chip cookies completed our decadence.

When we were laying in provisions in Camden, Diana had been furious with me when she unexpectedly returned to the boat and found an empty case on the dock with "Old No. 7 Sourmash Whiskey" printed on the side. She shouted, "If there's empty space enough to put that damn whiskey, then we should put rice in that spot!"

I said, "Diana, if you can find any of that whiskey, I will throw it overboard and replace it with rice." (I took ruthless advantage of her fear of electricity by burying it beneath a rat's nest of evil-looking wires. Scruples have no place in high affairs.) But now, up here and on her birthday, she did not protest too much when I offered her a "Hot Honey Jack." She sipped it and purred, "Oh my!" In fact, when it was gone, she coyly rubbed up against me, pointing out that the first had been rather small, after all. I told her I might just find another one after we tried the radio to contact her father in New Zealand.

Three hundred miles to our west lay the town of Resolute, where the Canadian Coast Guard maintains a radio station from June through early October. Knowing they would be shutting down in just days, we used Diana's birthday celebration as a last radio link with them and the outside world. A vibrant and cheerful French Canadian named Guy agreed to link our radio with a phone patch all the way to New Zealand. Diana sat at the chart table with microphone in hand, anxiously awaiting the first sound of her father's voice. This would cap a perfect day.

Diana's father had been a radio operator in the R.A.F.'s Lancaster bombers in WWII and was trained to the wooden military formality when on the open airways, so she beamed when he remembered her birthday and told her he loved her. She chatted on happily about our situation, then said, "Enough about me; how are you way down under? Over."

The pause that followed was so long I thought we had lost contact.

"Well, Di, not good, actually. Those bloody doctors have just diagnosed me with terminal cancer and given me three months to live."

Diana dropped the microphone, ran three steps, and crumpled in anguish.

She sobbed, "I have to go. I have to go." I knew instantly in my heart she was right.

I stood still, temporarily stunned. How could she remain aboard for a dark and difficult year with the knowledge that her father was waning away without her? Years earlier my father-in-law had lost his wife to a terrible cancer. He was alone and afraid. Diana was his only daughter. Faced with the serious needs of the family, our adventure paled into silliness. Our duty was clear and irrevocable, the consequences too vast to immediately absorb.

I grabbed the microphone, "Clive, this is Alvah. How copy? Over."

"Loud and clear. Go."

"Clive, we are so sorry. We are far out in the wilderness, so it may take time, but *somehow* I will get your daughter to your side."

He was a formal and prideful man, but he wept openly as he tried to express his fear that we might not have that time. Diana composed herself and returned to the microphone, encouraging her father to be hopeful and patient. When radio conditions deteriorated, we signed off into a somber silence. Although our duty was clear, how we would accomplish it was not. The boat lay trapped behind impenetrable ice, yet Pond Inlet, a hundred miles to the south, was still cut off by open water. We could not hike out, and no one could sled in. The following days were the most difficult of our lives.

I radioed John Henderson, a Scotsman we had met in Pond Inlet.

John owns and operates Eclipse Sound Outfitters. He had been helpful and informative and would certainly be knowledgeable about all aspects of travel in these regions. He asked that we give him two days to investigate our evacuation options, and we set up another radio schedule. His return radio call did not bring good news. He explained the government's policy; neither of us was in a life-threatening situation. Our situation might qualify as a tragedy, but not officially as an emergency, so their hands were tied. That left private operators. The last commercial helicopter had already gone south for the season. Even if we could have called it back, the cost was over eight thousand dollars and we had nothing near that. A local airline that flew Twin Otters between Resolute and Pond Inlet said they could divert a plane for a fly-over, but because it was too early in the season to trust the sea-ice, they needed a deposit of two thousand dollars just to consider a rough tundra landing. They cautioned John that they seldom set down in unknown areas for obvious reasons. Conditions would have to be perfect, and that was highly unlikely. John felt it would be a waste of money, but I told him I would go out and pace off possible runways and prepare flares and windsocks. We agreed to talk again in two days.

I hiked the tundra until the pain in my legs overrode that in my heart. Each time I thought I had found a possible landing strip, a boulder or ravine cut it shorter than the minimum thousand meters required. When I finally found one suitable in length, it was hemmed in between high peaks, forming an aerial box canyon. In my bones, I knew they would not risk it. Before they would touch down, they had to be certain, repeat, *certain* they could lift off. Expensive equipment and perhaps even lives were at stake. Who could blame them? I had to accept that it would cost many precious weeks, if not months, before we could get Diana out and home. I trudged several miles back to the boat. Tay Bay still lay at exactly 73° 30′ North and 80° 45′ West, but it was not the same place.

We held each other in the sleeping bag and discussed our options. We would wait until the sea-ice congealing over Eclipse Sound was marginally safe, then attempt Pond Inlet on foot. The road would be harsh and the risks dreadful, but sitting in dark isolation while her father suffered in loneliness would have meant a thousand deaths for

Diana. Only when we reached Pond Inlet safely could we consider whether I would try to return solo to the boat or carry on to New Zealand, abandoning our home to its own fate.

Would my presence be of more value in New Zealand than here protecting the *Roger Henry*? We did not think of ourselves as materialistic, having devoted our lives to action and ideas, not things. And yet, this boat we had saved so long to obtain and worked so hard on was more than "a thing." The *Roger Henry* was our home, our hobby, our work, our play, our partner.

What would we do with Halifax? We loved her like a child, but she could not go to New Zealand because of strict quarantine laws. And if I came back to the boat, certainly no one would accompany me. That meant me . . . here . . . alone. My heart beat with fear and excitement. I was embarrassed by both, because this wasn't about me. Every scrap of Arctic literature screamed one message, "No, never alone. It is too dangerous!" But what Arctic explorer has ever been faced with this dilemma? We simply stopped talking about it, letting the matter settle into our subconscious, seeking solution.

Guy from Resolute Coast Guard Radio listened in on all the radio conversations. He radioed the "Ro-zhay Ohn-rhee." His French accent was so heavy that I missed many of the words, but in our sad seclusion his message was clear and comforting to Diana. He broke the tradition of professional detachment and expressed his condolences and concern. One day he called and said, "I cannot say officially, oui . . . That eez to say . . . the Canadian Coast Guard cannot officially get involved een theze. But you should be ready, mes amis. You never know who might come to your boat tomorrow morning at o-eight-hundred."

This could mean only one of two things: a full-fledged icebreaker or a helicopter. Even if the word *rescue* was not appropriate, our elation betrayed how desperately trapped we had been feeling. For Diana, the news was bittersweet. She felt like a condemned prisoner pardoned at the last moment, but turning to see friends left to face their execution. We had not said it out loud, but she knew.

"You've decided to stay, haven't you?" she asked.

"Yes."

"I knew you would."

I put my hands on her shoulders. "Diana, we are a team, until today an inseparable one. But now being a team means we have to split up to cover all our responsibilities. Your father needs your love now. Turn your attention to him, and promise not to worry about me." I pulled her close to me, burying my face in her long, soft hair. "I made my decision when I thought about the Philippines and our wedding day. Remember? We left the boat for one night—just one night. They broke in and cleaned us out of everything—clothes, tools, food, pots, pans. Remember how we felt? Violated, because they didn't just rob the boat; they desecrated it. And if the ice shifts, or a leak develops, I'll be here. I can do something, or at least try. No, I'll stay and take care of our home and Halifax. We'll be all right."

Diana is a pragmatic woman. She understood, but understanding made it no easier. She threw her arms around me, dropped her head against my chest, and cried so hard I thought both our hearts might break.

"I'll worry myself sick over you—being alone, the darkness, the bears," she said. "I am going to find a radio contact so we can keep in touch."

Off Pond Inlet, the icebreaker CCG *Sir John Franklin* steamed through rough waters, escorting the ore carrier *Arctic Viking* on its last trip of the season to the Nanissivik mines. Lashed to the *Franklin*'s deck, a helicopter awaited flight for ice reconnaissance. The morning after talking on the radio with Guy, the captain suggested the flight crew reconnoiter ice conditions in the area around Tay Bay.

After a month of complete silence, the chatter of those blades shattered our nerves as the pilot spiraled down on the strange sight below. The chopper landed right next to the *Roger Henry*. I ran up on deck. Two plucky flyboys jumped out, leaving the machine roaring, and sprinted through the snow cloud to shake my hand. One shouted in my ear that they had only five minutes to spare. Diana and I were rushed. We were crushed. We went through the motions numbly. She grabbed a small bag of clothes, flung it into the cargo bay, and turned to me. We clung desperately to each other. I kept telling her that she had to get in and go, but I held on to her just the same.

The pilot saw us hugging and looked confused. "Wait—what are you going to do?"

Even as I opened my mouth, I was not sure which way my words would lead me. Then I heard myself say, "I'm staying."

"Alone? Seriously?"

Why tempt me? Why give me even a moment to reconsider? "Yes, that's my decision."

"Jesus, man!" he shouted. "You have no idea what it's like up here. We won't be back till next June."

Like stepping off a cliff, once it's done, it's done. "Well, I'll see you then."

He looked at his copilot, who turned his hands up and shrugged his shoulders. The pilot shook his head, saluted, and hopped in his helicopter. I kissed Diana good-bye through the window. She touched my lips through the glass as the tears froze on my cheeks. I thanked the crew and stepped back.

They rose in a snow cloud, turned, and were too soon a speck on the vast Arctic sky. I stood there staring for a very long time, watching the sun and my wife, both sources of warmth and light in my life, disappear over the southern horizon. I have never known such silence.

After a time, that stillness was broken by a soft sound behind me. I turned to Halifax and said, "You've been promoted."

Tay Bay

OCTOBER 1994

6 HOURS DAYLIGHT

Where you used to be, there is a hole in the world,
which I find myself constantly walking around in the daytime,
and falling into at night.

—Edna St. Vincent Millay

THE SWAMPY SPOTS in me wanted to protest. This was not fair. But in truth, this was so brutally fair, it might have been ordained. I had prayed for hard adventure, and that hardness in its final degree could be granted me only by removing the comfort and support of Diana. Mostly, I felt sadness for my father-in-law, for my wife, and a little for myself and the collapse of our plans. Fear would come later. I sat down in the snow, and the tension seeped out with tears that, once begun, swelled into chest-heaving sobs. When that was over, I got down to work.

There were now only a few hours of light each day, and those were waning quickly, so for the next three days I dove into a flurry of last-minute projects. My mind was absorbed. My body was exercised and tired—not tired enough, however, to sleep through that first shock of silence and solitude. No matter how often I reached out in habit, the space beside me remained empty.

I tried to impose upon my day the same rigid regime the English had used in colonial Africa and India, but my sleep patterns immediately became erratic. I lay awake all night and moved through the day in a druglike haze. Physical fatigue had no bearing on when or how I slept.

Time moved slowly. I wondered why I looked at the clock at all. What did it matter? I saw an arctic fox chasing a ghost white hare through the fog. Getting momentarily confused, I jumped below to tell Diana, but she wasn't there. The calendar stretched on into an unknown future, with no comforting mark on its pages pinpointing her return.

I jumped in fright and hope when I heard a human voice. My heart sank when it was only the marine radio.

"Ro-zhay Ohn-rhee, Ro-zhay Ohn-rhee. Zees is Resolute Radio."

"Resolute Radio, go ahead."

"Bonjour; I 'ave talked with ze captain of *Jean Franklin*. 'Ee sez 'iz pilot weel make one more reconnaissance flight over ze Navy Board Inlet. 'Ee wants to know if zer is a somezing zey can bring for you."

My instincts shouted, "No, nothing! Just the return of my wife to help me through this long winter ahead." If they brought supplies it would be misunderstood. The rumors would fly: An American tourist got himself accidentally frozen into the ice, totally unprepared, and now the Coast Guard has to bail his butt out with taxpayers' money.

I keyed the mike. "Resolute Radio. Thank you, but I need nothing. I'm fully prepared."

Guy dropped his voice. "Mon ami, let zem help. Zey are worried for you." He urged, "Somezing. Anyzing."

Hoping to diffuse the issue with a feeble joke, I replied, "Okay, Guy, I do need two things. Tell them to haul in a drum of diesel and a drum of Canadian whiskey for me."

Guy had a little laugh and then told me it was the station's final day on the air. He wished me well and signed off for the last time.

Four long and lonely days later I shouted, "Noise, Halifax! That's a noise!"

The boat started to shake. The air concussed in a machine-gun staccato. We looked at each other for an answer; then all went quiet. I heard voices. Halifax dove behind a pile of gear in the bow. I dressed quickly, crawled out the companionway, and opened the cockpit tent flap. The Canadian Coast Guard's red helicopter sat whining next to the boat. Three men in orange jumpsuits were unloading variously shaped containers and boxes onto the ice. I ran over to the flight crew, recognizing two of the men from the first landing. A third man trained a video camera on me. I was so excited, you would have thought I was being rescued after years on a deserted island.

I pumped their hands and shouted above the rotor noise, "Hello, hello! Welcome to Tay Bay. What's all this?"

"Jet fuel," the pilot shouted. "Not so good for yer engine, but inside yer heater she'll burn hot as a Saturday night in Yellowknife. We used up every darn container on the ship—empty paint buckets, cooking oil tins. There's over a hundred liters here."

We dragged the supplies to the boat. I opened the cartons and found cookies, peanut butter, instant soups, Cheez-Whiz, pickles, trash novels, and news magazines about the real world, hot off the press.

"Nothing could be better," I said.

The pilot grinned and from behind his back pulled out two bottles of Canadian Whiskey. He said, "Our whiskey doesn't come in steel drums. They only do that in Tennessee."

Amazed and embarrassed, I thought, *Ask and ye shall receive.*

We talked excitedly about weather, ice conditions, and animals. I could not bear to bring up Diana's name just yet. I was glad for the company of these hearty men. The pilot was muscular and weather-beaten handsome, with wide jaw and craggy face. His salt-and-pepper hair was cut military short. His copilot was younger, with an eager and innocent look, still excited about his new life up north. I invited them below. I was proud of our pleasant interior of shiny, varnished spruce and white enamel, and happy they had come when everything was clean and in perfect order. I sat them around the table, turned up the heater, and offered them coffee and fresh-baked chocolate chip cookies. They were surprised at the domestic normality of the scene.

"What did you expect," I asked. "Charred bones?"

The cameraman kept that lens pointed right at me, making me feel quite awkward. Was it my imagination, or were they all staring at me? No, not right at me—unfocused, or maybe just above my eyes . . . at my head? I instinctively put my hand to my head, and then burst out laughing.

"Oh, my hair! I forgot. I wanted to save water washing it, so I hacked it all off the other day. I haven't seen myself in a mirror."

They laughed, relieved that I was not yet as crazed as I looked.

Then they fell awkwardly silent. The pilot said, "Look, we need to talk. We took your wife back to our ship, and when we steamed by Pond Inlet, we flew her to shore. Man, word spreads fast up here. The Mounties in Pond Inlet asked us one hell of a lot of questions. They're not happy with you being out here. Hell, they even called Ottawa. Rumor says Ottawa wants 'em to pull you out." He shook his head. "Even the locals say you can't make it. It's just not safe."

My voice rose in anger. "Neither is skydiving or motorcycle racing. Am I breaking any laws?"

He held up his rough hands, "Look, it's not us. We're with you. Maybe the police are just covering their butts if something goes wrong. But, I gotta tell ya, one Mountie asked us to bring him out here today. We would have, but there was a rash of break-ins in town last night, and he missed the flight."

"Don't you see?" I pleaded. "That's one of the reasons why I won't leave my ship. Charlie Inoraaq told me times are changing, even up here. He warned me that there are hooligans in town. If they hear the boat is empty, eventually they'll find it and strip it. This is my home! Can you imagine coming back to your home in the spring to find someone had crowbarred their way in? Charlie said they'd crap in the corners. I don't know much about the laws, but I do know that I am captain of this ship, and every tradition says I must stay with it."

"It's the alone part. What if you get sick? The littlest injury? What if you die up here?"

"Look at me!" I said. I was fighting mad and had to defend my home and my plans. "Look me straight in the eye. I am not going to die up here. I have dreamed about this, I have prepared for this. I have two years' worth of food on board. Name any piece of equipment, and I'll show you two of them. I sail for the same reasons you boys fly—it makes life bigger. I know you understand. Don't let someone behind a desk in Ottawa take this away from me."

They looked back and forth at each other for a long time and then nodded.

The pilot said, "Okay. We'll tell the police how good things look up here. We'll talk you up. Maybe we just won't happen to have a spare seat available. Anyway, in two days we'll be going south for the last time. We're the only thing moving up here, so if they don't move fast, they can't move at all. I hate to say it, 'cause we're in the government ourselves, but if there's a decision involved, things don't move fast very often."

Standing outside beside the helicopter, they kept shaking their heads and shaking my hand very hard, reluctant to leave me behind. As they lifted off, the cameraman leaned out a window, zooming his lens down on me. I imagined the caption: "The last known photo of the American sailor . . ." They lifted straight up above the boat, cocked the craft, and waved good-bye. In describing these men—Guy, and the captain and crew of the *Sir John Franklin*—the word *gallant* comes to mind. The snow swirled around me, and when it settled, they were gone.

I was alone again, and given their news about the stir in Pond Inlet, I dearly wished I would stay that way. For three days worry churned my stomach. I monitored the southern skies for invaders and practiced my speech, designed to shame a low-level functionary into inaction. Days passed, and when a real ripsnorter blizzard began to blow, I knew I was out of the woods.

I had kept a strong and confident face for them. "Look me right in the eye." Did I really say that? What could I do, tell them the truth? "I agree, gentlemen. This is just not safe. You should see what's already happening in my head."

The nightmares began almost from the outset. Denied emotional outlet through the solitude of the day, I found that every otherwise insignificant insecurity or conflict flared up into a full-scale, cross-border war between reality and my subconscious. *I kick down the door and throw my hands around the throat of the bastard in bed with Diana. I squeeze past the pain of his punches, past his pitiful little thrashings, past his bug-eyed plea for mercy. I'm screaming, "You fuck with my life? Fight, you big son of a bitch. Don't just die! Fight me!" Diana is pummeling my back with her fists, screaming, "Stop! Stop! That's why I hate you. You're an animal!" She is scratching me, she is Halifax, Halifax is scratching me. That's pain. Am I awake?* Oh God, God, it's only Halifax. I'm thrashing, and she's just trying to get out of the sleeping bag. I'm sorry, Halifax; I'm sorry, Di; I just lost my temper. I'm not an animal. Forgive me.

I reach up to open the ice-encrusted porthole on the wall of my aft cabin cave. I punch a tunnel through the snow, and Halifax springs up and out into the cockpit. The boat acts as a guitar, and her footsteps in the dry snow reverberate through the cabin, sounding like a bear's. Thick air flows over my face like the River Styx. It freezes my sweat and shocks my lungs with my panicky panting. I remember other dreams: The boat was crushed; a bear was pulling out my intestines and I had to grab the slippery tube like a rope in a deadly tug of war. But I never once dreamt that I was cold.

Feeling cold meant I was awake. The heater was out again. Snow must have drifted over the flue pipe. Even though the end of my nose felt wooden with frostbite, I couldn't bear to pull my head back into the sleeping bag just yet. It was no darker inside than out, but the bag was shaped like a coffin. I pulled on my Darth Vader facemask and wondered if my eyes were open. My ears sucked in signals—Halifax was back. I let the shivering cat into the sleeping bag and lay awake until the rose-petal light of late dawn seeped into the boat.

I dressed quickly, hitting my head hard on the low ceiling while hopping around trying to pull on thick mukluk socks and jam my feet into frozen boots. My breath formed a thick fog, and I must have looked like a cartoon character with my thoughts written in that cold cloud, #@!!*^#*. I pulled on two layers of long underwear, a sweater, a fleece jacket, insulated bibs, and a khaki helmet liner.

The basket in the coffee pot was frozen solid into the dregs in its base. When I yanked it free, I felt a searing pain. I tried to drop it, to throw it away, but I couldn't let go. It stuck to me like a rabid rat gnawing at my fingers. The cold steel was smoking blue but burned my flesh exactly as if it were red hot. I turned to plunge my hand into the dishwater, but forks and knives stuck up out of the frozen water like glass shrapnel on top of a concrete wall. I knocked the lid off the water jug, smashed the ice on the surface with my other hand, and plunged my arm into the cold water. The basket fell free from my fingers and sank to the barrel's bottom, polluting three gallons of precious water. For the next three days, even the rice would taste like coffee.

I pulled on my crackling-cold parka, crawled out into the cockpit, and grabbed the plastic bucket full of ice chunks. I drove the stainless steel knife down in fast little chops, chipping off flakes that would melt more quickly. I heard a musical ting as the frozen tempered blade shattered into shiny little pieces. What is this environment where even steel is not strong? I grabbed the ice ax and swung down with its sharp piton end. My only plastic bucket split in two. I cursed loudly until I could not think of another body part or by-product, sex act, parental slander, or slur.

I crashed out of the cockpit tent and heaved the ice ax into the white abyss. It wasn't enough to exhaust my rage, so I threw some skis and poles after it. I grabbed the Japanese military rifle my father had given me for my tenth birthday and, grinding my teeth and muttering, stomped off for Navy Board Inlet with Halifax hard pressed to keep up. A mile out into the inlet lay an ambush area of huge ice boulders uplifted into confusion. I sulked through the maze, rounding sharp corners and seeking quick surprises. I was looking for trouble—call it trolling for bears.

I should have test fired the decades-old ammunition weeks earlier but had not, specifically because Diana had nagged me to do so. Smugly, I had said, "Diana, please, do not lecture me about guns."

I needed to make noise, break the back of this goddamn silence, get hold of myself and my bay. I shouted at the top of my lungs, "Bruno, I am here. I am staying here. Come if you want!"

I whirled, dropped to my knees, and aimed the rifle at a thick icicle, my mind's eye changing its whiteness into a charging bear. I squeezed off a heart shot, cool as you please. There was a little snick, but no thud on my shoulder or thunder in my ears. A dud. I leaned into the butt, looking forward to the pleasant punch of recoil, and fired again. A dud. And again, a dud. The ice and the ice bears were safe.

I thought, *Diana, how many ways am I going to find that I have relied on you? How many times has your judgment proved correct? How often have I been so full of myself that I barely heard your sound counsel or heartfelt concerns? Truly, you have been faced with a "my way or the highway" hardheadedness, haven't you? And still you stayed. Until now.*

I stood up and, holding the rifle lightly, casually fired again, expecting another misfire. The explosion knocked my feet out from under me. I lay out on the sea-ice, spread eagle. When the echoes faded, Halifax jumped on me to warm her paws. We lay there still as stone for a half hour, watching the bay pulse in red light leeching to gold, with green bands arcing horizon to horizon, holding up the lacy blue heavens. The mountains were close enough to touch, the air all crystals and clean. The beauty washed over me, and I felt warm and calm. The anger drained away to a vague shame.

Above us, a huge black raven circled in an endlessly empty sky. It spiraled down silently. Ravens are clever enough to know that a man standing on the ice is a danger, but one lying on the ice is dinner. Halifax crawled into my parka hood, clearly respecting the danger the large carnivorous bird posed. We remained still as the bird lit on an iceberg just above us. I recalled Steven Young's *To the Arctic*: "Omnipresent scavengers, predators, and observers of the Arctic environment, the raven is considered the most intelligent of all birds. It figures prominently in the mythology of northern peoples."

Indeed, the Inuit tell this story about the ebony bird: "Being close friends, the Raven and the Loon agreed to tattoo each other one day. They went to the igloo, where Raven created a delicate black-and-white pattern all over Loon. Raven stood back and said, 'Oh, make me look just like that.' But every time Loon pricked Raven with the tattooing feather, Raven yelped and flinched. Loon said, 'If you jump one more time, I'll pour this ink all over you.' Raven jumped. Loon dumped the pot over his head, and ran for the igloo tunnel. In a rage, Raven threw the ink pot, which struck Loon very hard in the legs. And that is why, to this day, the Raven is black, and the Loon cannot walk."

The raven is perhaps the Arctic's keenest judge of probable outcome. This lone bird had chosen not to fly south for the winter, and I thought I understood what that meant. I said out loud, "Listen to me, Raven, I'm going to live through this. If it's food you're after, then you better follow that sun south now, because there's no hope for you here. Halifax is smart, and I'm stubborn."

Staring at me intently, the bird tilted its head, opened its blue-black mouth and cawed, thinking, "I will start with his eyes."

It was now the end of October, and the last minutes of an Arctic day were already waning into perpetual night. Psychologists have done extensive studies concerning the effects of solitude on the human mind. Others have studied the effects of light deprivation, which are profound both psychologically and physically. To combine the two is to invite an unholy terror. Many an Arctic explorer who otherwise thought himself a happy man has turned a gun and scattered his skull to end his Arctic ordeal. Gurus tell us that our heaven is within. So too, then, must be our hell.

Still lying on the ice, I said out loud, "Halifax, I've been thinking. I'm already screwing up big time." To the Inuit, to lose your temper is to lose your dignity, and they have little else. They contain and control anger, as if letting the heat out allows the cold to creep in. The Bushmen of the Kalahari call whites "The Angry People." I wondered, *What is all this anger in me, all this emotion? The Arctic won't kill us—I will, with these impulsive outbursts, tantrums, and careless behavior. This will not be forgiven up here, not up here. In perfect control, I might just make it. Out of control, I'm as good as dead.*

I watched the skies fade to purple and felt the temperature fall. "Look, I know I'm going to drift toward madness, especially when the total darkness begins. I don't think I'll find the strength to resist it. I've decided not to fight everything—you know, let the least harmful things go. Save discipline for the important things. First, I am going to talk out loud to you all the time—both barrels, Halifax. People catch you talking to yourself, they lock you up. But you talk to your cat, and nobody thinks a thing about it. Up here, maybe it's healthy to talk to yourself. The problem begins when you start arguing with yourself—unless you argue with yourself so bitterly that you quit talking to yourself. Anyway, next I'm going to let my body determine our daily rhythms of sleeping, waking, working, and eating. But we're going to stay clean and orderly. We will bathe regularly, air our bedding, keep the equipment, the boat, and the galley in good order, make a nice environment."

I rubbed Halifax's head, now poking out of my parka. "We're going to eat like bears, keep a keen interest in food, and make it good and hot and varied. No more of this eating from the can. You get Di's share of the chocolate, but I get her share of the whiskey. Don't even ask. We're going to explore every foot of our new home, until it feels just like that, home. The Coast Guard was right: This is not an emergency. This is an *opportunity*. The boat is not a liferaft. We do not need rescue. Yet we are talking survival, here, and all we need for that is to be happy, because happy people are lucky people, and frankly, we'll need some luck to live through this."

I picked myself up off the ice and trundled back toward the boat. Halifax followed like a dog. At regular intervals she clawed her way up my back to thaw her paws. She leapt down to entice me to chase her around a small berg, then ran ahead to hide in the snow, and pounced on me as I passed. She was having fun, and that was no small thing. I might learn from her animal version of *The Unbearable Lightness of Being.* She stopped with her lips curled back, sucking up a cornucopia of odors from a big piece of frozen scat and yellow block of urine. She looked at the maze of tracks around us and then at me as if to say, "We're surrounded!" She loved those hikes. She lived for them. And soon, so did I.

From around the boat I gathered up the scattered skis, poles, and axes and lashed them to the aft rail so the next blizzard would not blow them away. I shoveled out the flue pipe on deck and extended it two feet higher with an old perforated pipe, repaired with duct tape. I crawled below, put water on to heat, dug out a knife of more flexible steel, and dragged out a large pressure cooker in which to chip ice. With boiling water, I thawed and cleaned the dishes, putting everything back in its place. I made very strong coffee and mashed chunks of frozen butter, raisins, and brown sugar into steaming oatmeal. In the cold, even eating can be dangerous, as the surface skim freezes while the underside awaits to blister your lips. I ate carefully, focusing on the mouthful and the moment, and then washed the dish and pan. Wearing thin gloves to protect my skin, I prepared the coffee pot for its next use by filling the base with ice chips and the basket with dry grounds. I dripped diesel into the heater's base, splashed preheating alcohol on its surface, and relit the heater. A hint of warmth filled the cabin.

I opened a can of gelled alcohol and laid big stick matches next to it on the galley counter. If my hands became too frozen to spin the little wheel on a cigarette lighter, the alcohol would be my ground zero source of heat from which to build. I practiced: I held the matchbox between two folded, pretend-frozen hands and lit a match with my teeth, dropping it into the fuel.

I couldn't always control my mind and moods, but for the moment I had that feeling of being "in the zone," that calm and crisp mental state with a fine, almost trancelike focus on the task at hand. Early seamen always found this part of the Inuit's behavior unfathomable. Now, faced with the same deadly seriousness of this environment, I understood it perfectly.

Diana hoped to find a ham radio enthusiast who would set up a regular schedule with me, and I had reluctantly promised her I would monitor a certain radio frequency. I understood that not knowing about my well-being would add an extra burden to the troubles she faced with her father. But for myself, if I had to be alone, then let it be alone. I did not want radio contact; I viewed it as an intrusion. Somehow, it compromised the adventure. I wrapped that core reason within a rationalized concern for the electrical consumption required to maintain a radio vigil. Yet on the designated day and time the radio crackled, "Whiskey, Charlie, Gulf, 4 3 7 7, Whiskey, Charlie, Gulf 4 3 7 7. This is X N R 7 9, Cambridge Bay."

"X N R 7 9, this is Whiskey, Charlie, Gulf, 4 3 7 7. Go."

A baritone voice said, "Very faint copy. I think you are out there in the ether. We'll give it a try. Hello, Alvah. My name is Peter Semotiuk. I'm in Cambridge Bay, about seven hundred miles to your southwest. I received a phone call from your wife, Diana. She got my name from the captain of the *Belvedere* in Camden, Maine. I have done some sailing on *Belvedere* and acted as the shore-based radio station when it went through the Northwest Passage. Diana is very concerned for your safety. I must say, since I heard what you are doing, so am I. She hopes that you and I may have regular radio contact. Over."

I bristled at that, so I slid sideways. "X N R 7 9, where is Diana now? Over."

"I cannot read you. Repeat, cannot read. You will want to know, Diana spent one week in Pond Inlet, flew to Ottawa, and then connected safely on to New Zealand. If you copy, key your mike three times."

I pushed the microphone button three times. Peter came back. "I have three keys. Good. Your signal is very weak. If you have a long wire on board, stretch it from your deck antenna jack up to the masthead and then out onto the ice. Try to point the end of the wire to within ten degrees of southwest. Do not let it touch the rigging or the ice. Start transmitting on your highest wattage setting, and then we'll shut it down to the minimum possible once we have established contact. Diana told me that you're concerned about your fuel supply, so I understand that you'll want to conserve electricity. I will try again, same time, same frequency, tomorrow. If you are well, key your mike three times now . . . I have three keys. Good. When we communicate, if conditions are poor, we will use three keys, and you can say A.O.K., Alpha, Oscar, Kilo, and I'll know all is well. Tomorrow, tomorrow, to-morrow. This is X N R 7 9, with W C G 4 3 7 7. Out."

As the cabin fell silent, I felt my heart beating fast. I did not want to break my vigil with chatty strangers, but this Peter fellow had been pre-cise and clever in overcoming my radio difficulties, and he seemed to speak directly to my concerns. I slid into the sleeping bag, muscling Halifax aside, and pulled the book *Arctic Passage* off the shelf. The au-thor, Dr. John Bockstoce, had attempted to transit the Northwest Pas-sage in a traditional hide boat called an *umiaq*. Traveling in the sum-mer months, he had tried and been repelled by ice for a number of years. As an archaeologist and ethnologist, he did not consider these at-tempts failures; he used the time well in studying old whaling sites. Ulti-mately, however, he wanted to conquer the Passage, and thus bought the enormous steel sloop *Belvedere*. Even with that strength and power, he was stopped for several years, laying the boat up on land at the end of each attempt. Finally, in 1989, conditions mellowed, and the *Belvedere* completed the Passage in its entirety. (For the record, that is from the waters of the Pacific below the Bering Strait to the Atlantic's Baffin Bay.)

Toward the end of the book, as *Belvedere* sailed home via Green-land, I saw a photograph of an enormous man standing on deck, look-ing out to sea. The caption confirmed that I had found the face of Peter Semotiuk to put with that deep voice. It was a strong face, with high cheekbones and a prominent brow hanging over a Roman nose. Thick, jet black hair fell over his ears. Between the ethnic look and the last name, I wondered if Peter might be a Native American.

Dr. Bockstoce wrote of a visit to a Defense Early Warning base: "While I was talking to Pat Murray, the station chief, a great bear of a man walked into the office. There suddenly didn't seem room for us all." I looked around my small cabin, and thought the same thing.

I got up, pulled on my insulated bibs and parka and oversized pack boots and climbed out on deck. One hundred meters south was a long ridge rising steeply from the sea-ice. At the crown of the ridge sat a large, lone boulder, silhouetted against the dim glow in the southern sky. There sat Raven like an old wizard, watching my every move. I cupped my hands over my mouth and cawed once. He cawed back. I cawed twice. He cawed back twice. I took comfort in knowing he was there, in spite of his purpose. Our exchange of signals filled a deep need in me. I had to ask myself, what was it *really* that made me so hesitant to establish contact and communication? Was it that my predecessors and heroes did not have this equipment? Did this gadgetry disqualify this as true adventure? If I called Peter right now and said, "I've just accidentally shot myself and I'm bleeding to death," what could he do? He'd say, "Oh, too bad. Maybe someone can make it out there next March to collect your body."

I went below and pulled up a floorboard, exposing the ice-choked bilges. I chipped free a plastic bag of old rigging wire. Unwinding the fine wire's kinky plaits, I planned to splice them into a hundred-foot length. To keep my fingers warm and functioning, I had to do the splicing below, in spite of the limited space. The spiraling wire spread about the cabin in tumbleweeds, the loops and whorls just far enough apart to prevent them from contacting one another—that is, until Halifax waded in. With two or three quick sorties, she tangled the wire into a rat's nest that overwhelmed the cabin. The more I tried to untangle it, the more entangled I became, like a cheap science-fiction plot. I spent the better part of the day taming the wire. (I was less successful taming the cat.) After many long splices, the wire was finally at one with itself.

Outside, I drove an ice screw into the surface far to the southwest and tied parachute cord to it as insulation between the wire's end and the ice. I connected the other end of the wire to the deck fitting that led to the antenna tuner. Forty feet up the wire I fastened the main halyard, then hoisted the wire aloft until it stretched taut, outside of all rigging, from the deck via the masthead to the distant screw in the ice. I tied orange, plastic-tape strips at close intervals along the wire to alert the likely bears and unlikely helicopter pilots to its presence. I stood back, pleased. It was a handy piece of jury-rigging, and I liked the bright orange tape fluttering in the breeze like Buddhist prayer wheels.

The next day, again precisely on time, Peter's voice came in loud and clear. He told me my signal was still faint but would be readable more often. He must have sensed my reluctance, because he never put me on the spot regarding regular contact. He suggested that he try me once a week but said he would monitor that frequency every night in case of an emergency—or, he added casually, in the event I just wanted to talk. He said just knowing he was there would make Diana feel better. He spoke of her with familiarity and concern and subtly coaxed me to consider her needs, without ever actually saying that. I told him I would contact him the next Sunday.

The following Thursday night, on a whim, I called, "X N R 7 9, this is W C G 4 3 7 7."

True to his word, he responded as if he had the mike already in hand. "Your mother called me. She cried, she was so happy to think that you were not really alone now. She said your Aunt Prudence is better. Diana called also. She's home now and says it is very warm down under, and green. I could hardly hear her through all the beautiful songbirds. Her brother Michael will be coming from Australia soon. Her father is doing surprisingly well, but they're waiting on some more tests. She sounded more rested."

That did it—the guy won me over entirely. He was warm, sincere, and concerned. He was not only my conduit to Di and my family, he was a commentator who could flesh out the meager tidbits with insight and paint her situation for me like a picture.

He said, "Let me check my notes of my conversation with her." (Notes! This guy was organized.) "Diana wants you to promise her that you will not go up on the glacier alone." (Three experienced French climbers had recently been killed on a glacier on south Baffin Island. Predictably, Diana and I had drawn different conclusions as to how that related to my plans.)

I joked, "Only Diana could find a way to nag me from ten thousand miles away."

Peter keyed his mike and bellowed a live, loud laugh. I had never heard anyone do that, laugh on the airways. The cabin seemed brighter.

"Peter, tell her I will not set one foot on the glacier until she returns. Tell her, please, not to worry about me, just take good care of her

77° 45' North. Turned back with Etah in sight.

Icebergs. We were dwarfed by their majesty, threatened by their power.

73° North, nearing Upernavik, on Greenland's northwest coast.

In a land of ice and stone, soil must be saved for an important community function. Maniitsoq, Greenland.

Charlie Inoraaq with family and friends. Pond Inlet, Baffin Island.

As hard as stone and equally silent,
Panoely prepares his team. Tay Bay,
Bylot Island.

Young ring seal.

September 12: Not
a day to spare as
we carve our way
into Tay Bay on the
northwest coast of
Bylot Island.

Nanook is always
there.

Chipping ice from a bergy bit. We would have only as much water to drink as we had fuel to melt ice.

Early October. Tay Bay, Bylot Island.

October 12: Diana disappears over the southern horizon, with the sun close behind.

Alone. Tay Bay, Bylot Island.

The *Roger Henry* disappears beneath drifting snow.

The long polar night begins.

Relative comfort before ice invades the interior of the *Roger Henry*.

Arctic fox.

On patrol, a female
and cub.

Limkee and Diana.

Diana in full traditional dress.

Inuit overbooties cleverly
crafted from polar bear and
seal skins.

Inexplicably, the *Roger Henry*
sinks inch by inch into
apparently solid ice.

The month of May brought
trench warfare.

Ground blizzards erase our
work.

Life on the edge: glaucous gull chicks.

Gyrfalcon fledgling, soon to be master of the northern skies.

Glaucous gull chics instinctively looking south.

Adult glaucous gull.

The first lead of an Arctic spring.

Arctic poppies.

Cotton grass.

Inussualuk Glacier carves deeply into the pristine interior of Bylot Island.

Tay Bay.

Dundas Harbor. Devon Island is 21,000 square miles of uninhabited wilderness.

The remains of the Dundas Harbor settlement.

Elijah, from Pond Inlet.

Musk ox bull.

August 1: At the mouth of Tay
Bay, looking out toward Navy
Board Inlet. The *Roger Henry*
must leave now or never.

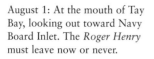

Matais and son visit from Pond
Inlet.

father and herself. Why don't we make contact in ... let's say, two days?"

Peter would be honor bound to honestly describe my physical and mental state to Diana. I decided I would never pick up that microphone unless I could at least fake a happy, healthy persona.

In part, that happiness and health required engaging my environment, not hiding below from it as if it were a malevolent enemy. On October 25, after being pinned below for four days by screeching winds and snow, I raced through my chores of cooking, cleaning, pumping up the heater's day tank, filling the lanterns, and chipping ice, and had the sled loaded for first light, which now came past eleven in the morning.

Leaving Halifax below, I set out for the head of the bay on skis with rubber climbing skins stretched the length of the skis' bottoms for traction. Skis were the safest if not the easiest form of travel, as the ski's length spanned the snow-hidden cracks and holes in the sea-ice. Through still air of ten degrees Fahrenheit, I pulled hard for two hours toward a razor ridge at the bay's head, which from the boat had appeared only a short stroll away. I simply could not adjust to the scale without even a tree to create a context of size. Where the rock ridge cut through the glacier's base, I staked down the sled, strapped the skis to it, and roped down my bulky parka, which I felt would be too warm and heavy for the uphill trudge. I pulled up my wind-suit hood and opened the zipper air-vents beneath each arm and at the hips. I stuffed the day-pack pockets full of survival equipment: heat-packs, fatty meats, a space blanket, and bear mace.

Everything I touched reminded me of Diana, the same Diana I had once considered coming here without. What a fool. We bought the bear mace in an outfitting store in Montana. I remembered that wonderful expression on her face when the cowboy sales clerk said to her, "If it don't work, bring it on back."

I started up the ridge, laughing out loud. The snow on the lower ridge cornice was wind packed and firm as a garden path. I made good time for what I guessed to be an hour, but then large boulders blocked the narrow spine and turned the hike into a scramble. I considered each footfall, aware how serious a fall or injury would be alone and this far from the boat. The ridge climbed steeply and arched north into valleys that ran all the way down to Maud Bight on Bylot's sheer northern coast. After another hour I crested the saddle, which acted as a continental divide of sorts. The ice cap split there like ice cream dripping off different edges of a cone.

The sky was absolutely cloudless, and soft, golden light washed over Tay Bay, a soothing salve for my loneliness. I had not brought a watch, and I quickly learned how nothing in the Arctic mirrors the experience of lower latitudes. The sun does not cross over the sky, but skids around or just beneath the horizon's rim. As the day wore on I felt a time vertigo; I could not even guess how long I might have been away from the boat.

I hiked as deep into the island's interior as I thought time and my promise to Diana about staying off the glacier allowed. I did not want to negotiate my return through the boulders and a thin cornice line without some light. I found a large boulder and crawled up to its high crown. The wind blew lightly off the massive, mile-wide glacier only one hundred meters to my right. The top of the glacier flowed gradually down into the bay, but its vertical sides dropped precipitously into a rubble moraine. The cliffs I stood on formed the opposite edge of a steep and narrow canyon. Carved into the base of the ice walls were cathedral-sized grottos and deeply sculpted caves. Those caves drew my attention with an inexplicable intensity.

Because Africa is acknowledged as the cradle of civilization, we forget that many of our roots lie with the advances and retreats of these great ice walls that swept up and down the Americas, Europe, and the Asian Steppes. By day we followed the mighty mastodons and woolly mammoths, cautiously evading the saber-toothed tiger. By night we retreated to caves, chewed on burnt meat, and huddled over smoky fires for warmth, carefully rotating our wooden spear tips in the flames so they would harden but not burn. We practiced sounds that would not only hone our communication and cooperation in the hunt but also stretch our limited understanding of ourselves and the threatening world around us. I experienced an exciting connection to the past when I realized that, many tens of thousands of years later, here I sat in this tumultuous continuation of the Ice Age, in that same attempt to stretch my self-awareness. I felt perfectly at home in an atavistic way that words will not describe. The ordeal ahead would become my solo microcosm of the great struggle of our kind. If I could remain alert and listening, I might learn much not only about myself but about the roots of humankind.

The time passed and the wind increased unnoticed, for I was lost in thought. I pictured those prehistoric times when evolving humans experimented with different survival techniques, roaming as loners or collecting in tribes. Those decisions are deeply ingrained in our subconscious, for even today if one individual human starts to vomit, those within earshot may begin retching automatically. This is because, back in those lost days and cold caves, if the tribe ate tainted meat or poisoned berries, the first person to react instantly triggered vomiting in all as a communal defense strategy.

I jumped up with a start. *I better head back down.* Tay Bay looked surprisingly small below me, and the *Roger Henry* was undetectable. How far had I come? I was only halfway down the ridge when the already dim light failed completely. I pressed on hard but started to slip and stumble. I decided that, if I had any hope of at least making the emergency sled, if not the boat, I would have to shortcut the long curve of the ridge. That was a mistake. It was all too easy to slide down the steep slope off the razor ridge, but it became a time-consuming, grueling crawl back out of the waist-deep snow in the hollow. For an hour I trudged back to the ridge line, trying unsuccessfully to gain ground without sweating. The possibility that I'd have to spend the night out there was increasing by the minute. My thin clothing was suitable only as long as I remained active. If I allowed myself to become damp and exposed, I would surely feel the cutting lash of the Arctic cold.

In the dark, I slipped over an icy boulder and fell heavily. I picked myself up and carried on. After several such falls, I crawled behind a rock for shelter from the increasingly cold breeze. I had to weigh the dangers of a sprained ankle or broken leg against not making it to the supplies on the sled. I had almost reconciled myself to the cautious choice, which was to wait the twenty-some hours until dawn, when I remembered the moon. I had not seen it in many days due to blizzards, but I guessed it to have been full two to three nights earlier. If that was correct, could I roughly calculate its rising time? Would it be the same up here? The full moon rises exactly as the sun sets, and then rises forty-eight minutes later each night thereafter. If I waited an hour and a half to two hours, could I expect some help from the moon on the trail down? If it clouded over, or if I had miscalculated, I would suffer a cold wait for nothing. Still, I lay behind the rock and slept for that time as best I could. Startled, I jumped awake, thinking someone was flashing a light in my eyes. But it was a fat and full moon, its glorious luminescence reflecting off glacier and snow. I do not exaggerate by saying I could have read by this light. The Inuit describe full moonglow more pragmatically: "One can pick lice off a shirt by it."

My lunar guide made the hike down not only safe, but marvelous. I strapped up to the sled, thankfully slipped into my warm parka, and hiked home through the single most beautiful night of my year in Tay Bay. The ice and snow sparkled and shone as if the night heavens had fallen to earth. My spirits were lifted for several days while I basked in the memory, even though I had to hunker down yet again from incessant gales.

Before we'd left America, Diana and I had gone to the Brookfield Zoo outside Chicago to watch a polar bear move. I'd turned sideways, stretching my peripheral vision, wanting to see that shape from different angles and train my eyes to pull it out from its perfectly camouflaged backdrop. An animal biologist was there measuring the hours the bear paced back and forth in its compound. She theorized that captive bears pace constantly to produce endorphins that relieve the monotony and depression of their sad situation.

I think my obsessive hiking was a similar attempt to relieve the stresses of being caged aboard the *Roger Henry*. At every opportunity, I walked as far from the boat as my legs would carry me; then, when I began to feel cold and exhausted and turned to look back toward the boat, I no longer thought of it as a depressing steel cave but rather as a relatively warm and safe haven from the darkness and doubt on the open ice. I pushed through weather conditions I should not have. I went out in the dark when it would have been prudent to remain below. I did not turn back when I discovered I was not the only lonely wanderer, finding enormous bear prints in the dark, because just being out there gave some meaning to my otherwise empty days. When I struggled back into camp after a grueling hike, I felt as if I had *done* something.

When loneliness seeped into my bones like the increasing winter winds, my perspective changed completely. I became more and more introspective. Increasingly what I *thought* and what I *felt* combined into what *happened* that day, and my diary dealt mostly with matters of the heart and mind, not my back and biceps. On high-spirited days, of which there were many, this was wonderful. But it plunged me into dangerous pits of despair on others.

As the sunlight began to fade in late October, moonless dark and shrieking gales forced me to remain below more often. Things began to go wrong. The novelty and initial excitement wore off, and the silence eroded both my confidence and my will. My mind wandered from its promised discipline and clouded with a dangerous inability to concentrate.

I recorded in my diary:

I'm going flaky and I've only been alone for a few weeks. Today I went for a long hike down the southern shore of Navy Board Inlet. Several miles from the boat I thought I saw movement behind some ice, so I unslung the shotgun and pumped a round into the chamber. Nothing happened. I could not believe it— me, the original Dan'l Boone, out here with an unloaded gun. Well, everybody makes mistakes, but I turned and headed back to the boat, never once thinking about the six rounds of ammo in the bandoleer on the rifle butt, literally at my fingertips. Yesterday, I left the kettle on the boil while I was out chopping ice and completely forgot it. When I rushed below, the cabin was like a sauna, dripping with a sooty rain. The day before, I was daydreaming while making pancake batter. I just kept pouring in the water until I had a thin soup. I told Peter I would come up on the radio Wednesday at a special time to talk with Terry Jesudason. He told me that she and her husband, Bezal, run the hotel and outfitting service in Resolute, and they wanted to meet me, so to speak. Right on time I fired up the radio and contacted Peter. I could tell he was a little miffed about something, so I finally asked him outright what was the matter. He said he didn't mind waiting for nothing, but when he organizes other people with a radio schedule, he'd appreciate it if I could at least show up as agreed. I was dumbfounded until later, when he said something else that confused me, and I realized I had somehow lost an entire day. It was Thursday. I can't help it, I'm afraid, because I can't put my finger on what's wrong with me. It's as if I've been poisoned. If I'm this disoriented already, how bad will I be by January or February?

I planned an outing to an alluringly shaped iceberg, six miles up Navy Board Inlet, thinking that getting entirely out of the bay might lift my flagging spirits. The ice terrain would prove easy, but the distance alone required many hours of travel, so I turned off the heater before leaving the boat. It would be better returning to a frozen boat than a boat in flames. The hike was too much for Halifax, so I locked her below to stop her from following. As I harnessed myself to the sled, I could hear a most unhappy kitten whining, scratching, and generally extracting her revenge down there.

I had vowed never to be caught out without a sled full of enough gear to make it through a blizzard. I left the skis strapped to the sled and laced on a pair of cheap ice creepers, which were far short of climbing crampons in quality but easier to hike with. For an hour I hugged the east shore of Navy Board Inlet, looking up new valleys, north to Devon Island, and south to the hidden peaks of Baffin. I should have been thrilled by this entirely new terrain, but I felt flat and dull. My legs felt like lead, and my pace was ponderously slow.

I came across a seal's hole in the ice, surrounded by blood. There was no offal and no clear bear sign, so I could not be sure what had passed. Still, the blood looked gruesome against the whiteness of the ice, and the brutality of it depressed me terribly.

I had to force myself over the miles to the berg. My steps stumbled wearily and my mind wandered. When I got to the berg, I could not find the boathook that I usually carried as a walking stick. If I fell through the ice, I would need a hook to grab onto the surface and pull myself out. *I had it in my hand. How the hell could I lose it?* Though I knew I would probably find it on the return route, my inattentiveness and lack of focus angered me.

In the drifted snows along the iceberg's base lay a clear trail of fresh bear tracks. The thirteen-inch paws pigeon-toed deeply into the snow, leading to an ice overhang that formed a small grotto at the berg's base.

A smooth surface of shiny ice and coarse tufts of hair indicated that the bear had slept there. The tracks then led out of the grotto, continued around the ice mountain, and abruptly disappeared, even though soft snow surrounded them. Inuit myths often mention flying bears. The Inuit also believe the bear can climb vertical ice walls, using its claws much as a human ice climber toe points with crampons. I looked up the sheer edge of the iceberg and again felt an inexplicable pull toward the beast I should fear most. Because of my inferior creepers, I found the easiest route up the iceberg by following fox tracks over the snow covering. I slowly crept up to the highest point, checking each hummock for the slight rise of breathing and the air for the telltale fog of warm breath. It suddenly occurred to me that I would be in deep trouble if I did find something up there. Nothing was there—but rather than feeling relieved I felt even lonelier.

We underestimate animals when we assume they do not appreciate beauty. Intellectually, I could see why both fox and bear would choose this high lookout, for the view from the top was both strategic and stunning. But emotionally, that haunting panorama only depressed me more. I worried that if I could not find joy in this, then I was facing a morbid time. An irresistible tiredness overwhelmed me. I lay down in a shallow depression and slept. When I woke, I felt even more tired, but I knew it was more than tiredness—it was a deepening depression pulling me down. *I'd better head back toward camp while I can.*

I took one step down the incline and felt the flimsy creepers twist off my feet. Things happened fast. I dropped the shotgun and grabbed my ice ax with both hands. I started sliding down the berg toward a sharp drop. I knew the fall itself might not kill me, but being killed outright might be better than the slow death of broken ankles five miles from the boat. I spun over onto my stomach and buried the pick into the fast-passing berg surface in a movement mountaineers call self-arrest. One hand grabs the crown of the ax and holds the body's weight; the other lifts the handle base to adjust the angle of attack of the curved ax point. In a hail of ice shrapnel, I ground to a halt on the steep grade. I could not dig my feet in and, with only one pick, could not hand-over-hand myself up or down. I felt utterly stupid, impotent, and impatient.

I couldn't hang there forever. Without careful consideration, I pulled out the point. The rasp of my nylon clothing began to hiss as I accelerated into the glissade again.

I flew over the drop-off and hit the ground with a sickening thud, even though I snapped into position to make a parachute-landing roll. A jolt of pain flashed up my legs. I lay on the ice, replaying the audio track of the fall in my mind. I did not hear any gruesome crack of bone. I was mainly concerned with the fact that I was not concerned. I had gone through the motions, even gotten them right, but I was detached, only mildly curious about what was going to happen to that guy falling off that iceberg. Somehow, solitude had sapped dry my raison d'être. There is affirmation in human company, a constant consensus over what matters. After only one month alone, without that company nothing mattered. I got up and limped in circles on sore ankles.

On a full run, the Bushmen of the Kalahari can follow a single animal's tracks in a large herd. Some claim they can read the signs in such detail as to tell you the animal's sex, condition, even mood. I wondered if my tracks and trails told my whole story. Would skilled observers bend over the disturbances in the snow and say, "How sad."?

I began searching for my brother Raoul's shotgun. It had taken three months of cajoling to get it out of him. I think he was joking when he said, "I don't care if they ever find your body, but I better get this gun back." It was clear that if I didn't head out soon, they would find neither.

I had dropped my boathook, dropped my gun, fallen off an iceberg. I was hurt, exhausted, and terribly depressed. Finally, I found the gun. Through the hours hiking home I could not keep my mind from fantasy. It kept detaching from my body. At first the feeling terrified me; *Not out here! Wait for the boat.* I tried to resist, but in the end I was powerless. *My father had not been killed in a crash! He landed his little airplane next to the* Roger Henry. *He was old now and could not hike far, but he reveled in the beauty, and we shared it deeply. He seemed so proud of me; he just glowed. He told me he had been wrong all along about the war in Vietnam, wrong to shout and scream at me so for not agreeing with him. I told him I had been wrong when I condemned his entire generation as suburban clones, driven by greed. They had en-*

dured the Great War, known hardships that we never will, done their best to make a safe home, community, and nation for us, all for us. We hugged. I touched the faded "Semper Fi" tattoo on his big forearm. "I love you, Dad. I love you, and I respect you. You were tough, but you were steady and true. You knew right from wrong. You preached duty and responsibility." I was saying all this out loud as my trail wove drunkenly. Emotion choked me, and I fell to my knees. The fantasy was bordering on real. With its hallucinogenic intensity, it was so compelling that I replayed it scene by scene, making pleasing adjustments, as if I could rework history to make it so.

I must have begun walking again because I almost stepped on the boathook. I could have passed right by a bear and never have known it. The dark cliffs that formed the entrance to Tay seemed to get no higher. I felt so tired. I wasn't sure I could make it back to the boat. Increasingly, as I would see the next day, my trail wound more and my tracks staggered. I lost track of time and even forgot where I was walking to. When I came upon a mast sticking out of a snowbank, it took me a moment to understand what it was. *Oh yes, this is my grand adventure.* I unbuckled the harness and left the sled untied and exposed to high winds. I dropped the shotgun in the snow and crawled below.

The cabin was empty, cold, and silent, and I hated it. My ears were ringing, my mind racing, my stomach filled with fear. *What is happening to me? I think of myself as being as tough as they come, and apparently that is not going to do me one damn bit of good. Just how bad will this get? To what ring of Dante's Inferno will I fall?*

I forced myself to cook pancakes and smoked bacon, and I washed it all down with two highly illegal shots of Jack Daniel's. I crawled into the bag and slept dreamlessly for twenty hours. I woke in a refreshed, vibrantly happy mood—humming zippity doodaa, zippity-ay, my-oh-my, what a wonderful day.

My mood swings were extreme, uncontrollable, and unpredictable. One thing was sure: This was going to be one hell of a ride.

S E V E N

Tay Bay

NOVEMBER 1994

ZERO HOURS DAYLIGHT

To go into the dark with a light is to know the light.
To know the dark, go dark. Go without sight,
And find that the dark too blooms and sings
And is traveled by dark feet and dark wings.

—Wendell Berry, "To Know the Dark"

IN THEORY, THE SUN would lie due south at my *local noon,* which is the exact time the sun reaches its zenith in the sky. To establish this, I added to twelve o'clock four minutes for each degree of longitude I was west of the meridian that began my time zone. However, the southern horizon was buried deep behind the jagged edges of steep mountains, and from early October on, only a shadow of silver light gilded the peaks like a photographic negative. Based on my latitude, I calculated the exact day the sun would fail to break the real horizon for the first time: November 3. Like most such exercises, it was meaningless. If I had asked an Inuk hunter, "When will it be totally dark?", he would have laughed at me and said, "When the sun is gone."

Still, I could not help myself. Early on the designated day, I headed out across the sea-ice, over the rolling tundra, and up the southern slopes. Three hours later, I slipped and sweated up a scree slide at the steep summit. I threw myself on the ground, panting, when I crested the ridge. When my breathing quieted, I turned slowly toward the south, hoping to fill my senses one last time with that heavenly sight. There was just a smudge of orange leeching into a purple sky. The sun was gone.

For any people on this earth other than the Inuit, the total loss of the sun is cataclysmic. I am not Inuit. My mind knew it must return one day, but my heart doubted. Below me, I saw a single mast sticking up from a snowbank, a small dome tent, and forty thousand square miles of uninhabited wilderness. If ever I was to execute a panic pullout, now was the time, for soon an impenetrable cloak would be laid upon this land. A dissenting voice within me said, "Give it up. Go get the sled and make for Pond Inlet. No one will fault you. People were never meant to be alone. Not even the Inuit go it alone."

I knew this to be true. Many years before, in the highlands of Papua New Guinea, I had set off alone into the jungle toward the headwaters of the Ramu River. By foot, raft, and finally a broken dugout canoe, I spent ten days pushing my way down the river to the first village. When I walked up the worn trail, the villagers came rushing out around me, trilling, and tugging at me in obvious anguish. In Pidgin, they wailed, "Oh no! What happened to your friends? Are they all dead?" It took me some time to convince them that no one was dead or even missing, that I was traveling alone by choice. They shook their heads in disbelief; this was inconceivable. Never, ever, do they spend significant time alone. To be alone is punishment for a crime. They have no prisons, only the threat of fellow villagers turning their backs. Banishing offenders to the agony of a life alone deters social disorder. Wholeness is found in the tribe, not the individual. From primitive jungle dwellers to urban modernists, we structure our lives around this herding instinct. Forget the "rugged individualists"—even they form clubs. So do the buffalo on the plains, birds in the sky, and fish in the sea.

On the long climb down the mountain, an internal debate raged. *You never said that your goal was to winter alone. People will understand.*

Yes, they will, but will I? Remember what I prayed for off Nova Scotia? I asked, Please, let me keep my courage and do my best. Would leaving now be doing my best? I knew it would not. Right, then. Into the breech, Lad. Get down to the details.

Back at the boat, in the dulled pewter light, I rechecked everything. Sled load by sled load, Diana and I had collected a mountain of freshwater ice to last us through the winter. Now, I found that its enormous weight created a sag in the taffylike sea-ice, and seawater had somehow been forced through the ice, filling the hollow. Snow had drifted between the pieces and acted like a wick to pull salt up into the pile. The entire supply was fused into a contaminated brick. No doubt any Inuk child could have warned me that this would happen. My tuition for this Arctic lesson was the loss of weeks' work. At each such mistake I thought, "Well, next time I'll know," and laughed, knowing that not even the eloquence of Daniel Webster himself could talk Diana into a "next time" up here.

I decided to start over by building a storage igloo for my ice. I sawed blocks from the snowbanks surrounding the boat, but they invariably crumbled or split. I went below to consult the Inuit masters, pulling out an old Arctic exploration book. I read of an elderly Inuk describing for a Kabloonah where and how to look for the perfect building material. Mimicking that story, I walked back and forth over deep snowbanks beneath the black granite cliffs that paralleled the boat and faced the prevailing winds. I listened carefully to each footfall. It had been difficult for the old Inuk to describe the specific sound with words, but I knew it the moment I heard it because it was the same tortured screech produced by walking on Styrofoam. I dug out the front of the snowbank with a camping shovel, shaping a vertical wall ten feet long. I leveled the top of this wall back two feet, then cut out a huge block using a rough-toothed snow saw.

That first block spoke to me. I sat in the snow as it told an entire chapter of the Inuit's amazing saga. When the wind blows across this land, the need for immediate shelter is extreme. The travelers look around, but there are no sheltering forests, only snow, and more snow, all seemingly the same for as far as the eye can see. But if they are keenly attuned to every nuance of nature, they will see a living and logical process. The snow lies in different depths with changing pressures, has varying amounts of moisture, and is packed or loosened by the prevailing winds and fluctuating temperatures. To be able to find the exact intersection of these forces is to survive in the Arctic. For here is found a building material that is plentiful, easily shaped, surprisingly strong, yet incredibly light. It allows hurried construction of a shelter that is efficiently insulated and totally windproof. This structure rises easily out of the snows when one needs it, and is just as easily left behind. In the wake of the Inuit rest no pyramids or Taj Mahals, for spring erases their efforts like footprints washed by the surf. But ask any engineer what building shape is considered the most sophisticated, and he or she will tell you it is the spiraling dome, for it requires no beams, struts, or supports. It is eloquently integrated into itself, much like its Inuit inventors.

I loaded the sled and hauled it from the bank to the boat and back again. With a little trial and a lot of error, I constructed a crude igloo.

For hours I stacked, beveled, and chinked with snow. The walls looked good, but my skills were not up to the traditional spiraling roof. I lifted the flooring above the sea-ice by paving it with thick blocks and covered these with a plastic sheet. I filled the roofless igloo with freshwater ice boulders, then covered it with a bright blue tarp. I weighed the tarp's corners down with full cans of jet fuel. My hardwater well, if you will, lay only five feet off the starboard quarter of the boat, so I did not think it was necessary to mark it. After all, where could it go?

When the outside temperature sank to a dangerous thirty, then forty degrees below zero Fahrenheit, maintaining a warm cabin required more fuel each day. To quantify exactly how much fuel I had, I sounded the keel tank with a long wooden dowel. When I withdrew the dowel, the wet/dry line lay beneath the half-tank mark. Certain I had more fuel than that, I assumed the stick had snagged and not reached bottom. I pressed it down again, but the line did not change.

I rushed about counting the liters scattered through the many jerry cans, and added to that sum the small amounts of specialty fuels, such as gasoline for the outboard and white gas for the camping stove. In spite of the Coast Guard's contribution, no matter how I juggled the numbers, at my present rate of consumption there was no formula that could stretch my supply through the eight months until breakup.

I pored over the logbook records, tallying the hours we had run the engine, the number of times we'd filled the lamps and stove. It was important that I understood my error, at least. I found that, like most disasters, my fuel shortage resulted from a series of mistakes that were of small matter individually but combined to produce serious consequences.

We had burned too much fuel getting to and then into an ice-encrusted Tay Bay. An undetermined amount had squirted through a loose fuel line. Cooking required more fuel than I had anticipated. Melting ice into water consumed not only a major part of the day, but also a major part of the fuel. The diesel drips falling into the cabin heater's burning chamber were slow, but ever so continuous. The alternator mounted to the homemade generator in the forepeak was rated at 50 amps of output. Due to resistance in the long lines leading back to the batteries and a faulty regulator, the actual output was a mere ten amps, which rocketed up the cost of keeping the batteries well charged.

I might construct an excuse for each error, but there was no escaping the bottom line: I was running out of the one thing on which everything else relied—fuel. I was facing a serious challenge and knew that the clarity of my thinking now would weigh heavily in my eventual outcome.

With Halifax in tow, I climbed over the broken ice boulders at the tidal fracture zone and up the snow-drifted shoreline. Through the dim twilight we hiked westward up the tundra, postholing through the deep snow. Perched on the edge of a shear cliff overlooking Navy Board Inlet, tucked between overhanging cornices of drifted snow, stood my Thinking Rock. The cornices looked as if they could defy gravity no longer and would any second explode in avalanche. This created a natural tension, an air of expectation and calamity that was somehow exciting. I did my best thinking there.

I sat still, looking across the five-mile-wide Navy Board Inlet. The cliffs of the Borden Peninsula rose vertically out of the sea, relaxed momentarily in a short plateau, then began the steep climb up again to ragged peaks. Cold air perpetually rolled down the mountains, fell off the cliffs, and created a vortex at the base. High wind and dense fog are normally mutually exclusive, but on the Borden they literally boil together in maelstrom. I sat only five miles away, and yet a completely different weather system surrounded me. The lay of the land in Tay Bay melded in a way that brought what peace was possible during this troubled time of year.

A ptarmigan cooed close by. I could picture its fat little snow white body, shiny black eyes, sharp beak, and special, feather-fluffed feet, but in the dim light my eyes could not pierce its perfect camouflage. Halifax had it fixed on her radar, but her tail thumped in frustration because Raven had followed us, and the kitten knew she dare not wander too far from my side. Ptarmigan, like all members of the grouse family, are considered a stupid bird, but in fact they can be crafty. When finished feeding on exposed willow bark, they fly high into the sky, twist earthward, and divebomb directly into a soft snowbank, leaving not a track nor trace for foxes or wolverines to follow. Buried deep within, they find warmth in the insulating snow.

I pulled my parka hood out into a long tunnel, forcing my body heat to pass by my face on its flight upward into the dark skies. My breath crackled as it hit the frigid air in a sound the Siberian native people describe as "the whispering of the stars." I watched my breath crystallize on the fur fringe until my mind settled, then I focused on my problem.

It was time to think the unthinkable—Diana might not return. If the doctors were wrong, as we dearly wished, and her father hung on, she would rightfully remain at his side. That would leave me alone to try to navigate the boat out of the congested ice the following summer. Without her help, I needed to anticipate more motoring than sailing. Worse yet was the possibility that I would not break out at all the following year. Prudence required that I set aside a large reserve for these contingencies. To binge now and rely on resupply later might cost me dearly.

But how best to ration? In my mind I listed the basics of life in order of importance. In the Arctic winter they all required the use of fuel. Water meant melting, food meant cooking, and shelter meant heating. I turned the list upside down and began my economizing there.

I hiked back to the boat. Below, I stripped off my heavy outer wear. For thirty long, luxurious minutes I bathed in the warm cabin air. Then I pulled on a second set of long underwear, some thick felt leggings, a balaclava hood, and gloves. Reluctantly, I turned the heater down to its lowest setting. I had to trust in the Inuit beliefs that heating the air around you is wasteful; that the human body is the best furnace and fatty foods the best fuel. To bridge long periods of cold with limited resources, they eat heavily and insulate efficiently with clever clothing. They do one more thing: They adapt. That is, they adjust their comfort level, and in so doing adjust their survival level. They harden themselves to the harsh realities of their world, and so must I.

I changed my entire living regime. I began cooking only once a day but ate enormous amounts at that one sitting. An extra dollop of butter or chunk of fat floated on top of every stew or soup. In fact, my craving became such that other food groups became only convenient systems through which to convey fat to my mouth.

No more did I boil water whenever I fancied a cup of tea or coffee. A single morning boil-up had to cover my first cup, clean the dishes, fill two thermoses, brush my teeth (shaving was suspended), and melt the various malfunctioning pieces of equipment. Every action required spending the precious energy units called "ergs," and I horded them stingily.

For both safety and economy, I turned the heater off when I climbed into the bag to sleep, relighting it each morning—or better stated, each time I woke with the intent of rising, for there was now no morning nor afternoon, only night. I kept the heat so low that it took the entire day to bring the cabin temperature up to "radioactive" level, the temperature at which the liquid-crystal display in the radio emerged from frozen inertness. Only then could I use the equipment without risking damage. Then the heater went off again. Thus, it was not light but heat that defined my day. Through the heater's mica window, only an inch and a half in diameter, I'd gaze at the red flicker of flame that drew me in with the hypnotic effect of a campfire.

Of course, the interior temperature fell well below freezing and remained there for the next four months. Ice invaded my already small space, filling the bilges and glazing the ceiling and walls. The sharp cabin corners now arched with smoking ice. In Diana's clothing locker hung a bit of frilly lace suspended in an ice cube, like an insect in amber.

I tried regularly to clear the cabin of ice, until I was forced to accept that I could not keep it at bay. Ironically, heat became more of a problem than cold; if I let the cabin warm up too much, the ice veneer melted and rain fell on my bedding, clothing, and equipment. That moisture was more than an inconvenience. It was a danger, for wetness destroys the insulating properties of most materials.

A factor in the tragic loss of Robert Falcon Scott's entire South Polar party was their failure to minimize the buildup of moisture in their clothing and tents from perspiration, breathing, and cooking. After a long day of sweaty, grueling toil manhauling heavy sleds, each night they used their precious body heat to thaw their way into their ice-clad sleeping bags. This sucked out their remaining energy, and they woke more exhausted than when they went to sleep. Slowly, they wore down, diminished their supplies, and awaited their deaths, only eleven unattainable miles from fresh supplies.

In contrast, Scott's rival, Roald Amundsen, made a relatively easy time of reaching the South Pole first by precisely imitating the actions and materials of the Netsilik Inuit, which he'd learned during his successful attempt on the Northwest Passage five years earlier. His team did not sweat by pulling; rather, they let their sled dogs shoulder the load. Amundsen donated a precious hour of travel time each day to the airing and beating of bedding and clothing. It was time well invested, for his party beat Scott's to the Pole by three weeks and returned without loss of life or limb.

I, too, tried to imitate the Inuit, but my ventilation system did not work as well as the igloo's, which has a low entrance tunnel sloping up from the outside. The moist, warm air inside rises out the ceiling vent hole and pulls in fresh, dry air from beneath, while a clump of dried grass in the vent hole regulates this flow precisely.

The *Roger Henry*'s hatchway had to act as both the air intake and outflow. If I opened the hatch too widely, heavy, cold air poured down the companionway. If I didn't open it enough, trapped moisture below formed ice rapidly, especially at the confluence of the hatch itself. I had to clear the heavy buildup daily. Should I get lazy, drift mentally, or even sleep too long on the wrong day, I'd be sealed below in a dark coffin.

I used the twelve-volt electrical lights sparingly, except for holidays and timely celebrations. The kerosene lanterns had the advantage of giving off both light and heat. The dim lantern light, however, did not beat back the borders of darkness very far. Any mechanical, electrical, or otherwise intricate work required I use a battery-operated headlamp strapped over an insulated helmet liner. This freed my hands and focused a beam of light on the task at hand. The batteries for this required constant recharging, forcing me to be very disciplined in rationing their use.

I often sat in the dark for a couple days to save up energy and then really splurged by lighting two lanterns, perhaps even a candle. The light was glorious. It cheered the atmosphere and warmed my soul. But most importantly, I could read, exercising my eyes and mind. Compared to the continuous blizzards and average outside temperature of minus thirty-five degrees, I found my refuge acceptable.

Halifax disagreed. Mostly, she huddled deep in the sleeping bag, emerging only if her keen ears detected the sounds specific to me thawing out her block of milk. When one sleeps in a heavy hat, gloves, and thick clothing inside a tightly tapered sleeping bag, space is at a premium. We often had territorial disputes. She usually won, for she was better equipped to dig in when push came to shove. If I tried to force her out of the way, she would curl her lip, flex her claws, and give me a "go ahead, make my day" stare.

One day, as she walked from the bag bottom over the length of my body to get out for some fresh air, I noticed that she felt surprisingly light. I had not stocked much cat food, thinking that she could eat what we ate, but no matter her hunger, she would not touch the smoked meats. I turned on an electric light and saw that she was alarmingly thin. In the energy-demanding Arctic, one can starve to death almost as quickly as one can die of thirst.

I searched for the best medium with which to convey fat into her little stomach. For the baking of bread, the *Joy of Cooking* told me to "let dough rise at room temperature for two hours." I took one look at the thermometer and devised Plan B. I took the full mixing bowl into the sleeping bag, hoping to use my cocoon and body heat as a proofing oven. It was a slow process. I fell asleep, rolled over, and spread the gooey mess everywhere. I woke to Halifax licking the slop off my face. For my next attempt, I wrapped the dough bowl and a hot-water bottle in a woolen blanket. Maybe I checked its progress too often, because the result was a loaf with the texture of oak through which even feline fangs could not cut. The effect of the gas blowtorch on the next globule was equally discouraging.

Finally, I put the dough in a body-warmed bread pan, put it in the insulated oven, placed a lit candle beside it, and closed the oven. This worked too well. The goo grew like an alien life form and filled the oven to its blackened confines. I scraped out the sooty mess with a spatula. Experimenting, I adjusted the amount of yeast to an exact length of candle stub. Just as the candle went out, I turned the oven on. In this way, I economically produced some handsome loaves of white, wheat, oat, cornmeal, onion flake, and combinations thereof. Halifax did not offer up a purr easily through those dark days, but a bowl of warm diced bread saturated with butter and oily tuna evoked at least a hint of grateful rumble.

This learning process heightened my awareness of the relativity of resource. I had only as much water to drink as fuel to melt it and matches to light it. I had only as much bread to eat as candles left in the box. In the wider world, the relationships may not be as clear, but they are no less pertinent. I looked up *resource* in my Webster's pocket encyclopedia: "Materials that can be used to satisfy human needs. Because human needs are diverse and extend from basic physical requirements, such as food and shelter, to ill-defined aesthetic needs, resources encompass a vast range of items. The intellectual resources of a society— its ideas and technologies—determine which aspects of the environment meet that society's needs and, therefore, become resources. For example, in the nineteenth century, uranium was used only in the manufacture of colored glass. Today, with the advent of nuclear technology, it is a military resource."

To anyone who would listen, I shouted, "We have taken the use of uranium from making windows to breaking them, and we call that progress!" I looked up *progress,* and then *irony,* which appeared around the *Iron Age.* The lantern flickered near empty, and I was startled to think that I had been playing this game for hours, which led me to the natural conclusion that *time,* "the continuous passage of existence, recorded by division into hours, minutes, and seconds," was *the* most valuable of human resources. Whatever else I lacked, *time* I had plenty of, and that was my problem—too much of a good thing.

I used increasing amounts of that time on the radio with Peter, and I happily made sacrifices elsewhere in fuel consumption to do this. He instructed me patiently in radio tricks of the trade: combining certain weather conditions with lower levels of the ionosphere to bounce my weak radio waves to him, selecting differing frequencies at different times of the day, and tuning my antenna to optimum efficiency.

Security codes demanded he not go into much detail about his work, but over the course of several radio conversations I construed this much:

He was a civilian supervisor of a radar maintenance team on a military base two miles outside the small community of Cambridge Bay. I do not know who signed his paychecks. He had come to the Arctic from Manitoba twenty years earlier as a young electrical technician. On the base he met, fell in love with, and married his coworker Alma. For a period they worked on base and lived off base in Cambridge Bay, but when she lost her job the cost of town living became too much for a single salary. Peter moved back to the base and she went south to set up their home in Winnipeg. He joined her for what vacations and holidays his work allowed. Being childless, it must have been a lonely life for them both.

Having me as a responsibility seemed somehow engaging. He said many of his coworkers hated the Arctic; they thought it bleak and boring, even if very profitable. He disagreed with all his heart. Above all else, he loved the light and photographed it with passion.

He had another passion: cats. He talked often of his and Alma's cat, Merlin, and he related to the species closely. When he heard about Halifax, he was delighted. I was reduced to a supporting cast, for he always inquired after her well-being first. I liked that.

I sat on the wooden stool at the chart table with the microphone in my gloved hand. The lantern illuminated only the radio area, leaving me to stare out into the darkness as I listened to Peter talk excitedly about the specific dates migrating birds or animals left or returned. He knew the exact order in which the many species of wildflowers would paint the tundra first purple, then yellow, then white.

He was enormously curious about our boat and expedition, asking for every last detail. I'm afraid on some nights I went on in more detail than required, but he kindly responded as if it were all of utmost importance. Most rewarding for me was that he laughed at my jokes. In a decade together, rarely had I tickled Diana's dry sense of humor into an open chuckle.

On November 12 I recorded in my diary:

Diana has been gone for one month. The darkness is now complete. Even at noon the southern horizon does not offer a dull glow to draw my gaze. A very hard blizzard blew. When it was over, I crawled outside to fetch some ice from

my storage igloo, but I found nothing but an enormous snowbank. I dug down and down and still the blue tarp evaded me. I dug to the left, and then the right. I got confused and very upset. I am learning the hard way that the Arctic is all about shift and drift and illusion. Now I have to forage in the dark for freshwater ice. Male polar bears do not hibernate. They are out there, and they have to eat.

During our next radio contact, Peter relayed the Arctic news. Mostly it was a body count, for the season had taken a heavy toll. "Nine men from Iqaluit drowned while out walrus hunting in big leads off Frobisher Bay. One survived to tell the story. They left port in a leaky little trawler. Out in the ice, it started to go down. All but the one survivor scrambled for the canoe they kept on board. The survivor clung to the trawler hull when it turned turtle. When the nine tried to scramble into the canoe, it capsized and sank. The cold water pulled them down one at a time, they couldn't even swim back to the big boat. Over."

"Roger that, Peter. It must have devastated the village. What else? Over."

"Before the freeze-up, four American scientists died of hypothermia off southern Baffin Island, even though they were wearing life jackets, when a whale capsized their inflatable. Over."

"I copy that, Peter. These seas look so beautiful, but they're just liquid death. Over."

"The land is no safer. An Inuk hunter from Baker Lake went missing in October. Even though they still had some daylight down there, a ten-day search couldn't find him. Finally, someone came up to a small orange flag sticking only inches up from the snow. They dug down to find the man sitting upright on his snowmobile, looking perfect, but long dead. Over."

When Peter heard about my lost ice supply he expressed grave concerns about the bears and cautioned me never to underestimate them. I explained that what might appear as my underestimating animals was really my willingness to accept the risks of interaction with them.

I relayed to him a story told to me by a game warden in Namibia, in southwestern Africa. The warden was commissioned to do a game count far off the dirt roads. Dutifully, he left his pride and joy—a shiny and expensive new Land Rover—parked at the trailhead and hiked off into the veld. At night he returned to find that in his absence a tribe of baboons had been using his vehicle as a perfect lookout. They had defecated and urinated all over the roof and hood. After a few days of this, their urine actually blistered the Land Rover's shiny new paint. Something had to be done, but because he could not stand guard all day he thought he would employ the superior native intelligence of the *Homo sapien* against animal ignorance. He bought a realistic rubber replica of a black mamba snake, the baboon's feared enemy. The next day he left his menacingly coiled deterrent on the Land Rover's hood and confidently hiked away.

When he returned from the field he found his prized truck totally destroyed, all the windows smashed, the doors, hood, and roof deeply dented. The baboons had gathered in the bushes and, from a safe distance, hurled huge stones at the snake to drive it off their favorite perch.

Peter laughed so hard we had to suspend radio contact for the night.

The days flowed by seamlessly, emotionally some good, some bad, physically all dark and difficult. Normally only two national holidays hold any meaning for me—Thanksgiving and Martin Luther King's birthday—but I was looking for excuses. I would have celebrated National Hemorrhoid Awareness Day. On Thanksgiving Day, I cooked up a sumptuous feast. Halifax knew something was up, so she hung on my shoulder like a fur collar to watch my every move. I mashed canned turkey with dried vegetables and made a meatloaf shaped like a bird, surrounding it with mashed potatoes with gravy and soaked, dried cranberries. I baked pumpkin tarts and poured my last can of cream over them. Halifax ate two, then curled up contentedly on my chest.

W.C. Fields once said, "There I was, trapped in the wilds with nothing but food and water." I had planned more carefully, which is to say that I got a little drunk, but that was okay. I had saved up my rations for that very purpose. I turned on the cassette player, electrical consumption be damned! Champion Jack Dupree was a southern black blues singer and prizefighter. He'd roll into a town, and if he couldn't find a fight, he'd play the piano in some smoke-filled, sleazy honky-tonk. His simple, sad music flowed right through me. Emmylou Harris sang my feelings for me, "The last time I felt like this, I was in the wilderness, and the cabin caught on fire. I stood on that mountain, and I watched it burn, I just watched it burn." Hank Williams, Jr., wailed, "I'm so lonesome, I could die." I knew what he meant.

I read the historical account of the Pilgrims' feast with the Native Americans. For a time there was peace and cooperation between the two cultures. I wondered if our history might have gone some other way. What might our land and culture look like today had we been less fierce, or had there been fewer of us. What if we had we melded our two outlooks on life?

I read the famous "From where the sun now stands, I will fight no more, forever" speech made by Chief Joseph of the Nez Percé, as his people were surrounded by the U.S. Cavalry. He was noble and wise, a man who tried his best to avoid violence in protecting his people and their land. When he was forced to fight, he did so skillfully and honorably. Even his enemies recognized this. For eighteen months, his 250 warriors held off the seven-thousand-strong cavalry, but ultimately they were caught just forty miles short of their escape over the Canadian border. Those of his people who were not starved, shot, or frozen to death were exiled to Oklahoma in clear violation of the terms of their surrender. He mistakenly thought that words meant something. The Chief never saw his native land again. I closed the book and cried so hard I thought my heart would break just as his had. In the darkness, in my loneliness, I had never in my life felt more closely connected to humankind. "Ask not for whom the bell tolls." It tolled for me, as if the Nez Percé's tragedy had happened yesterday, and mattered.

I cleaned up the feast's debris, blew out the candle, crawled under my pile, and in my mind's eye replayed each flavor, sound, and emotion. I counted the days until the equinox on December 21, which would be my next party. I would celebrate the turnaround of the sun and its passage back north. It is a pagan feast, if we define pagan as that which is connected to earth, sun, moon, and stars.

I slept in the cavelike starboard aft cabin. The chore of constantly climbing in and out of the berth from the bed's head was offset by the cabin's opening porthole, which allowed me to let Halifax out without getting up. In theory, this was a considerable savings of precious heat because it took a long time to rewarm the bag if I had to get up. In practice, Halifax soon learned that if she knocked down the hinged upper board beneath the main hatch, hypercold air would fill the boat. My nose would freeze, and, no matter my reluctance, I would soon have to get up and close it. There she would sit on the galley counter, looking back and forth between me and her frozen milk.

I woke one night or day—there was no telling one from the other—and tried to roll over. I felt only a dead tug and panicked. *I'm paralyzed! My legs won't move. I know I'm awake, because I am cold . . . very cold.*

E I G H T

Tay Bay

DECEMBER 1994
ZERO HOURS DAYLIGHT

Someday should you wander away from the beaten path
You might chance to find your Self . . . before the cavern of your soul
"Dare I enter?" You ask yourself, "What might I find therein?"
Once decided, then best look to your supplies
The usual spelunking gear will do no good inside
Mortal lights won't pierce the dark. Hemp rope will serve no guide . . .
Take love for food, and faith for light, and leave security behind
For only then will you safely return, from your journey to the inner caves
That births the wellspring of the silent stream of eternal unconscious mind . . .
If you have the courage, and if you have the time
To go spelunking spiritual, without any line

—Charles Wiggins, *Dreams of Life* (unpublished)

PARALYZED, PETRIFIED, I felt around my thighs. *What is this, is it ice? Am I sleeping in a pool of freezing water? Is the boat sinking? No, how could the boat sink? It's in solid ice. Calm, stay calm . . . think.*

Slowly, I realized what must have happened. The cabin walls had been glazed with a half-foot of ice. I had fallen asleep with the lantern burning. In this confined space, the heat would have melted the ice. Water had run down the cabin walls onto the berth, which had a waterproof sheet on the mattress. The water had flowed to the low spot beneath me, and when the lantern went out, the cabin had cooled and the water had frozen.

My frozen clothing and bedding had me pinned down like Gulliver in Lilliput. My normally mild claustrophobia gave way to panic, which gave me the strength to rip myself free. I stumbled into the main cabin, dragging a train of frozen fabric stuck to me. My body was numb. My mind was the dangerous kind of sluggish that comes when the body's core temperature drops precipitously. Exposed to the frigid cabin air, my wet clothing quickly started to freeze. I stripped naked while I could and stood there mumbling stupidly in the dark. In a daze, I crawled into my insulated overalls. The nylon surface of that clothing was searing cold and sucked heat right from my center. Spots on my skin instantly frostbit. I rubbed them back into softness. I shivered hard, rubbed myself, and rocked from foot to foot, but I could not get warm. My teeth chattered uncontrollably. My hands shook so hard I could barely get into my boots, facemask, gloves, and parka. The coat was large enough to serve as a day pack, and in its pockets, fortunately, I had stashed food, hand warmers, extra gloves, and shotgun shells. I shoved a piece of fatty sausage into my mouth and put my clacking teeth to use.

I knew walking was the only way to warm my body and blood slowly. Sitting doesn't burn enough fuel to restart the inner furnace, while the exertion of running forces you to suck in huge amounts of cold air before your muscles are truly warmed. I climbed out of the boat, somehow remembering my shotgun but barely noticing that the night was clear and showed no threat of a blizzard. Because the snow is so dry in the desert air of the Arctic, the slightest wind whips up a blinding ground squall, and navigation is hopeless. I stumbled out across the broken sea-ice at a slow but steady pace. I pushed hard for an hour, walking until I could think, then until I could feel a severe but comforting pain in my feet.

Each footfall sounded like a cannon shot in the absolute silence surrounding me. Each rumble or shift in the snow might have been a precursor to a charging bear, but I could not concern myself with bears just now. I had to deal with my problems one at a time, starting with the most pressing: regaining warmth.

Disoriented, I had to pay close attention to the lay of the land to establish where I was and where I was going. The tundra sloped left and was blown nearly clear of snow. That meant I was on the windward side facing southeast. If I followed it downhill it would lead me to the cliffs off the vessel's starboard beam. I was relieved to find my mind now working clearly.

But when I came to what I thought was the spot in which we had first tried to anchor, I was confused, for a huge uplifting of ice boulders rose above me in the shape of Stonehenge. *Wait, this should be sea-ice outside the tidal fracture zone, only moderately rough, not cliffs or boulders!* It took discipline to calm myself and think it through. If I was where I thought, then some disturbance, a ledge or boulder, must be hidden beneath the water's surface. As the ice thickened, this caused uplifting right at our anchoring location. Assuming that to be my position, I cut off at the angle that should lead to the cliffs beneath Raven's Rock. When those cliffs appeared, a flush of relief flowed through me. But still I felt unsettled when I realized that, had we remained where we originally anchored, the *Roger Henry* would have been severely damaged.

I came up to the cliffs, which cut a high swath even darker than the night behind them. I climbed up the rocky slope of a gully to the cliff top and followed the rim around toward Raven's Rock. The air was perversely cold, near forty-five below zero and compounded in its deadliness by a rising wind, yet there the old black sorcerer sat on top of his rock, fully exposed against the starlight that the ancient Inuit believed the bird had a hand in forming.

Ravens, unlike ptarmigan, snowy owl, musk ox, or bear, have no outer protection from these extremes. But they, like other Arctic birds, do have the special adaptation of a countercurrent circulatory system in their legs that maintains their body heat at 104 degrees while their legs and feet fall to close to freezing.

I did not think of the Raven as my enemy, nor did I find his black countenance forbidding. He was more like a fellow gambler sitting across the table from me—an opponent, but not an enemy. Make no mistake, this was a game with high stakes, and there had to be a winner and a loser, but it was a game we both enjoyed and to which we were inexorably tied.

The Raven sat there unsuspecting, deep in his own thoughts—perhaps profound thoughts, for again we underestimate our fellow earthly species. We have maligned their intelligence by calling anything apparently stupid a "bird brain," based on our simple logic that a small cerebral cortex equals a smallness of smarts. But recent studies discovered that bird brains do not function at all like ours. Their cognizance is centered in the hyperstriatum, which mammals lack. Researchers were startled to find that the *Corvidae*, the family including crows and ravens, possess brain-size-to-body-weight ratios equaling that of dolphins and nearly matching ours. In addition, Corvid brains were found to be

packed with an enormous number of brain cells. In the mid-1800s, the
Reverend Henry Ward Beecher said all this sooner and simpler: "If men
had wings and black feathers, few of them would be clever enough to
be ravens." Of course, native people have always credited this bird with
a cunning intelligence, as their many legends about the great trickster
attest.

I slipped up out of the darkness. It was important to the game that
I put on a good face, so I shouted, "I'm fit as a fiddle, old buddy."
Startled, the Raven leapt up and cawed a holy hell of protest. It was
wonderful to hear a voice other than my own echo across Tay Bay. I
cut off from the cliffs at the angle I knew would lead to the boat. The
tidal fracture zone extending one hundred feet out from the land had
become a chaotic field of splintered ice sheets and ice boulders, one
tossed upon the other. The bears never walked directly across the bay
but stuck to the fringes of this tumble, looking for seal lairs. Without
incident, I wound through the boulders onto the smoother sea- ice,
found my way to the boat, and slid below.

I lit the heater and hung the frozen bedding in front of it on a long
cord. Our salon table is offset from the centerline to port and is surrounded by a U-shaped settee of cushioned benches. The table is on a
collapsible pedestal, which I dropped to seat level, creating a wide bed
when I laid the back cushions on the table. I rummaged through the
dirty clothes bag and layered myself with some disgustingly dirty long
underwear. As each piece of bedding dried, I peeled off a layer of clothing. It took two days to regain complete control.

I surrendered the aft cabins to the cancerous ice by shutting the foil-
backed doors. This shrank my already small world, but it reduced the
space I had to heat. In my Western orderliness, I had not wanted to eat
where I slept—here for cooking, there for sleeping—but that was an ex-
travagance the Arctic would not allow. Within one day of living in my
new arrangement, it struck me yet again how highly attuned the Inuit
are to their environment. I had accidentally come to the same conclusions they had made millennia earlier. My sleeping platform, which
they call an *ikliq,* was now well above the flooring, and being just those
few inches higher than the aft-cabin berth made it noticeably warmer.

Also, by creating one living space I concentrated the effects of my body heat, kept all the equipment of daily life easily at hand, and found a psychological lift in the relative expansiveness of the main cabin.

The day or date became less relevant in tracking the passage of time. Nature provided more meaningful milestones. Dreadful temperatures, howling blizzards, and total blackness pinned me below. Besides the drudgery of daily chores, there was little to do. Thinking became my sole entertainment, and I grew playful. In the darkness, with no external distractions, it was easy to focus my mediocre mental amperage on a single subject. What I could not cut through with brilliance, I bludgeoned with persistence. I decided to mop up some of the world's most often asked yet lingering questions. I started with:

Q. Which came first, the chicken or the egg?

A. Our Western insistence on the strict delineation of species means that, in evolutionary terms, there was a precise moment when a very-nearly-chicken animal laid an egg, within which developed the first true chicken. Thus, the egg came first. Why the chicken crossed the road remains a mystery.

Q. If God is omnipotent, can He create a rock so big that even He can't lift it?

A. As we define God as Spirit, and acknowledge Him to be the creator of the material universe, we have established a cause-and-effect order and, clearly, a case for the superiority of Mind over Matter. Therefore, God can lift any rock he can create, but He should remember to bend at the knees and always wear His support belt.

Q. How many angels can dance on the head of a pin?

A. None. There are serious religious duties to attend to in Heaven, and pinhead dancing is strictly forbidden.

When one blizzard blew itself out, I boiled up a thick beef stew, poured it over a cookie sheet, and laid it up on deck. A half hour later I pulled on my overalls, big pack boots, and stuffed parka and crawled out into the black cockpit with a lantern in one hand and a hammer in the other. I smashed the frozen stew once with the hammer, and it shattered into small pieces that fit nicely into meal-sized plastic bags. I laid these up next to the stack of soup bricks. If I fell sick or injured, or if the diesel gelled into wax in the stove's fuel line, I could start up the camp stove, hacksaw off a nice thick slice of soup, and be warm and fed in minutes.

Staying ahead on my water supply was even more critical, and that meant venturing out to find and chip freshwater ice. The tunneled hood of my parka kept my face warm but severely restricted both my field of vision and hearing. With hobbled senses, I became apprehensive about my surroundings. As I sat in the cockpit, waiting to make my move into the unknown, the thin fabric of the tent constituted my last line of defense. I sat absolutely still for ten minutes, trying to pierce the darkness with my ears, probing for the faintest sound of a bear lying in ambush outside. On some days I burst out the back of the tent. On others I threw something out first as a feint. On still others I slipped my head out as quietly as a church mouse. I did not want to establish any pattern of behavior. Initially, I wanted to throw Halifax out there first, armed only with her keener senses. But as our friendship and partnership grew, I could not bring myself to do that. My life had no more inherent value than hers.

There were times—especially the ones when I dramatically crashed out onto the ice, whirled, and prepared for mortal combat with empty air—that this all seemed silly, tempting me to just get up, go out, and get my damn ice. That would be okay ninety-nine out of a hundred times. Then one day, a crushing blow would smash my head like an overripe papaya. The big beast would then hold my corpse down with one ponderous paw and with his massive jaws snap my head from my body like a berry from a bush.

Fortunately, this night was one of the ninety-nine. After gathering ice and returning to the cockpit tent, I sat there for hours chipping ice boulders into fine flakes. I had experimented with melting times of different-sized ice bits and concluded that minimizing them was well worth the extra effort, considering that I had lots of time and little fuel. I stopped, pulled back my hood for as long as my ears could take the cold, and listened for bears. I pumped up the pressure lantern. Its dim light filled my tent, and its comforting hiss broke the silence. My hands chipped, chipped, chipped, as my mind wandered the world. Occasionally, I slipped below to add a bucket of chips to the melting water on the stove.

Back in the cockpit, my mind wandered to some balmy beach. Condensation formed on the outside of the pot, then ran down to the burner and doused the flame. Soot and toxic smoke filled the cabin, forcing me to open up the boat and release my precious heat into the night air. I regrouped, vowed I would concentrate on my task, and began again. When the pot filled, I carefully poured it into the insulated water barrel. I laid up a full six gallons of water, which would cover my every need for four days and should span any blizzard.

To reward myself, I fried several slices of smoked bacon and dehydrated eggs, then poured maple syrup over the lot. For dessert I crawled between the covers of a good book. Exactly a century before my Arctic vigil, Norwegian explorers Fridtjof Nansen and Hjalmar Johansen left their icebound ship *Fram* drifting in the Arctic Ocean pack ice and made a bold dash for the North Pole. Turned back short of their goal, they were forced to winter on a wilderness island. With a walrus-hide tent, skins to sleep under, blubber to burn, bear meat to eat, and some luck, they had everything they needed to survive. But when asked what they missed most, Nansen replied, "Oh, how we longed for a book." Forewarned is forearmed. Cocooned in my sleeping bag, I began devouring *Endurance, Tundra, Kabloona, Arctic Dreams, Arctic Grail,* and three more feet of bookshelf.

First I tried to read the "Gee, what a guy" novels, to save my good biographies, histories, and travel books, resources that were no less vital than food or fuel. I invested two hundred pages into one mad genius's plot to destroy the world. The President reluctantly told his cabinet, "There is only one man who can save us now." They called in the chiseled-jaw rogue agent, Lance Sterling, who, through episodes of cool gun play, gratuitous sex, and unbelievable co-coincidence, crushed the forces of darkness. I lost it completely and shouted, "Fuck you, Lance Sterling, and the man who wrote you! Life is too short, even if I do have time to burn. I need intellectual meat, not cream donuts!" I angrily threw the book into the black void. I heard smashing glass. Lance had just crushed the forces of light—my spare lantern. My raw nerves and intense emotions always cost me something. The next day, to be sure my opinion was perfectly understood, I wiped my butt with the pages of that book. Take that, Lance.

I raided the spot on the shelf earmarked for February. I tried to read slowly, stop early, but the books were just too damned good. My gloved hands clumsily plowed through thousands of pages. William Manchester's *The Last Lion,* covering Winston Churchill's early years, filled me with wonder about this giant of an era. I sank into the plush leather chairs of mahogany men's clubs, tasted the claret and Highlands whiskey, smelled the cigar smoke. I rose in jubilation and fell into despair with Winston through his changing fortunes. And when I laughed, which was often, or cried, which also was often, I thanked gifted authors Pierre Berton, Steven Ambrose, Arthur M. Schlesinger, Jr., and Michael Caro for touching my day.

I read until my nose froze, and then I slipped under the bag and thought about what lay between those lines. If I were Winnie, what would I have done? Could I have stooped so low to rise so high, as L.B.J. had? Is it goodness of heart that makes men seem simple of mind? As a senior at West Point, Dwight Eisenhower stopped a plebe to haze him, as tradition demanded. He said in a sneering tone, "You don't look like a soldier. You look more like a barber." The plebe, standing at terrified attention, flushed red and said, "Yes sir, I was a barber before I came here." Eisenhower went to his room and told his roommate, "I have just mocked a man for the way he makes an honest living. It is the worst thing that I have ever done, and it will never happen again."

Breaking a lantern did not break the tension. A good laugh was better for that. I do not mean a little chuckle, I mean a belly-aching, knee-slapping, tension-snapping laugh, set off by something that might otherwise have been only mildly amusing but in my solitary confinement became hilarious. Example: While Winston was in his rabidly conservative days, he walked into the Parliamentary urinals only to find his very liberal archrival, Attlee, standing at the trough. Churchill walked down to the far end to relieve himself. Attlee teased, "Feeling a little stand-offish today, are we, Winston?" Churchill replied, "Naturally Sir, every time that you see something big, you try to nationalize it." I spit out my tea, and it took me five minutes to catch my breath.

WITHOUT LIGHT AND DARKNESS to define time, I cannot say how long I sat and read, wrote, thought, or did absolutely nothing. Once, I drifted off to sleep with the ship's clock saying six o'clock. (A.M. or P.M.? It mattered little, anyway.) When I woke, it still said six. Had I really slept twelve hours? I couldn't believe that, so I warmed up the cabin and turned on the satellite navigator for a time update. It was worse than I thought; I had lapped the clock and slept through a full twenty-four hours. That depressed me so much, I went back to sleep. When I woke to that same six o'clock, I panicked. Was my life flashing by in nanosecond days? I vowed to quit looking at the clock, but two days later I weakened and turned my headlamp on it. Sure enough, six o'clock. A vague fear gripped me. I lay still in the darkness, listening to a silence too absolute. Then it hit me: *The damn clock has stopped. I am being toyed with like a mouse.*

Allies and strategies helped control my waking moments, but when I fell asleep, those excruciating nightmares still racked me. I dreamed Diana was cruel to me. *It had started almost the day after the wedding. I had grown used to her infidelities, but never her indifference. I begged her to tell me why she had shut me out physically and emotionally for years. What had I done? Why had she married me if that was how she felt? She just sneered, knowing that my not knowing was killing me. She walked away.* I woke up sweating and breathless. I was convinced it was not a dream; it was a psychic premonition. My mind raced. After all, she had not contacted Peter last Sunday. Where was she? She would be distraught and lonely and would need someone to talk to. She is an attractive woman. Men would want to help her, men who would not ask her to camp out as a permanent lifestyle, men who would not drag her into war zones or the dens of wild animals, men who had professions, prestige, income, and fine things, who offered security, who would give her that garden behind a nice house. She would be home and happy. Who could blame her?

I felt nauseous with a chilling certainty that all this was occurring as I sat there, helpless. A hiss of murderous jealousy swept up my spine. I screamed, "You bastards! I could hike out of here, fly to New Zealand, and get my hands on you. You excite Diana only because you're new. In six months she'll discover that you fart in bed and tell the same jokes over and over." My mind covered every mile, my taxi pulling up unexpectedly, me barging in, fists clenched, and there . . . there . . . would lie my dying father-in-law beside my grieving wife. *My God, am I going insane? This poor woman is* not *on vacation. You have to stop this, Alvah. You have to stop.* I was afraid to fall back asleep for fear the dream would repeat itself.

I got up and went through the cumbersome exercise of dressing for the minus-forty-degree cold outside. With a kerosene lantern in hand, I crawled out onto the buried deck. Fox prints covered the snow. Halifax followed me, her tail puffed up like a raccoon's. She was mad at me; after all, a deal is a deal. It was my job to fend off the foxes and bears so she could take her daily constitution. She dug a hole in the cockpit snow, squatted over it, very smartly did her thing, and dove below.

I stayed on deck—or, more precisely, on the hummock of snow that hid the deck. The wind was still, the air crystal clear, and the sky could not have held a single star more. Above me sparkled an entirely new cosmos; new because it has been viewed and named differently by the native people of this land. Our Big Dipper is to them *Tuktu,* "the caribou." Our Pleiades scampers across their mind and sky as "the Little Foxes." And of course, everybody knows that our Milky Way is really the tracks of Raven, made when the universe was fresh and everything was possible. I walked away from the boat, my footsteps unnaturally loud in the stillness. I lay down on a snowbank. Just those few yards flushed me with the joy of freedom. A Muslim moon bounced a shimmering light off the glacier. The night was many shades of beautiful black. Its beauty calmed me, and the fresh air woke me.

I wrote my diary entry right there in my head, knowing that I would not forget a single word, comma, or period.

December 10: Two months alone. Look, I can handle the cold, the threat of ending up bear shit, the idea that, if I get sick, I die up here alone. I can take this, but these dreams are tearing me up. It is like fighting water, like falling. If it's not Diana, it's Jon's death. If I could have just found his body, if I could have put my fingers in the wounds made by his speedboat propeller, like Doubting Thomas placing his in Jesus' side, if I could have thrown the first clod of dirt on his casket . . . But he is out there, part of the Atlantic Ocean.

In my dreams, I find Jon alive. A tall, athletic man catches a Frisbee in a park, and I know it is him because I know how he moves and I recognize his unique handsomeness. I dreamed he faked his death to avoid the draft or because he was gay or HIV-positive and could not tell his wife and family. In each dream I create another reason. In each, when I call to him, he tries to run. I catch him and we wrestle. Jon was always bigger, stronger, and faster than me, but he could never beat me in a fight because he was the nicer man. In the dream, I always punch him hard, just once, for the pain he caused me, then I hug him with all my soul. Then I wake up and can't tell where I am or if the dream is true or not. Then I feel the cold, and I know, and I cry.

It is not just me going crazy; Halifax's behavior is altering noticeably. The snow leopard is well suited to the cold but lives near the equator, so it never has to face extended darkness. Felines are not natural Arctic dwellers. Why *wouldn't* Halifax go as crazy as me? She has the classic symptoms of cabin fever. She whines and wails all the time. She is broody and petulant. How can you quarrel with a cat? But I do. She waits for me to watch, then she destroys things with obvious rage. She'd rather risk my wrath than be ignored. It is a dangerous game she is playing, because my temper is terrible, uncontrollable, and I don't know why. She was determined to lure me out of my bag by tearing up the foil on the backside of the forepeak door. I was determined this would be the last time. I had to teach her once and for all. I lit into her with the blind fury of a baby shaker. I could not believe that it was I doing this. I love animals. I have never been a cruel man. For the next two days, every time I tried to pet her, she bit me.

My back is hurting and my eyes are failing. Unless I come out here in the starlight or moonlight, everything I see is no more than two feet in front of me. It doesn't matter, because I cannot write worth a damn. It's all this angry drivel. I heard on the radio that Boris Yeltsin said the Russian troops were in Chechnia to spread peace and harmony, but if the Chechnians resist, they will be annihilated. Words disgust me. They stink of piss or sting like poison. There is no truth in anything we hear. Who asked me anyway? Why do I keep working with words? A mason uses bricks. He builds his wall. It is what it is. It has lasting purpose. But ... I agonized over a nearly finished short story for fourteen hours. I read once about an author telling a friend that he had a busy day—he took a comma out in the morning, then put it back in the afternoon.

The dreadful cold interrupted my thoughts. I had been lying in the snow for several hours, and I started to shake. There was no avoiding it—I had to return to the boat, and I had to fall asleep eventually and face my dreams, so I got up and shuffled back through the dark. I crawled into my bag and, when I was warm enough, I fell asleep. But the next dream was different. I ran over sparkling snow dunes. I came upon a mystical fox, all fluffy, white, and pure, with soft brown eyes. We recognized each other. We were old friends, the kind that find sheer joy in each other's silent presence. We played and played, he deftly nipping my heels and me chasing him in circles. Then the fox sat on his haunches and stared at me with serious concern. He cocked his sharp little head and yelped little burps and barks, trying to tell me something very important. I could not understand. He tried so hard to make the sounds of human words, and I tried so hard to understand. I grew frustrated, then agitated, then afraid. This could be terribly important. I thought I would burst from turmoil, when suddenly a golden light washed over me, and I was filled with a peace I had never known. The message was somehow clear; I was just not yet ready for what the fox was trying to teach me. Everything unfolds perfectly and in its own time. I patted the fox's head and scratched his chin. I thanked him but told him it was more important that we play in the moment and leave the future to itself.

In mid-December, Peter radioed with the sad news that his ninety-one-year-old mother had fallen very ill and was not expected to pull through. He was going south on extended leave to be with her; he anticipated an absence of eight weeks. I offered sincere condolences, for even though we had never met in person, I now thought of this man as my close friend. He was concerned about me, but I tried to play it down with weak humor.

Peter had been a voice of reason, and having to mask my madness from him had, in fact, helped me keep it in check. Now I was left truly on my own in the darkest and coldest of times.

William James defined religion as "the feelings, acts, and experiences of individuals in their solitude." My need for constant talk, action, and adventure indicated my babe-in-arms spiritual immaturity, an immaturity I would gladly have clung to. But now I was left no option but to turn my whole attention inward.

Above all else, mystics prize silence and solitude. From cloistered cells to mountaintop retreats, in isolation they find inspiration. St. Augustine's search for the mystic began with a meditative state he called "the cloud of unknowing." The setting he created to encourage this differed little from mine, except for its temperatures. Mother Teresa laid out what she called "the Simple Path." It has five steps but is bedrocked on the first: "In silence there is prayer, and in prayer, peace." Yet powerful religious institutions have traditionally been in outspoken, flesh-burning disagreement. Priests, parsons, rabbis, and elders sternly warned us that "an idle mind is the Devil's playground." Did they fear that, left to ourselves, we would each naturally find our own God, a God who did not demand obedience to a manmade structure nor contributions to maintain its earthly edifices? In the Far East one finds keener insight into the relationship of time and self. The Buddhist philosophy inverts the Western phrase, "Don't just sit there, do something!" into "Don't just do something, sit there!"

And so I sat, through moments and months, through elation and despair, through hissing mental clarity and numbed, beast-of-burden stupidity. On my climbs to the emotional peaks and frightening falls to the valley bottoms, I passed a specific midpoint of perfect balance, but I moved so fast I could but glimpse it: ephemeral, simple, comforting. Now if only I could quiet the white noise, still my chatterbox mind, a natural spring of well-being might fill me, and, if left in peace, begin to pour out.

I recalled my treks through the scorched plains of Africa; climbs in the high, thin air of the Andes; paddles down verdant rivers of Borneo. I had seen third world disease, disorder, and death. But beneath it I had also seen the grace of unhurried human movement, noticed the serenity of acceptance reflected in elderly but unfretted faces, heard a ripple of laughter too light to be called hilarious, for native people do not seem to store the tensions necessary for that. I wondered if the reasons for this might be no more complicated than the pace of life, the quiet time to process the natural signals from without *and* within. These people might not spend time alone, but they do spend time with themselves. I thought about times I had said, "I really enjoyed myself last night." What I really meant was, "I really enjoyed some person or activity outside and other than myself last night." I was beginning now to feel as if my whole life had been outside and other than myself.

At first I was frightened by my solitude. There were moments, difficult to describe, that I would not wish on anyone. But whenever I could slow my train at this midpoint stop, I felt content, fulfilled and, surprisingly, often more alone than lonely.

On a very still day in mid-December, I closed my useless eyes and listened hard. There was only the wispy sound of a zephyr, or *is that my breathing? Being here is like dancing in the dark. It is the Zen sound of one hand clapping. If a tree falls in the woods, and there is no one there to hear it, does it still make a noise? Is our definition of personal self formed from within or by the collected impressions of how others perceive us? There is no one here to perceive me, nor has there been for a long time. I feel as if I am coming apart, becoming transparent, light, unreal. Sometimes, I see my hand move in the dim light and I wonder what it is. But is there really no one to see me? What if there is a God? What if I am in the eyes of God right now? I was taught that not a sparrow falls from the sky that God does not see.*

Think about that, but not too much. I intellectualize everything into mush. Take that phrase, In the eyes of God. It could mean exactly what it says. Not God, standing back, watching. It could mean we are in his eyes. No, that is still vague. Get it precise. We are his eyes. We are not being watched, we are the process of watching. I tried to open my eyes but could not. Something was happening. For a fleeting moment, I saw something—no, I knew something. But my mind could not hold it. I held out my hand in the dark trying to grasp it physically, but it swirled away.

Start from the beginning. "In the beginning was the Word." What word? Maybe not a particular word, but a sound, a vibration. To find the building block of all matter, physicists have probed deeper and deeper into the atom. They find only energy, and when they peel back the onionskin layers of energy, ultimately they find only vibration. The brute paw that might crush my head is made of muscle, blood, and bone, which are made of molecules, which are made of atoms, which are made of electrons, which are made of sparks and quarks, which are made of nothing that can be measured or weighed. Everything is made of nothing! My head will be crushed by illusion. My illusory brain will drip onto the illusory ground. My death itself will be an illusion and therefore so too must be my life. In the beginning was the Word.

The Word was God. God is that vibration, that vibration that creates form through visualization alone . . . Well, shake, rattle, and roll, Big Daddy! Is this *my grand conclusion?* I cringed at its triteness. My mind flickered like the lamplight, and I tried again, and again.

As my days of darkness passed, a duality started to form in my consciousness. I became actor and audience. For my every thought and action, I was both creator and critic. My present play received endurable reviews, but when I drifted back into my past with astonishing power of recall, the critics savaged me. I could remember what shirt I wore on the day I committed a particular unkindness or infidelity. I'd had so many opportunities to do good, but each opportunity was but a brief moment, and I'd missed many. I felt terrible. I found no atonement in sorrow or regret. I tried to shrink my heart to avoid the pain. I sneered, "Yeah, well nobody's perfect."

I turned on my headlamp and grabbed a travel book off the shelf, impatient to rid my mind of all this. A card fell out. I picked it up and was stunned by what it said.

> Lord, make me an instrument of your peace
> where there is hatred, let me sow love
> where there is injury, pardon
> where there is doubt, faith
> where there is despair, hope
> where there is darkness, light
> where there is sadness, joy
> Oh divine Master, grant that I may not so much seek
> To be consoled . . . as to console
> To be understood . . . as to understand
> To be loved . . . as to love
> For it is in giving that we receive
> It is in pardoning, that we are pardoned
> It is in dying that we are born into eternal life.
>
> —St. Francis of Assisi

I yelled, "Leave me alone, damn it. I'm just an ordinary adventurer, not some fucking saint. Anyway, I don't even believe in you."

I was spitting angry. Increasingly, what I wanted to do with my life was to write one thing of lasting value. Instead, I dabbled and dribbled, and I knew it. Even if I could cast aside its message, this passage was the most perfectly written I had ever read. The cadence and balance were masterfully crafted and lyrical. It mocked my mediocrity. "Stuff it!" I yelled into the dark. "So you devote your life to achieving that perfection and what do you get? Birds shitting on your shoulder!" But an inner voice said loudly, "Wrong. What you get is one bright shining moment, one chance to create something of lasting value. Francis, this simple man in sackcloth, sworn to poverty, was so at peace with every living thing that foxes followed in his footsteps and birds perched on his shoulders. This simple man painted with a few pen strokes the path to peace, to heaven on earth."

Seven hundred years later his words fell out of a book I opened specifically in an attempt to escape the very uncomfortable awakening of my spiritual self. A man too young for such wisdom once told me that anyone who believes in coincidence is not paying attention. Down deep, I knew that events outside my control were aligning themselves. In this journey, rough spots had been inexplicably smoothed, dangerous mistakes had been forgiven by nature. I felt I had been led to this specific place and time. It was eerie, and I was afraid. I didn't think I was ready, but some stubbornly resistant strand in my willful ego snapped.

I could accept the idea of burning bushes on the road to Damascus, but in the Arctic? If the rough terrain of my psyche could be mapped, this moment would mark a watershed. The collection of events that I called my life flowed from this high spot backward, and the man and person I could become through this difficult, black experience trickled forward as a new river seeking outlet in a body of water larger than itself.

Each time I woke after that day, I found myself feeling less alone, more purposeful, and deeply grateful just to be alive. Daily, that gratitude escaped my lips with an audible "Thank you." Then, as now, I have no earthly idea who it is I am thanking. But I think I know what it is I am thankful for: the privilege of being a small, frail, faulted, but integral part of the magic and mystery of life on earth.

You can do worse.

NINE

Tay Bay

DECEMBER 25, 1994
ZERO HOURS DAYLIGHT

In memories we were rich. We had pierced the veneer of outside things. We had suffered, starved, and triumphed, groveled yet grasped at glory, grown bigger in the bigness of the whole. We had seen God in his splendors, heard the text that nature renders. We had reached the naked soul of Man.

—Ernest Shackleton

I T WAS CHRISTMAS DAY, but a blizzard howled outside, leaving little peace on this piece of earth. On the stove the pressure cooker chattered away, a comforting sound. Inside the pot bubbled my unique recipe for "Bedouin Beef." Any educated traveler will now protest that the Bedouin do not have beef—which is why my recipe is unique. In water, put one cup of dried beef jerky, one cup each of dried prunes, dates, and raisins, ¼ cup dried onions, ¼ cup sun-dried tomatoes, desiccated coconut, curry powder, ginger powder, and one dried chile. Cook it just short of forever. Serve it over couscous and you can smell the camels outside the tent.

I gave Halifax a whole can of tuna, unadulterated. I let her eat it up on the normally *verboten* galley counter as a treat. She slurped up the oil until the can shone in the candlelight. A month earlier I had found a gift from Diana marked, "Do not open till Christmas." I opened it now to find a small box of Fig Newtons, a special treat for me. I taped her card next to the radio and read it a hundred times. It said, "I love you. Diana."

I lay in the sleeping bag with the drawstring pulled tight around my face, and I thought about Jesus Christ. I felt a little hypocritical celebrating his birthday, but I admire courage, and whatever else one believes, Jesus' courage was heroic. A minister once asked me if I was a Christian. I told him I did not know. Irritated, he demanded, "How can you not know? Do you or do you not believe in Jesus Christ?"

I said, "I believe Jesus, but I do not know if I believe *in* Jesus. What does that make me?"

"A fool," he snapped.

Christ, Buddha, Mohammed, Krishna, Yahweh, The Great White

187

*Buffalo, must I choose between them? Who am I to define the divine—
say it is this and nothing more? On this day, alone here in the dark, can
I just take to heart their similar messages concerning peace on Earth
and good will toward all men and women? And can I add to that list
the creatures of the forest and the deep, the flowers and the trees, the
wind and the sun, the snow and the rain?*

The wind howled outside, the boat shuddered, Halifax purred. I
thought about my family at home, together, perhaps sitting down right
then to a home-cooked meal, and my mind created before me the feast.
My mother's honey-clove ham steamed at the head of the table, my sister's garlic-herb mashed potatoes were piled high on the heavy china
plate being passed. The aroma of hot pecan pie wafted in from the
kitchen. Everyone was laughing, even though it was the exact same
story being told as was told last year and the year before.

I felt around for my headlamp and pulled it on over my bomber's
hat. I turned it on and pulled a blank sheet of paper from my writing
file. Sitting up in my bag in the dim light, I wrote my name and the
names of my mother and my four brothers and four sisters in a circle
on the page. Then I drew a line representing a relationship from each
name to all the others. When it was done, the sketch looked like a
beautifully faceted jewel—the family jewel, if you will. I put the pen-
point down on a line at random and traced it to each end of that relationship. How long had it been since Prudence had shared any time
or closeness with Raoul? After thinking through several scenarios, I
counted the lines. There were forty-five separate relationships, not including the in-laws, nieces, or nephews. Just one family, and yet its dynamics were complicated and delicate, sustainable only with patience,
love, respect, and a sense of common cause.

I had a good Christmas, sober and reflective—perhaps a Christmas
as they used to be, before we counted the shopping days leading to the
blessed event.

As I scratched all this into my diary, Halifax, who had escaped the
sleeping bag, had scratched her thoughts into the soft spruce wood-
work and waited in mischievous anticipation of my charge. In the holi-
day spirit of goodwill, I switched tactics. She is an intelligent animal.
When she wanted a drink and could not lure me from my bag to thaw

her dish, she unscrewed the large lid on the water barrel. Her little paws pushed the cap counterclockwise until it was loose. Then she shoved the lid to the floor. She stuck her head down in the barrel for a chilly slurp. This became habit, and I have collaborating eyewitnesses to prove it true, although when I told Peter Semotiuk, who knows cats well, he demanded photographic proof. *If she is this damn smart*, I reasoned, *she should understand at least the intonations of this little poem I have just written in her honor.* She stared at me as I read it aloud to her with dramatic flair:

> "Halifax, my cat, was furry and fat.
> Oh, a finer companion could not be.
> I was trapped in the Arctic,
> My life was so stark it
> Had no other warm company.
> And so side by side,
> the dark months we did bide,
> Huddled as bleak blizzards blew.
> And when the food ran out,
> At eight pounds thereabout,
> she made a fine and filling meat stew."

The day after the Christmas blizzard, Halifax and I were huddled below when we heard the sound of footfalls approaching the boat. From their volume, I assumed they belonged to something very big— a thousand-pound bear, at least. Halifax puffed up like a porcupine. Right over our heads paced a tremendous crunching, as both our heads swept back and forth like radar tracking enemy sounds above. Whatever was up there had our undivided attention. I waited for the beast to rip the hatch away. Then I noticed that the footsteps were rapid, unlike those of a lumbering bear. I swore, realizing we were the victims of an Arctic audio illusion.

I crawled out of the bag, got dressed, and poked my head out the companionway. Standing perfectly still in the cockpit, two feet from my face, was my belated Christmas present—a personal visit from an arctic fox. He did not run, but stared directly into my eyes with an intense inquisitiveness. His eyes reflected emerald green in the light of my headlamp. He looked like the fox from my dreams—pure white, fluffy, keenly intelligent. For a moment I was not sure it was truly happening. I said out loud, "Hello, my friend." This did not startle him. In fact, he sat down serenely. I crawled out into the cockpit and sat myself down next to him.

Beneath his thick, rich coat hid a small, specially adapted body. To preserve body heat, his ears and legs were shorter than those of fox species to the south. Fur covered the bottom pads of his feet for insulation and traction. arctic foxes are clever opportunists. They hunt continuously through the spring and summer, gorging on lemmings, fish, birds, eggs, berries, and occasionally, seal pups. As the summer wanes, they carefully lay caches of dozens of birds and eggs in neat lines and piles for later use. During the bitter times of want, they follow bears, patrol beneath gyrfalcon nests, and scavenge any kill or camp they can find, returning to their cache only if all else fails. In their incessant search for food, they cover many miles and fall prey in great numbers to the steel jaws of traps, for their pelts are still highly prized.

In mutual fascination, we stared at each other until my headlamp faded and the cold drove me below. It was a wildlife encounter like none I have had.

For the next two days he visited the boat often. Halifax began wailing; she had to get out to do her business but dare not as long as I let this intruder hang about. When Halifax hissed, I knew the fox was visiting. It was a beautiful animal, but full of fast fangs and driven by extreme hunger. I had also been warned about a high incidence of rabies in the arctic fox population. I imagined the progression: He gives it to Halifax, she gives it to me, I foam about the mouth more than usual and die in agony. I knew what I had to do.

I crawled out to see scattered across the snowbanks the frozen food supply I had stashed on deck. As an animal lover I wanted to be patient, but when I saw my homemade burritos ravished, that was it! I chased the fox off the boat, screaming that the three-alarm chili would serve him right! He was not frightened and did not retreat far. By lantern light, I chased him round and round the boat, entertaining him and exhausting me. My emotions ran too high. I screamed at him. He sat happily. I threw things at him. He dodged them nimbly and sat excitedly waiting for the next missile. Angry, I pulled the large can of bear mace from under my parka.

"Don't make me do it!" I screamed.

The fox sat just a few yards in front of me. I aimed the nozzle, ready to give him the searing hell of the strong pepper gas, but those emerald eyes seemed to see into my soul. His head tilted as if to speak. Was I ready to hear his message? I hesitated, open to the moment.

Then my mind slammed shut in disbelief. "This is ridiculous!" I aimed again, but I could not squeeze off a shot. Halifax's enemy or not, this *was* the fox from my dreams. I couldn't do it. I decided to spray to his right and let just a little of the gas drift down on him; he would get the message and take off in search of more natural fare. I squeezed, and a jet stream shot out and drifted down. Some of the gas hit him. He dove under the snow, burrowed horizontally for ten feet and sprang up in a sitting position. He looked at me happily and unfazed. But when I aimed again, he understood. He started to run to my left. I turned and led him with a squirt. In a flash, he leapt out of the falling spray's range.

Suddenly, my face and lungs exploded in pain. In tracking him to my left, I had shot directly upwind, and so reaped what I had sown. No one could have been more deserving. The gas choked me and burned, and I fell to my knees. As terrible as the pain was the guilt I felt for having tried to do this to the fox. Learning by example, I planted my face in the snow, and the pain subsided.

I brushed the snow off my face and stood up, thinking, *I can't kill him, I don't want to hurt him, but I have to drive him off.* I chased him again until my lungs felt ready to explode. Obsessed, I finally danced in delight when a well-thrown ski pole prodded his behind. He yelped and dashed into the darkness. As I climbed below, I couldn't help but feel I had missed an important opportunity. I scratched with mitten-distorted writing my diary entry for December 28:

Dad always used to warn me, "Son, you'll never make eighteen." Even though I turn forty-four today, in some ways he was right.

ON NEW YEAR'S EVE I threw a party, and everybody came. I baked a pizza, turned on the lights, cranked up the stereo, and cracked the bottle of brandy. I chased Halifax around the cabin, teased her with a raven feather, and let her tear up one of my charts. She careened off the walls and whirled in mock battle, clearly having a wonderful time. She passed out under my knees and purred so loudly it woke me. For a terrible moment I thought a helicopter was coming. *Why can't they leave us alone?* Then I knew it couldn't be—they do not dare fly in the inky, Arctic night—and I felt happy.

A blizzard was wailing, and I listened as I drifted back to sleep, feeling safe and snug. A strong gust sent a shudder down the mast and through the entire craft, and I felt like I was at sea. For the hundredth time, my mind sent me sailing south into the arms of my beautiful wife.

I woke to a silence too complete and knew immediately what had happened. I jumped up, rushed to the hatch, and crashed into it with all my might. It did not budge. Snow had drifted over the boat and sealed me in. I pushed against the small galley hatch, knowing it was too small to crawl out of but that it would at least let air in. It was frozen shut. I ran to the middle hatch, then the foredeck hatch, to find the same situation. We had greased all the gaskets with a silicone paste, the makers of which swore it would not freeze until sixty below. That paste and the weight of the snow acted as an epoxy, sealing me below. My exertions only made me gasp more for precious air.

Settle down, now. Be calm. Think. Go slow, be methodical. I sat down on my *ikliq* and recalled the many Arctic stories I had read, until the pertinent one came to mind. Separated from his party, Danish explorer and prolific author Peter Freuchen dug a trench in the snow to escape a blizzard. He lay in the trench and slept. When he woke, he found himself buried beneath the snow and a thick, ice-encrusted surface. He tried to sit up, but the ice pinned him down. He clawed at the underside of his ice coffin until his frozen fingers were bloody, but he could not scratch it away. All his equipment lay uselessly above him on the sled. Without a digging tool, he was certain he would die. He carried absolutely nothing he could use as a tool . . . or did he? He slid his arms down the back of his fur trousers and defecated into his cupped hands. He quickly formed his own warm feces into a chisel shape, with a wide, slightly curved, sharp end. He pulled it out into the cold air, and it instantly froze as solid as steel. He dug his way out with this dung chisel. He ultimately lost one foot, but not his life. The Arctic is cruel. It demeans, and it demands innovative use of every resource at hand.

I rushed to the forepeak and foraged around for a pine plank I had found floating and added to my junk pile of jury-rigging material. I laid the end over a raised ship's frame and stomped down hard on it with my heavy pack boot. The four-by-half-inch plank snapped loudly, creating a splintered, sharply serrated edge similar to a wood saw. Try as I might, I couldn't squeeze my makeshift tool through the slender crack between the top hatch and the companionway boards. I didn't want to reinjure my back or force heavy breathing that would consume my air supply rapidly, but these were risks I had to take. Crashing into the main hatch repeatedly, I compressed the snow on top of it and opened a one-inch gap. I slid the board out and probed for precious air. I pushed straight out, then swung the butt back and forth in an arcing motion, cutting a swatch three, four, five, six feet wide but finding no atmosphere. Finally, with just the final stub of board to hang onto, I felt it swing smoothly, without resistance.

I had broken the tension of the snowbank above the hatch, but I still had to deal with its dead weight. With every fiber of my muscle, I lifted the hatch enough to force out the hinged washboards. The gap created was just wide enough to sink the camping shovel into the soft underbelly of the snowbank. I pulled the snow behind me and down the companionway ladder into the boat, like a prisoner secretly tunneling. The snow fell onto my face and down my sleeves and back, instantly melting, but I kept burrowing up and out to freedom. I stuck my head out of the snow and sucked hard on the fresh, oxygen-laden air. I felt around with my hands and was shocked to find myself at the far back crown of the tent, which was tightly packed to its peak with snow. The *Roger Henry* had disappeared entirely beneath a white mantle.

I crawled out and turned my energy back to the drift. I shoveled until I felt my arms would fall off, but still there was more. When I'd emptied the cockpit, I dropped back below, where I had to remove the snow in two stages, shoveling it first up into the cockpit and then overboard. It took hours to clean up the mess in the cabin.

I set a doubled layer of insulated-aluminum bubble-pack sheeting over the open hatch, then laid a wool blanket over that and weighed it down with snow. The soft material would not slow down an intruding bear but, if I was buried again, I could cut through it with a machete and dig my way out.

ON MARTIN LUTHER KING, JR.'S BIRTHDAY, I feared I would repeat my emotional outburst of Thanksgiving. No American outranks Dr. King as a hero in my mind. Even under normal circumstances, I am always filled with rage and sadness when I think of his tragic but somehow inevitable end. By low lantern light I read everything I had on board about the Reverend. I felt he spoke to me directly when he stated, "The ultimate measure of a man is not where he stands in moments of comfort and convenience, but where he stands at times of challenge and controversy." Then his rich voice rose in righteous power, "I have a dream. I have a dream that this nation will rise up and live out the true meaning of its creed. . . ." How long, how long? I was moved deeply, but I kept control. The bell still tolled for me, but in softer tones. I thought, *Maybe I have exhausted my intensity, passed through this crucible, and now I'm emerging on the other side.*

Several days later I woke to total darkness with a terrible migraine-like pain in my eyes. I reached out of the bag and flipped on a small light above my head, but it didn't seem to be working. At first I assumed the bulb had blown, but in the intense cold my hand could detect the heat of even that small light. I put my fingers directly on the bulb, and within seconds pulled them back burned. My heart sank. The bulb was fine. It was me—I was blind. I jumped up in panic, but a wave of nausea knocked me back down.

I could not think clearly. *What is happening? I have read too long in very low light. I took my laptop into my bag and wrote in eighteen-hour, possessed frenzies. Maybe, just maybe, it's only severe eyestrain.* I sat up slowly, put my face right up to the bulb, and looked into the light again. This time I saw a dim glow but went dizzy and started to vomit immediately. When I closed my eyes, the nausea stopped.

I wrapped my eyes with a bandanna and tried to sleep, but worry would not let me be. I dressed by feel and began stumbling through my most essential chores. I pumped up the day tank, but I didn't think I could control the heater, so I let it sit cold. I toured the entire cabin with my hands, growing more confident with each reaffirming contact. As on any shipshape yacht, every item had a place and was usually in that place. My memory and hands, working in unison, could locate most anything on board. I lifted the water barrel—*Good, I have plenty of water and I think there's a whole pile of ice chips in the cockpit. Let's see . . . I left the chipping knife in the port cubby hole and the ax lashed to the starboard aft rail. There's a huge hunk of ice on deck next to the antenna. I have to be most careful with the stove. Pump up the pressure; there, it feels right, okay. Go slow, pour the alcohol in the burner base, one—one thousand, two—one thousand, three—one thousand. Right, now light the match. Good, good, it sounds like it lit, now drop it in the liquid. Damn, damn that hurts! Did I burn myself? No wait—it's worse than that. I put my finger in subzero liquid alcohol. Ooohhh, that hurts! Try again, and don't burn down the boat, stupid. Yes, yes! That sounds right. The burner's humming perfectly. I never realized it, but I know that specific sound. Now get some water into the kettle. There, and get some coffee—no, too complicated, switch to tea, lots of honey; no telling how soon I'll get the hang of cooking food.*

My senses of smell, hearing, and touch immediately amplified to fill the void. I learned that if I did not think about an action but rather jumped in with a normal motion, letting muscle memory take over, most things went well. But I got overconfident, and my next mistake was a serious one.

To generate electricity, I had to first pull-start the generator, then flip two of three large T switches, one for the field input to the alternator and the other to open the charging output to the batteries. I got the system running without the slightest hitch, but when I shut the system down by feel, I accidentally turned off the charging output switch while the generator was still at high output. The internal diodes vaporized, killing all capacity for charging. I knew instantly what I had done.

It was critical that I hoard what battery power remained for starting the main engine in the spring. *If my sight comes back*, I told myself, *there will be no more of this bingeing on twelve-volt light and certainly no more amperage-sucking radio chatter.* I was panicked by the thought of not being able to read, but less upset by the loss of the radio.

After careful consideration, however, I could see what the probable outcome of this would be. Peter would return from his long vacation, fail to contact me, and deduce that something had gone wrong—a mechanical failure, medical problem, or accident; I might be lost in a whiteout; *ad infinitum*. He would feel obliged to err on the side of caution and punch the panic button. The powers that be would be notified, and although they could do absolutely nothing about it, one hell of a hullabaloo would surely follow. Extra! Extra! Read all about it! Tenderfoot American Tourist Missing! "Fenton Wadsworth the Third was quoted today as saying, 'If I was Chief Minister of this province, which I hope to be by this time next year, this would never have been allowed to happen.'" I cursed. *I never should have started this radio thing in the first place. If I can get this thing up and running, the first thing I'm going to do is come to an agreement with Peter. I'll say, "Do or die, all alone—no help, Peter. You have to promise me that."*

Somehow I had to get the alternator off the main engine and adapt it to the generator. In my blinded state, I could not read wrench sizes or trace wires by color, so I had to do it all by feel, with stiff, numb fingers. Before I could touch a tool with gloveless hands, I first had to warm it close to my body. The procedure would have bettered the patience of Job. I elongated the holes in the mounting brackets with a file and hacksawed off interfering corners. Had I not handmade them once with sight, I could not have done this now, blind and sick. When I had tensioned the alternator and rigged the wires, I set the throttle on the generator and heaved on the starting rope. The engine roared to life. I crawled back to the switch panel and very carefully traced the three switches with my hands. Holding my breath, I flipped the switch and listened. I heard the engine labor, which meant it was producing power.

Tension dissipated into relief, then deep, cold fatigue. I shut down the engine, fumbled around the medical kit for the familiar shape of the aspirin bottle, and dropped a handful of the pills into a glass of whiskey. I held it up in salute to the blind and drank it down. I chased it with a quart of water, then crawled back into the bag. I tried to calm myself with memories of my grandmother, who, although blind, was one of the happiest people I'd ever known. Then a terrible thought surfaced that made the idea of living through this blindness every bit as frightening as dying from it: *For the rest of my life, I will have to depend on other people for everything.* A voice within me responded, "You always have, Alvah. You just would not admit it."

T E N

Tay Bay

JANUARY 1995
ZERO HOURS DAYLIGHT

'Tis solitude should teach us how to die, it hath no flatterers, vanity can give us no hollow aid; alone—man with his God must strive.

—Lord Byron, *Childe Harold's Pilgrimage*

HALIFAX WOKE ME two days later, persistently pushing her paws into my face. I was so used to waking to total darkness that, for a moment, I forgot about my problem. Then I bolted upright and grabbed for a flashlight. I passed the beam over my eyes. It hurt like hell, but I could see! I had to ease my way back to the sighted world; every time I tried to read for even a minute, that terrible wave of nausea washed over me. Fear persisted in spite of my relief. Reading and writing had become my only anchors in the turbulent ocean of time. To cast those away would set me dangerously adrift.

I did not understand then what had happened to me. What I thought was eyestrain was in fact something far worse. For the time being, however, I knew only that the symptoms slowly subsided, and I went back gratefully but more cautiously to my reading, writing, sleeping, and deep mental drifts.

In late January, Orin, a teacher, helicopter pilot, and radio enthusiast from Baker Lake whom Diana had called upon Peter's advice, relayed the sad news that my father-in-law had passed away. Orin said it had been a long ordeal for Diana—a series of emotionally charged ups and downs, denial, talk of clinics in Mexico, then false hopes dashed by a rapid decline.

Through heavy atmospheric interference, I dictated a message to Diana, letter by letter: "Mike Yankee, space, Lima, Oscar, Victor, Echo, comma . . ." Orin faxed it to her on the other side of the world. I have often thought that, no matter our age, real adulthood begins at the death of our last parent. Until then we are someone's child; afterward, we are alone in a way that can never be corrected.

I lay in the bag after a round of chores. To reward myself, I decided to create one of my fantasies, bringing Diana to life before me like an image on a screen. But her face was foggy and far away. I could not remember her exactly, and that saddened me. I got up and dug through a small wooden box of souvenirs. Under the rattlesnake skins, stingray spines, boars' tusks, and photos of old friends, I found a picture of her sitting on some beach in the Mediterranean, taken before I met her. She wore a large, floppy hat and was bare skinned, beautiful, and carefree, basking in happier times. Now she faced bereavement. In one sense she was more alone than I, for however you cut it, I was not there when she needed me most.

Once more I sank into a black funk and could not shake the negative thoughts chasing each other around my brain. The chatter was driving me mad and I had to hike it off, no matter the forty-five-below cold. I kitted up and set out through the moonlight with Halifax on my heels. We had hiked before at these temperatures, and she loved it. I couldn't understand why this time she lagged behind, whining. "Come on, Puss. Come on!" I urged as I hiked toward the shoreline. I looked back, and she remained far behind. When I called, she came halfway and then sat down in my tracks. Angry, I shouted, "You wimp!" and stomped off up the hill to Thinking Rock. She hated to be caught out too far from me, so normally if I outpaced her early she turned back to the boat. But we were past her point of no return, and I was sure she would follow. Halfway up the long hill I looked back through the dim lunar light. She was a little black speck in the snow, immobile. I knew something was terribly wrong.

I ran down the hill to her. She sat stiffly, staring at me, seemingly half-frozen to death. I picked her up and tried to push her into my coat. Her right ear cracked in half and hung down on her cheek. *My God! What have I done?* I ran all the way back to the boat. I took her below, put her in the sleeping bag, and lit the heater. I tried to get her to drink some warmed milk. She lay stupidly still. I pulled her ear back together while she still had no feeling in it. As she warmed, the pain started; she howled in agony, and my heart broke with pain and guilt. *Just when I think I am doing so well, I do something so stupid! What is wrong with me, shouting at a cat that she is a wimp? How can a cat be a wimp? The signs were there. The wind freeze-dried her ears, you fool. That's why there are only dogs up here—cats can't drop their ears. She tried to tell me, but I wouldn't listen.* I hugged her in the bag. *Please, Halifax, just heal, and I will take care of you for the rest of your natural life. I'm not like this normally. It's being out here. You get scrambled, you make mistakes. Forgive me.*

Her pain grew worse as the days passed. Her ears puffed up, wept, and finally scabbed over. The broken ear seemed to be growing back together, although with a permanent droop. She shook her head as if she was crazy and furiously tried to scratch off her ears. I had to hold her little paws while we slept. Those were long days for us both. When she fully healed, her jet black ear tips had turned a permanent, snowy white. To this day, they act as a reminder to me that, in nature, all I need to know is there if I simply look and listen.

The intensifying cold of thirty, forty, then fifty below zero Fahrenheit affected everything. Camera batteries froze, inert. The film became too brittle to advance. To take a single photograph required careful planning. I wanted an image of that indescribable night sky, so while below I placed a cap over the lens and opened the shutter on the manual mode. Outside, once the shutter had frozen open, I took the cap off the lens for the time I estimated the proper exposure required. I replaced the cap and took the camera below and placed it on the stove as I prepared my meal. Thirty minutes later I heard the thawed shutter slap closed. It was a crude but necessary adaptation.

The cold's effect on the pump shotgun proved more than an inconvenience. At first I tried to keep the gun below and close at hand, but the condensation on the cold steel jammed the inner moving parts with ice. After disassembling and cleaning it a dozen times, I finally began to leave the gun in the cockpit. To be certain this had solved my problem, I tried to test fire it one day. I pointed the muzzle out the tent flap, pulled the trigger, and felt the release of the firing-pin latch, but nothing else happened. The trigger was depressed, leaving the firing-pin spring frozen, still in tension. Because of the internal mechanics, I could not pump out the round, put on the safety, or in any way change the situation. It was like standing on a live landmine. If I took the gun below to work on it, the firing pin might thaw and release, discharging the weapon. The noise and concussion alone would be a danger in that confined space, not to mention the ricocheting lead.

I crawled below and put on all the clothing I could find, including

three hats, two facemasks, and my goggles. Then I rifled through the
tool box for Old Ed's set of miniature screwdrivers. I crawled back up
into the cockpit and, by dim lantern light, with double-thick gloves and
blurred vision, I began disassembling the tiny screws on the muzzle
underplate. Shaking from the cold, I found it impossible to work with
a jeweler's precision or a bomb squad's deliberateness. Eventually,
though, I was able to slip a wedge of plastic between the firing pin
and the primer in the shell casing. I completed the disassembly and
cleared out a solid block of compacted, drifted snow. My nerves were
shot and my body racked with cold before I finished.

Back below, I turned up the heater and ran the generator longer than
usual to charge the batteries and create some warmth. For the next few
days I remained incapacitated in my bag. I attributed this to the shotgun episode, but when it persisted, I was forced to recognize it as more.
I entered in my diary:

My heart has been racing at 110 beats per minute at absolute rest and feels as
if it might burst. It is a terrible sensation. I can actually feel the blood coursing
through my body. I have a crippling headache and a loud ringing in my ears.
Clearly I have a serious medical problem. Heart attack? I've lived hard; I'm in
my forties. I wouldn't be the first. It has always been possible, but now it seems
probable that I will die up here, alone. Death, however premature, is somehow
more acceptable if we have loved ones at our side. They can't accompany us on
our journey, but at least they can calm our natural terror and wish us well on
our way. Two or three months ago I would have been terrified. But I have been
alone too long for that now.

But if I do die, then this diary will fall into Diana's hands. Cooped up together in this small space during difficult times, we had our frictions. I tried to
bite my tongue and used this diary as a vent. She would not understand, and it
would hurt her. I should burn it, but I don't think I can do that. I must at least
include this page.

My Love, if you have reason to read this, then there is something that needs
saying. I did not write these pages intending for you ever to read them. They
reflect my pettiness, my daily dissatisfactions, and perhaps some larger disap-
pointments. But they do not tell our whole story. Please forgive me. Please for-

get how hard we have been on each other. Forget how far we have drifted from each other at times. Forget that we have let our love wither. Remember that we have never let it die, that we have never given up trying. Know that I have loved you from the first time that I held you, love you now, and will love you forever. If I do not get to rip up this page and tell you this in person, know that this love did not die with me. We will be together, whatever happens. I am so sorry for the time lost, for I am now so anxious for time together, in love and happy in each other's embrace. You are the love of my life. You are first, foremost, and forever on my mind and in my heart.

I closed the diary and turned my thoughts to Halifax. If I died, she would wither away or be forced out to forage and fall prey to foxes. It was an unbearable thought. Next to Diana, she was my best friend on this earth. We had come so far together. What could I do? I thought hard, then I smeared a dab of honey on my stomach, which she licked off. I smeared again; she licked again. If I could get her to associate my stomach with food, she had a chance. I would die in the bag with her curled up next to me. Her own heat would keep that part of my corpse thawed. She could then get at my soft underbelly for a lasting supply of food. Still, I knew her chances would be slim. Once my body was discovered and the truth of her survival obvious, she would be shot in disgust. How could they understand? They were not locked in our realities. Halifax, Raven, and me—we understood.

My heart rate rose and fell and did not normalize for two months. I had no heart attack, as I had speculated, but I was weak and ill often enough that I should have reacted with logical attempts to identify and solve the problem. It may seem I accepted my fate passively, but my reaction was well precedented by victims of crash, crisis, and war, who often develop a lie-down-and-die approach to the mayhem around them. In addition to that, I had fallen prey to an insidious poison whose first effect is a serious erosion of the mind and, therefore, sound judgment.

History was a living force throughout my Arctic ordeal. I felt such empathy with and connection to the struggles of those before me that, in a sense, they spoke to me, inspired me, and guided me through troubled times. As Chief Seattle said, "The dead are not altogether powerless." I had read so voraciously about the Arctic that I did not have time to cross the equator and research the annals of Antarctic history. If I had, I would have read Admiral Richard Byrd's account of his four months of frozen solitude, aptly entitled *Alone*. Instead, months after returning from this Arctic year I would sit stunned by similarity as I read my private experiences of depression, paranoia, impaired reasoning, blindness, nausea, heart palpitations, and migraines described in the voice of another. How I now wish that Byrd's chronicle had perched on my bookshelf then.

Alone in his underground hut on the Great Ice Barrier, the physically ill and emotionally shattered Byrd wrote: "I don't know what is keeping me down, but I suspect a subtle enemy is the cause of my dark morale." In part, the Admiral discovered that enemy when he passed out in a narrow snow tunnel while running a generator, one he thought was properly vented and safe. He was saved only because he fell to the cold ground beneath the warmer, poisoned air. When he regained consciousness, he crawled inside the hut and slid into his cot in such a collapsed state that he could not feed himself or tend to his fire. Days later, he scratched into his diary that he felt death was imminent. He survived, for his loyal men at the main base risked their lives to rescue him from the outpost, but he was completely dispirited and physically incapacitated. He never regained his vigor.

In my case, the warming elevation of my *ikliq* exacerbated the dangers of the deadly carbon monoxide gas gathering in my cabin. I became vaguely aware of a pattern. After running the generator, I felt a dreadful malaise for two days, but in this dark underworld it was impossible to separate physical and emotional decline. On the third or fourth day, just as I was climbing out of my torpor, it was time to charge the batteries again. My mental acuity kept falling short of the simple and logical conclusions necessary to save myself.

A rare northerly wind broke the cycle, pumping the cabin full of fresh, bitterly cold air through the crack in the hatch. I woke feeling strong and clear headed. I lit the cabin heater and noticed the flames were brighter and the burning hiss more aggressive than usual. For some time I had begun talking to things as if they had their own living spirit, and this flame was an especially close ally. *Oh, so you too are feeling better today, my friend*. And then it hit me that I had been look-ing down a double barrel of deadly trouble: oxygen deprivation and carbon monoxide poisoning. The engine had sucked in more oxygen than the cabin intake could supply and had given it back as a colorless, odorless, murderous gas.

I draped Diana's sleeping bag over the forepeak door, hoping to slow the seepage of gases aft. Then I dug out the deep snow on the fore-deck and used a small blowtorch to open the bow hatch. By stages, I found ways to more safely heat the cabin and charge the batteries. I'll never know exactly what influence the carbon monoxide had on my state of mind in the long darkness, but considering how soon and se-verely the psychological problems hit me, I suspect it was substantial. Probably the generator's exhaust hose was porous from the start, de-spite its wrapping of asbestos and duct tape. The effects might therefore date back into October, subtle at first, intensifying as the boat was sealed by drifting snow. Once again I had been lucky.

Richard Byrd took the same terrifying journey into the bowels of darkness I did, but he did not emerge whole. Beneath the Hollywood hype lived a terribly troubled man. At the time, he alone knew he had falsely reported the very event that propelled him into fame: the first flight over the North Pole. He alone knew he was participating in a stunt, not a study, for he had intentionally maneuvered the events lead-ing to his supposed last-minute decision to send other members of his Antarctic party back to the base, leaving him to winter alone. He was a man hungry for redemption, in an age hungry for heroes. Commercial commitments and debt had plagued his expedition. Had he accom-plished a solo winter, he would have had a legitimate historical first and, perhaps, an escape route from his many problems.

There is no setting more conducive to a bitter rendezvous with one's true self than a solo polar winter. When your soul is stripped bare, the answer to "Why am I here?" becomes either salvation or destruction. Byrd's answer almost destroyed him; my answer is what got me through.

However, for all my spiritual arousal, for all the days I found bal-ance and joy in the natural beauty of Tay Bay, and even with clean air to breathe, the perennial darkness clearly was eroding my mind. Little things upset me, and my confusion frightened me.

Standing in the galley one long, dark day, I held a flashlight like a pretend microphone. I ran through a stand-up comedy routine that would not stop pestering my mind until I acted it out. I had written the lengthy and ribald skit in my head and, if I do say so myself, it was very funny. My laughter got rolling, and I couldn't stop. I laughed and laughed, gasping "Oh, that is just too funny!" Yes, it was—because I had crossed the border from the hilarious to the hysterical and kept going. I could see what was happening but was powerless to stop. I collapsed on the cold floor and howled myself into tears, barely able to catch my breath. I laughed until my stomach ached, until I was exhausted, and still laughter erupted.

In the dark, Halifax offered a little mew as if to say, "Pull yourself together, man!" That struck me as so funny that I laughed even harder. I howled, then sobbed, and finally quieted to pitiful whimpers. I lay on the floor, cold, exhausted, and as ashamed as if caught masturbating. I made my way to the bag and crawled inside. The episode was over but not forgotten, for I never fully regained my previous confidence. I was always on the alert for some snap in my behavior, always fearing a tailspin into delirium.

Some part of me watched my emotions and reactions as they not only amplified in intensity but became increasingly inappropriate to reality. I had built a life around the belief that, when presented with an obstacle or challenge, you grit your teeth, lower your head, and charge. This approach no longer seemed to apply. At times an acrid smoke clouded my thinking. Fear flooded me both emotionally and physically. My mind raced, my heart palpitated, and loneliness flowed through my bones with an ache.

One day in late January, I cried into the blackness, "I can't take it anymore." I chided myself out loud. "Hey, Einstein, what are you going to do, go home? Missed your chance. Now take it, or die trying." I got up, turned on a light, pulled a shotgun shell out of its box, and placed it on the shelf next to the shot glass. Because I usually filled the shot glass with whiskey on Wednesday and looked at it lovingly until Saturday, I knew my headlamp would fall often on the printed message: Double 00 Buck Shot, Magnum Load. Translation: If you want to splash your brains all over this cabin, this should do it nicely. Just do it. Otherwise, quit your weeny bellyaching.

Robert Service wrote, "When you're lost in the wild and scared as a child, and death looks ya bang in the eye, and you're sore as a boil, it's according to Hoyle to cock your revolver and die. But the code of a man says fight all ya can. Self-dissolution is barred. In hunger and woe, oh, it's easy to blow. It's the hell-served-for-breakfast that's hard."

Hell served for breakfast?, I asked myself. Hardly. A strong boat wraps itself around me, sheltering me from screeching gales. Our coffers are filled with food, medicines, and tools. Out there waits a lovely and loyal woman who has endured a decade of me. Out there are four sisters, three brothers, and a mother who have always supported me. In the mountains of Montana is my friend Blaine Wright, who once, when I worried about where my long road was leading, said, "What you are doing matters, for this is your life's work." Few people have impacted me so with a single sentence. In the sleeping bag, right smack in the middle of my spot, is my little pal, Halifax. Even up here, even alone, I have more than most. I just have to hold on, live, and learn.

I had almost forgotten about a world bathed in light when, in early February, the first blushes of light appeared, hardening to midday shadows as the days rolled by. Celebrating, I waved to my shadow, and it waved back. To tease Halifax, I locked my thumbs and spread my fingers, flying a shadow raven above her head. She crouched in a sunken footprint in the snow.

I climbed the southern ridge, and then, keeping my eyes closed, turned slowly, ceremoniously. As I opened them, there to the south, ripping clear of the horizon, that distant star, our sun, the center of my universe, met my eyes for the first time in a hundred days. A simple sunrise filled me with happiness, hope, and awe. This was the turning point. Upon reaching the summit, a climber actually still has half the distance to go, but it is all downhill from there.

I opened my arms to the sun's golden light. Even at fifty degrees below zero, I felt a healing warmth from those rays. Life-giving light caressed my face and leeched through my closed eyelids, rushing its good news to every cell in my body: I'm here, I'm here!

ELEVEN

Tay Bay

FEBRUARY 1995
1 HOUR DAYLIGHT

I arise from rest with movements swift
As the beat of the Raven's wings
I arise
To meet the day
Wa-wa.
My face is turned from the dark of night
To gaze at the dawn of day,
Now whitening in the sky.

—Inuit poem as told by Edmund Carpenter in *Eskimo Realities*

O F COURSE, after that first sunrise, the periods of light remained minimal—twenty-three hours of darkness to one of soft light—but that was enough to fix myself in time and define a day. I planned everything around that moment and was up and out, ready and waiting for each exciting photon.

Light *from* the sun, however, was *not* the sun itself. Hidden beneath those mountains, I could not yet see the sun from the boat, so a few days later I climbed to the ridgetop again. I had not heard nor seen Raven for many days. I worried that he had lost his big bet. Beneath those black feathers, denied his prize after so long a wait, had he wasted away to nothing? Yet according to Inuit legend he could not be dead, because it is the Raven who brings back the light. As I hiked the tundra, I looked everywhere for my friend so that I could give him a proper burial.

I lay perfectly still on the mountainside, in a frigid imitation of sunbathing. High above me in that immense Arctic sky, I saw a black speck circling downward. Sure enough, Old Raven had seen me lying there still as a stone and, thinking I'd finally given up the ghost, wasn't a minute behind schedule. I lay very still, luring him to me. He landed close and hopped toward me, like a vulture. I opened my eyes wide and said, "Thank you for the sun, Raven." He puffed up in surprise and squawked up a storm. But I was sure that, down deep, he was happy I was still around to keep him company.

In early March, the temperatures dipped to their lowest point yet—minus sixty degrees Fahrenheit, and that without any windchill. I threw a cup of hot coffee into the night air. It crackled and hissed, then exploded into crystal vapor, leaving nothing to fall to the ground. At such temperatures, flesh freezes on contact with the air. If you hold an exposed finger up for just one minute, you will lose it. Needless to say, before my hikes I was careful to urinate below decks.

During the night of March 6 or 7, I heard a voice calling my name. I was not alarmed—by that time I had been hearing voices on a regular basis—but Halifax also heard this one. When she dove behind a pile of gear in the bow, my cold skin started to crawl. I dressed, grabbed the lantern, and creeped out into the cockpit tent. Peering into the night, I found no one. I felt both relieved and disappointed. Then I heard my name again and saw movement in the dark. Well back from the boat stood two heavily fur-clad people. I was too confused to speak. I thought I could make out a snowmobile and large sled just behind them. They did not approach.

An unusually tall Inuk called out, "I have fresh meat under my anorak and a letter from your wife."

I shouted back, "Bring the meat first."

The two cautiously approached the boat. My heart raced with excitement. *Is this real? Are they here? Actual people!* I ushered them below, thinking I would wake from this dream soon.

When the tall man shook my hand and placed his other hand on my shoulder, I knew I was awake and this was real, for there was something unmistakable about that human touch. He introduced himself as David Pitsulak and said his friend was Michael. From under his anorak he handed me a thawed loin-strap of caribou. I quickly cut off Halifax's share, and then, as I was deciding how to cook mine, I shocked myself by jamming it in my mouth and eating it raw where I stood. David showed no surprise; quite the contrary, he had known exactly what I would crave most, so saw to it that red meat was the first thing I got. David knew, he really *knew* what I had been through. I moaned in ecstasy as the bloody meat slid down my throat, filling a deep need. I licked blood off my fingers, not wanting to miss a drop.

I put on coffee, poured them each a whiskey, and sat David down at the table. Michael, in his early twenties and (obvious even through his thick fur clothing) barrel chested, either spoke no English or was too shy to try. I turned on the electric lights to get a good look at them both.

Michael did not want to sit. Acting the host, I tried to usher him close to the heater, but he kept withdrawing, I thought from shyness, or politeness, not wanting to get my floor wet. I pushed him close, my own voice sounding strange, like that of an elderly man, "Here, here. Get warm, my friend." He mumbled and retreated toward the hatch. After several such attempts on my part, he protested to David in Inuktitut. Then he abruptly turned and climbed outside. I was confused and, irrationally, hurt. David explained to me in perfect English that Michael would normally never wear his caribou furs inside. If he let them thaw, they would get wet and cold, and in these temperatures that was dangerous. Michael had come below only because I had insisted.

David had left his fur anorak outside and beneath wore clothing of Western fabric. At first I found conversation difficult, stumbling over the simplest ideas, but all too quickly my words started to blow at a hundred per minute with gusts up to one-forty. David smiled when he physically could not answer my questions as fast as they flew.

He had a rugged face, softened by quiet intelligence. He was thirty-six and was married with three children, the eldest fifteen. He smiled with pride when he described his children. He worked in construction for the government housing department. When he spoke, his words were inflected evenly and spaced at equal intervals, as if no one word had more worth than another. He said nothing obvious, nothing that was already known, and he did not repeat himself. I suspect the Inuit silence is not often broken with "Cold today."

David did betray a deep emotion when he said his lifelong dream was to grow a vegetable one day. His eyes shone as he talked about wanting to go south, way south where it is warm, and buy a farm. When I asked him where, he replied northern Quebec.

David told me that he and Michael had drawn the very last bear-hunting permit. The entire region issues only fifty per year on a lottery system, and his name had eluded the draw for many years running. He smiled and said, "This will be my first bear." I found that foregone conclusion to their upcoming hunt rather optimistic. When trying to write a dictionary of Inuktitut, Knud Rasmussen once asked an Inuk to define happiness. The man replied, "To come upon fresh bear tracks and be ahead of the other sleds." I understood David's excitement, but still my sympathies were torn between David and the bear. By this time, I knew I would not shoot a bear, no matter what, for I could not go out looking for a bear and then blow it away, falsely claiming self-defense.

It is different for the Inuit. To them, the bear hunt is the only true test of manhood, and they value it highly. Even though tourist hunters will pay the small fortune of fifteen thousand dollars for a permit, few permits are sold, so few of the Inuit's precious bears adorn luxurious livingrooms worldwide. The bear ends up dead regardless of whose barrel smokes, but there is a difference. The Inuit will eat the meat, wear the fur, adorn their necks with necklaces of fangs and claws, but they will not have defeated the bear. They know that, without a gun, man is a pitiful little thing, slow on the run, offering harmless punches. They stand in awe of the great animal. They have studied its intelligence and know its cunning, its dazzling speed and thunderous power. They are proud of the ice bear.

Before pulling the trigger, old hunters ask permission of the bear to use its life to ensure their own. After the bear's spirit rises, the hunter thanks the animal with reverence and ceremony. In olden times it was believed that certain hunters were great not because of their skills, but rather because of the degree of respect they offered their quarry. Animals presented themselves to the respectful hunters' spears and muzzles with full understanding of the necessary cycles of life.

I had to coax out of David that this area may or may not be the best for bear hunting, but the townspeople had wondered and worried about me. They urged David to stop by and see how I was fairing. He admitted that he and Michael had reservations and had not approached closely to the boat at first in fear that, half crazed, I would blaze away at them with a twelve gauge.

"So, now you've seen me. Am I crazy?"

He smiled to soften his directness. "A little."

After twenty minutes, I noticed that Michael had left his hat and gloves. I jumped up in fear. Exposed like that, I would have been dead by this time. I expressed my concern to David, who just laughed. I hurriedly dressed. Outside, I couldn't see Michael on the boat, so I padded across the darkness toward their sled. Through the glistening starlight I saw a bobbing red glow. Casually lounging on top of the sled and gazing intently at the stars, Michael smoked a cigarette. He did not hear me approach.

He started to softly sing a little chant. "Ahh yaa yaa, yaa . . ."

I cleared my throat. Even in the dark I could see his smile. I asked what he was singing.

"It is my Ah ya ya."

"Can you tell me the words?"

"Yes, but my English is not so good. I am singing to the sun, to bring him back. I am telling the sun that this land is too cold. In the dark, this land is not real. He must come back. He must make this land real again."

I found this strikingly similar to the beliefs of the Australian Aborigines, who sing their Song Line. Travel author Bruce Chatwin described eloquently how, as the Aborigines move over the desert, they believe they must sing up the terrain that appears before them. If they do not sing, it does not materialize. Down each line they travel, there is a specific song that creates that certain hummock or dry riverbed. In the Aborigine's beginning, also, was the *Word*. The vibration from that word collects and directs energy into the usable form of earth before us. In this interactive view of creation, all things exist because we *think* one another into existence—trees, rocks, waters, animals, and people. We are not being watched—we are the process of watching.

Michael and I sat out there for a long time, me thickly bundled yet cold, Michael bare-handed and bareheaded, as at home as if he were lounging on a beach. I sat silently watching the starlight multiply on the crystal snow. Michael sang his soft song, perhaps using his ancient ah ya ya to ensure that my favorite mountain remained capped just right in glacier ice, that Tay Bay would appear each day just where it should be. I was grateful, because I had come to love this land more deeply than any other spot on earth. I could not bear to think of it with a single stone moved. This healthy, hard young man, casually wandering this dangerous wilderness, on his way to face the great bear without fear, was taking time to call back our sun. For a moment, I believed it would not come back to this land unless it felt appreciated, unless

Michael begged it to do so. Together with the Raven, they would make it right.

I remembered an ancient ah ya ya sung by the old men:

> I have grown old. I have lived much.
> Many things I understand, but four riddles I cannot solve.
> Ah - ya - ya - ya
> The sun's origin, the moon's nature,
> The minds of women, and why people have so many lice.
> Ah - ya - ya - ya

I stood up and shook Michael's hand. It was too dark to see into his eyes, but I would probably find only confusion there anyway. I was a Kabloonah, a white man, and he would always see me in that dim light. But for a short time, we shared something, and I felt I learned as much about this land in these brief moments of Inuit company as I had in five months alone.

David and Michael decided to sleep on board before the great chase. They offered me a cigarette, but I told them that I do not smoke. Michael asked David something in a worried tone. David turned to me and said Michael would sleep outside because he could not sleep through a night without a cigarette. I told him that I wouldn't hear of it—he could smoke as much as he wanted below. But when I saw the pace at which Michael sucked them down, I couldn't help myself. I told David about my father-in-law's terrible demise due to tobacco. I somehow thought this graphic description might sway them, but David dismissed me with a wave of his hand and a matter-of-fact "smoke like a man, die like a man."

After they went to sleep in the icy aft cabins, I opened Diana's letter. I read it slowly, squeezing the maximum meaning from each word. She described her father's last days. As a young radio operator in the R.A.F., he had watched in horror as most of his friends were blown out of the sky around him during air raids over Germany. He came home cold and hardened. The warmth of a fun-loving woman brought back to him human emotions, but when Diana's mother died of cancer in her early forties, his life was destroyed. He closed his heart in bitterness and for thirty years had let no one touch him emotionally. Finally, near death, he had cried in regret. He found the capacity to love openly just months before he died, but it was too late. Time had been lost. To the wail of a Scottish piper, old military friends looked on while the family carried his body to a hill overlooking the ocean waters where his wife's ashes had been scattered.

Diana wrote that she had asked her brother to remain in New Zealand to tend to all the affairs of the estate. Although she was emotionally exhausted, she felt she had to come home—and home was on board our boat, wherever it was. She hoped to make arrangements for a return as early as mid-March. This was the woman I had doubted in my darkest moments! This was almost too much, too fast. First David and Michael and then, perhaps just two short weeks later, Diana. I suddenly felt very nervous about her return.

In the middle of the night, Halifax crept out from her hiding spot. She had met only a few humans in her short life and was normally terrified by them. To my surprise, she walked past me into the aft cabin, climbed up on David, and fell asleep right on his face, clearly concurring with my opinion about this fine man.

The next morning the sun rose near noon. I fed my friends great gobs of hot, fatty food to see them off. Outside, I helped pack the sled—well, I *tried* to help. They politely retied my efforts. They worked together, silently and efficiently, each diamond lashing exactly the same and the tensions carefully regulated. I asked if the hide rope was ring seal. Michael smiled. David explained patiently that this rope had to be made from the hide of the bearded seal. It produced an incredibly strong lashing, but more importantly, it contained oils that kept it supple and ice-free no matter the temperatures and conditions. Even the best of Western technology has not bettered this product. Our ropes stiffen and our knots freeze. A thing as simple as a knot that will not untie can lead to serious consequences.

On their sleek snowmobile, they would cover in minutes what had taken me hours of hard hiking. Our traditional roles were reversed, for I had never driven a snowmobile, and I ran my hands over theirs in wonder. They knew every moving part and could strip and reassemble it out on the ice. I was as full of questions as the early Inuit upon seeing the great ships of the Kabloonahs.

I asked if I could jump on the sled and catch a ride for a few miles toward Lancaster Sound. I held on to the bouncing *quomitik* as their machine whined up Navy Board Inlet. If I combined all the sounds I had made or heard in the previous five months of solitude, it would not have matched even a moment of this discordant screech of internal combustion and grinding steel. I stayed on until we reached the iceberg from which I'd fallen almost five months before. Then, saying nothing, I rolled off the moving sled and watched them disappear into the rough ice nearing Lancaster Sound.

This time the long walk back home was a wonder. In my mind I replayed the entire encounter, thinking that when there are few people with whom to interact, the nature of each becomes terribly important. No two people could have better broken my solitude than David and Michael. I was elated by their company and comfortable demeanor around me.

David promised he would come back when travel was bright and safe. I asked him to tell all the hunters that our home was their home. When that anxiously awaited period of sun-soaked, distant travel returned, when the air was still wonderfully cold and the ice still thick and safe, every man, woman, and child would be welcome. They could use the *Roger Henry* as a base camp. Here we had a radio, food, repair material, and medical supplies. Our presence this far afield would extend their hunting range. It would also provide the kind of interaction for which I had waited so long. I had paid my dues, and now when we talked it would be with a common language formed by a common experience. When they said "cold," I could say that I knew cold. Dark? Yes, it is a force unto itself. Lonely? My friends, how can it be otherwise in a land such as this?

Strangely, I regretted that my long and lonely vigil was nearing its end. Through five months I had made so many mistakes, wasted so much time. There was so much more to explore, so much to learn. Alone in the dark, I sensed that hidden in my dreams and depression lay a message. At first it was spoken too softly, in the muted tones of an alien tongue. Now it flirted with me from the edges of my quieted consciousness, just out of reach. This message was what I had come so far for. And if I could open my eyes, ears, and heart a bit more, I might yet hear it, and understand.

TWELVE

Tay Bay

MARCH 1995
8 HOURS DAYLIGHT

> The longest absence is less perilous to love than the terrible trials
> of incessant proximity.
>
> —Ouida (Marie Louise De La Ramée)

PETER RETURNED TO THE ARCTIC and agreed to emphasize my message to Diana that she should take her time and come back only if and when she was truly ready. She had not had time to grieve properly and, understandably, would be emotionally exhausted.

He radioed back, "She won't hear a word of it. She's coming, and that's that."

Counting the days until Diana's return would have been bad enough, but Halifax and I counted the hours. In my mind, I followed her long journey—the drive through the verdant grasses to Auckland, the tearful good-byes, her plane's thirty-thousand-foot arc across the dateline, then over the equator to the opposite shore of earth's largest ocean. In Vancouver she would change to a midsize jet to pass over ocher plains to Ottawa, on to the gray granite of Frobisher Bay, and then transfer to a commuter for those long, icy, and inert miles to Pond Inlet. From there she would organize whatever people and method would best get her safely to the boat through those last but most difficult one hundred miles.

The human contact with David and Michael had been like a splash of cold water in my face. I snapped out of a strange somnolence and rejoined the brightly lit world with clarity and vigor. I turned to myself for some much needed maintenance. I scrubbed my soot-stained parka and insulated overalls, let them freeze outside, then beat out the soapy ice with an ax handle. I combed the hood's long fur back into an attractive fringe. As delicately as my cold fingers allowed, I sewed the many tears in my gloves, pants, and thick, felt mukluks.

I turned on the forepeak light and looked into the washbasin mirror for the first time in many months. I turned away in disgust. In the dark, I had begun thinking of myself as mind and soul—light, free, somehow having "slipped the surly bonds of Earth." Instead I saw what one might realistically expect: a rough-looking character on the wrong side of forty, with a weather-beaten face and the hollow, haunted eyes of a returning veteran.

Trying not to cut off my ear or poke out an eye with the sharp scissors, I clumsily cut my hair, seeking to reverse all that I saw. I wondered if that was what would be required to re-welcome my wife into my life. Could I talk of the trivial again? Could I use chatter to fill a silence I had grown to accept and knew to be infinite anyway? Could I touch her and not feel the terror of possible rejection or the pressure to perform something I had not performed for five months, five eternities? Sex—how ludicrous is this bone-bending mattress mambo. How futile is this pushing and pulling, expectation and demand, this trying to find through another person what can only be gained on one's own. *Why am I worrying so? I love this woman from the inside out. I have pined for her these many long months. Why am I not just excited and happy for her return?*

I felt confused and guilty because, simply said, in a small way I did not want her to come back. A part of me did not want to reenter the society of humankind, could not handle the complexity of a relationship. Events I had not planned for had propelled me into aloneness; to survive I had adopted an emotional autonomy. David and Michael—and soon, Diana—had begun breaking that autonomy, bursting through my private door with firefighter's axes. Only now can I see that theirs was a timely rescue mission, for I was approaching a point of no return, that place far from the madding crowd from which the hunted, the hurt, the highly enlightened, and the deeply disappointed do not return.

The outside thermometer had long since shattered, but my skin was finely attuned, and I could decipher the temperature to within a couple degrees. When radio conditions allowed, a weather report confirmed my estimates that Diana would be coming from a balmy New Zealand summer into temperatures as low as sixty degrees below zero, plus windchill. She would surely suffer.

I hiked out to Thinking Rock. Where the noise of David's snowmobile had torn through the stillness like a dull knife, now silence lay on the land as smooth and delicate as new skin. I watched ice boulders barter hues of cobalt, lapis, sapphire, and ultramarine in the day's rapidly increasing hours of light. To the north, the ice cap on Devon Island hung in the sky like a low cloud. No matter how often I had seen them, my imagination was immediately pulled to those distant summits. I thought of Kipling's *Explorer*: "Something lost behind the ranges, lost and waiting for you." *Perhaps after breakout, I will find what is waiting for me there.*

I wondered if Diana would see our Tay Bay in the same enchanting light as when we first arrived. Or would the remaining months held fast in the ice be demeaned into an act of duty and an endurance contest? That question was answered when, back on the boat, I tuned into the popular Iqaluit CBC radio station. I might have missed it, except my attention was caught by a news item. A prisoner had just escaped from the Iqaluit jail. I laughed at that, wondering just where in this under-populated, roadless wilderness did he plan to run? Then the announcer, Winston White, said, "Stay tuned for an interview with a most amazing woman, Diana Simon, who is returning to her husband and boat, frozen into the high Arctic wilderness."

My heart pounded through the agonizingly long commercials. I grabbed the chart of Baffin Island and, with parallel rulers, marked off the miles separating us—a mere seven hundred as the Raven flies. Winston welcomed Diana to the studio, explaining to the audience that he had heard of her return and met her at the airport in the hopes of a live interview. She had some layover time and agreed, provided he wouldn't mind first swinging past a grocery store for thirty-five pounds of cat food, the last item on her shopping list. Halifax of the North was a big hit, and Winston made good humor about her being the Canadian representative in the expedition. He asked Diana to describe our purpose, journey, and the events that had separated us. She did so with no embellishment or hype.

Her beautiful voice brightened the cabin like a light. Halifax sat on my shoulder, staring at the radio, her little head cocked in question. First commenting on how fast news travels in the North, Winston said that everyone who had heard about our situation had expressed grave concerns. He asked if Diana thought our adventure was too risky, perhaps even reckless. She said that, in fact, she was proud of our adventure, our purpose, and preparation, and was anxious to get back to her husband and home. She did not say "boat," she said "home"! The force of it hit me squarely.

The *Roger Henry,* her home, was buried to the boom in hard snow, a wisp of smoke its only sign of habitation. The outward serenity of the scene was marred by a dangerous problem. Through the dark, so slowly that I hardly noticed the change, the boat had rolled three degrees to starboard and the bow had risen. The stern had sunk into apparently solid ice. Walking from the stern to the bow was becoming an uphill trudge. Diana would be justifiably concerned, and I had no comforting explanation. I assumed these were forces well beyond our control and resigned myself to whatever the eventual outcome might be.

Putting that aside, I hurriedly readied the boat for her homecoming. I dug for two days, rested, then dug some more, leaving only a foot of snow for insulation on the deck. The boat now rested so far below snow level that I had to scallop out snow steps so Diana would be able to walk down to the aft deck entrance through the lifelines. Inside the boat, I whacked the larger chunks of ice out of the cabin corners and, a potload at a time, hauled them on deck. With buckets of meltwater and plenty of soap, I scrubbed the sooty walls, floors, and ceiling of the cabin until my fingers ached from chilblains. I aired the kerosene-rank curtains and carpets and scrubbed the pots; then I smashed all the tin cans flat and cut up the plastic refuse, laying it all tightly into large garbage bags. I forced open Diana's locker to find her clothes still suspended in a solid brick of ice. I tried to chip them out, but the first garment came free pockmarked with knife wounds. I wondered if Diana, ever practical, would try to haul with her a drum of diesel. It was best to assume nothing, though, so I decided to maintain my moratorium on heat; the cabin interior would have to stay frozen until Diana's return.

Outside, I sawed out snow blocks, rebuilt the wall around the latrine dump site, and neatly arranged the forest of ice chisels, mountain axes, skis, poles, shovels, and guns standing upright out of the snow. Finally, I walked around the boat proudly. The sight that would greet Diana could not be called inviting, but it did look relatively less forlorn.

Peter's news in his next contact alarmed me, even though I should have known it was coming. My brother Phillip and his friend John

Bleicher would be arriving from Missoula, Montana, into Pond Inlet sometime in the beginning of April. They planned to ski to the boat, estimating a ten-day trek at ten miles per day. Both Phil and John were athletically fit and experienced winter ski-campers, but the Arctic is the Arctic. I worried that my many pleas for caution, via Peter, would go unheeded. Phil's reaction was much like mine when I was warned about bears: "Yeah, yeah. I know." You cannot know the true danger until the coldness of your first Arctic gale sucks the living warmth from your lungs.

In a roundabout way, I was responsible for their coming. In the language of the self-help movement, I was the *enabler*. When I was a teenager burning with adventurous desires, I had made a solemn pact with my two younger brothers, which we had called the "Tierra del Fuego Accords." It stated that, regardless of age, stage, or situation in their lives, should any of the signatories receive a telegram containing only the words *Tierra del Fuego,* they must immediately drop everything and rendezvous within thirty days at the forbidding tip of South America—at that time, the edge of our conceivable world. We were young, but not too young to know that all the forces of the adult world wanted to shape our lives into nine-to-five predictability, herd us into relationships heavy on responsibility and light on laughter and love, and move us away from each other and down roads too well signposted—at thirty you should be here; by fifty, there. Nothing terrified me more. Thus, our *deus ex machina* would keep the wild spirit of abandon hanging over our lives; it could, at any moment, extract us from those tender traps. In spite of thirty years' passing, I still held onto the Accords as a point of honor, albeit moot (but then, I suffered from retarded development). Others move on, mature, assume more important and realistic modern responsibilities. What child has not huddled in a fort or treehouse and sworn a secret blood oath to adventure, sworn it for life and meant it, and then discovered girls (or boys) the next summer or moved away, leaving the gang's sacred pledge to collect the dust of other childhood rituals? My brother had his lovely wife and three children, his home, his job. He should have known it was just a joke when I had Peter send that cable bearing only three words.

I fussed about, preparing for the coming crowds. The next week's weather was settled. The sun was climbing above the peaks into pastel blue skies; the glaciers shimmered white, silver, azure, and green. The *sastrugi,* corrugated-pattern snow drifting across the sea-ice, rolled away like miniature Ohio hills. I hiked as far as my legs could carry me, soaking up the last of this lonely beauty. At the same time waiting eagerly, I cherished every last moment of the solitude I had at first feared, then wrestled with, and finally come to see as the most powerful and positive experience of my life.

Halifax hiked beside me, mile after mile. We wondered over a rotten seal flipper two miles inland, and we squatted over a bear track two hand-spreads long. We sniffed the air and looked around carefully, then back at each other. I wondered what this experience had meant to her. Why had I even once thought of myself as being alone? Every five minutes Halifax leapt on my shoulder to warm her paws and hitch a short ride, then something spectacular like a feather or fox track would lure her down.

Back at the boat, we continued our vigil, awaiting word of Diana or my brother. The ship's radio crackled, and Peter's voice reported: "Whiskey Charlie Gulf 4377, XNR 79. Diana will leave Pond Inlet in three days with Charlie Inoraaq. [Wonderful news. If anyone could deliver her safely, it was Charlie.] She will bring a drum of diesel. [What a woman.] Your brother Phillip called. He wants me to tell you, quote: 'Quit acting like an old lady. It's not fair that you should have all the fun.' [He's right.]"

AS SHE MADE HER WAY BACK to Tay Bay, Diana chronicled her journey in her diary.

MARCH 9TH,

From a mile in the sky I could see a solid sheet of white ice paving Baffin Bay from coast to curved horizon. Tons and tons of thick sea-ice. Hells teeth, how will we ever be able to sail out of here? In such a short, cold summer, how will this enormous frozen sea possibly melt? And if it does not? We have provisions, but it would be slim pickings. Cross that bridge if you get to it, Di.

A rather spectacular flight up the east coast of Baffin Island. Still heavily cloaked in winter, expansive valleys of snow broken only by lethal granite peaks—the ultimate in rugged and remote. Touched down briefly at two Inuit settlements, Broughton Island and Clyde River. Clusters of tiny houses shadowed by a formidable landscape. Life on the edge, quite literally.

Plane skidded to a halt on Pond Inlet's ice-encrusted runway. Outside temp.: −53°F. Our "hostess," a burly, bearded bloke in fur-lined parka and mittens, informed us the plane doors were frozen shut and would take time to thaw. With my first mouthful of icy air, my unwary lungs seemed to contract sharply and my Roman nose, protruding beyond the confines of my hood, felt instantly frostbit. No wonder the Inuit have small ones. Retreated into my fur-trimmed hood and took short, shallow breaths through my nose. Read somewhere this would warm the air en route to my lungs.

Met by outfitter John Henderson. News not good. My intended guide, Charlie Inoraaq, is ill, so another will have to be found. Suppose a little time to acclimatize would be good, plus I need to buy a drum of diesel and some final treats—tuna for H., Fig Newtons for A., and . . . well, perhaps a little chocolate just in case.

MARCH 10TH,

Awoke disorientated. From my mound of sleeping bag, the view of Bylot's snowy peaks reminded me I was in another season, another world, thousands of miles from New Zealand. No matter what I face north of here, it cannot be more difficult than these past five months of Dad's illness and painful death. He died with so many regrets. Live for today—who knows what cards will be dealt tomorrow. Just one hundred more miles to go.

Phoned Peter and asked him to relay to A. news of my delay. Dressed in two pairs of long-johns, wool jersey, inch-thick polypropylene bib trou and top, inner and outer socks, insulated size-9 boots, inner gloves and outer mittens, thin balaclava under fleece-lined bomber hat, down coat, and, finally, a wool scarf. Stuffed facemask, ski goggles, and two chocolate bars into pockets and was ready to face the outdoors. Hiked out over sea-ice toward a huge iceberg trapped in Eclipse Sound. Never made it. In the clear air and without a point of reference, distances impossible to estimate. Snow on the sea-ice incredibly brilliant—must remember my glacier glasses next time. I see why snow blindness caused by reflected ultraviolet rays is common up here.

Still −50°F, and that without any wind! Amongst the fractured ice on the shoreline two small boys played with toy dogsleds, cheeks a rosy glow. Showed

me their teeth, warning me to keep away from the real sled dogs staked out on
the ice. Breathing is an odd sensation; the frigid air feels solid and spiky and
crystallizes in my nose, leaving a frosty rim. Looking over to Bylot, the light
was incredibly beautiful, mauves and pastel shades, colours I have never seen
before. Vistas most beautiful to the eye yet somehow chilling to the soul.
Heard loud cracks echo across the inlet—gunshots or expanding ice? Mistrust-
ful of my surroundings, felt in constant anticipation, as if something dramatic
might happen at any moment. Retreated to my cabin for tea.

MARCH 11TH,

Limkee has agreed to take me, but I wonder how we will communicate, for his
English is limited and my Inuktitut more so. He looked me up and down and
clearly did not like my layers of polypropylene. In sign language he told me I
could freeze to death in one hour and that his wife would loan me her traditional winter clothing. At his home, my dress rehearsal was an event for the village. Women with babies snug in their oversized parka hoods came to see as
Limkee's giggling wife pulled and pushed me into her furs. First chamoislike
top and trouser inner liners. Next, calf-length caribou pants, then a fringed
caribou anorak reaching my knees. Sealskin mukluks, also lined, were pulled
high up my calves. On all these the fur was to the outside to shed the snow. Finally, outer booties with the fur on the inside and a pair of oversized mitts.
The stiff and heavy skins restricted movement to a waddle, but I was cozy
warm for the first time in three days. As I looked at my outfit, something Alvah
said many years ago flashed through my mind: "Stick with me, honey, and
someday I'll have you dressed in furs!"

MARCH 12TH,

Day of departure. Weather clear and sunny; seemed settled but still very cold.
−45°F. Diesel delivered on time and loaded onto the sixteen-foot wooden sled
attached by a long tether to a snowmobile. Another setback: The field radio,
for communicating back to Pond, was not operating. Would I go without?
Looking at Limkee's face and seeing the wisdom and courage of his forebears
convinced me—yes, let's go. My two bulging seabags were stashed, a bloody
caribou hide thrown over to insulate my seat for the journey, and we were off.

First few hours were exhilarating. With my temperate-climate upbringing I
sat in awe of the frozen seascape around me. We made good speed over a well-

worn track, but nearer to the SW tip of Bylot the track went east, and the smooth ice became ridged with hard, packed snow, haphazardly sculpted by the wind. The sled slammed into these frozen "waves," and the diesel drum broke loose. Had to offload entire sled to retie.

Felt quite the fool when I yelled excitedly to Limkee, "Look, foxes." He grinned, shook his head, and spread his fingers next to his head, indicating the animals were caribou. The Arctic's illusory nature was playing with me again. At times, this region is transformed into a realm of fantasy where the senses are befuddled by the strange actions of cold air and drastic temperature extremes. Mirages are common. Why, foxes may even look like caribou.

Pushed north up the vaguely familiar Navy Board Inlet. Ice surface increasingly more difficult. A bone-shattering bump broke wood planks under the diesel drum. For the third time the entire sled was offloaded and, this time, diesel moved forward. I noticed Limkee showed absolutely no frustration, completing what needed to be done without complaint. Another mug up (tea for two). I remind myself not to drink too much, peeing being quite a chore, not to mention somewhat precarious in these temperatures. But what about dehydration?

Noticed a heavy fogbank to the southeast rapidly rolling toward us over the sea-ice. Looked like a radical weather change. Packed up quickly, hoping to keep ahead of it. Half hour later, ground-drift stopped us in our tracks, wind picked up the old snow and threw it thickly into the air where it seemed to hang suspended, reducing visibility to a mere one hundred feet. Without explanation Limkee detached the snowmobile from the sled and sped off into the whirling snow. I could hear the snowmobile but could not see it. Then, silence. I was utterly alone, and it was totally, strangely quiet. My mind raced; "Is he crazy? He is always grinning." Or did I offend Inuit custom when I had to ask him to help retie my caribou trousers at our last stop, or worse still . . . No, that's ridiculous, he's just a little disoriented. Remember, you have read how the Inuit often use nature's signposts to navigate. Over time, the wind blowing constantly from a prevailing direction creates drift patterns resulting in an unending series of low, fluted ridges of rock-hard, packed snow—a built-in winter compass for Limkee in these conditions.

Wind increased (probably 15–20 knots), hurling more snow into the air, reducing visibility to about 50 feet. Fur trim on my anorak hood became encrusted with snow; scarf was iced to my nose. Felt colder. Stand up, move about, keep warm. I wondered if there was food on the sled? Why didn't I check? I cannot believe I did not check! There was a Coleman stove, but did I know how to light it?

Limkee returned. The sun was merely an area of brightness in the snowmass overhead. I pointed to it, thinking it might help with his bearings. He grinned and nodded and we were once again speeding across the sea-ice into the unknown. An odd sensation—to speed, with no control, into white oblivion. While inner voices cajoled me to trust Limkee, all my senses put brakes on.

After about an hour's travel, we passed over our tracks! Had we been traveling in circles? We stopped and Limkee once again disappeared into the opalescence. I walked around the sled to loosen my limbs. When Limkee did not return, I couldn't help myself. My mind wandered back to all that reading I did in Camden. Hypothermia begins with shivering when the body-core temperature begins to drop below normal 98.6. Clouded consciousness and loss of memory follows at a body temp. of 93.2. The absence of shivering at about 91.4 indicates the body has given up its defenses against the cooling. A state of unconsciousness follows, and soon thereafter, death. They say the end comes peacefully.

To fuel my furnace I ate a peanut-laden chocolate bar and walked around the sled. Uncertainty sets the imagination afire. My mind continued in wild debate. Bears . . . what about bears? Limkee had the only gun. As if it could protect me, I jumped back on the sled and rummaged for a weapon—something, anything to give me a fighting chance. The teapot and a metal spoon—make a racket, they hate unfamiliar noises. Who the hell said that?

After an incalculable length of time my guide reappeared, still smiling, icicles hanging from his moustache. He drew a map in the snow indicating Pond and Tay Bay. Pointing to me, he put a mark where he estimated us to be (about 60 miles from Pond); then he drew a triangle out to the west. He kept pointing from me to the triangle. I was confused. Going west would take us away from Tay Bay, and with all the extra fuel we had burned . . . Then I remembered seeing on a topographical map an Inuit hunting camp on the Borden Peninsula. Yes, he was telling me we were going to this camp to find shelter. Knowing there was a plan, I relaxed, a little.

Moving west across the packed snowdrift made travel easier. Quite suddenly, a hill and then three cabins rose in front of us. Limkee had found the camp in conditions where I hardly knew which way was up. I wanted to hug him.

Greeted by excited children and howling dogs. Taken to a small house. My furs were left outside amongst a chaos of skin and cloth. I later learned that leaving them frozen helps prevent shedding. Thickly warm inside. Adult faces, weather worn and shy, stared at me curiously. Ate a meal of plain rice. Watched Flora making a pair of polar-bear and sealskin booties, using an *ulu* (women's knife). From her collection she chose one and gave it to me. Must remember to send a gift for her—some chocolate and one of my miniature Chinese cleavers, perhaps?

After five months, I can hardly believe I will see Alvah tomorrow. I wonder how he truly is. I am dog tired. What a day. Was it only one day?

March 13th,

Awoke early, anxious to be "on the road," but the Inuit do not operate on a tight schedule. More rice, tea, conversation, and laughter—always lots of laughter. Left around ten, still very cold, but weather clear and sunny. Limkee's niece and nephew, Denise and Sam, joined us, just for the fun of it. Traveled north along the coast of the Borden Peninsula, weaving our way through a labyrinth of trapped bergs and enormous upheavals of ice. Could see for probably fifty miles. Feel so minuscule in this powerful landscape. Lots of bear prints. Denise explained they were not recent because the prints were raised above the surrounding snow. The bear's weight compresses the snow. Then wind-blown granules of hard snow erode the surrounding soft snow, leaving a replica of the paw print in bold relief.

Once we were headed northeast across Navy Board Inlet back toward Bylot, the ice was smooth and the traveling easy. Hard to believe that just six months ago we had sailed these frozen waters. Five miles to the north, I saw the long finger of dark rocks I remembered marks the entrance to Tay Bay. Then, suddenly, Limkee stopped for a mug up. Tea ... with just five miles to go, he stops for tea ...

I SAT ON THE SNOWBANK just behind the boat, my parka hood turned toward the south to scoop up, like a bat's ear, the slightest hint of sound. Did the Inuit designers know how useful these hoods could be for this? Of course. My face was growing wooden, but I could not go below. I might miss something, some sign of a sled approaching, bringing her home. Halifax flicked her head sideways and fixed her eyes on the southern slope. I heard nothing, but I had faith enough in her superior senses to ski across the sea-ice, through the broken ice boulders, past the sheets heaved upon the shore, and then strap climbing skins on the skis to trudge up the tundra to the cliffs above the inlet. I turned my hood south and sat silently. *I hear Raven . . . a ptarmigan . . . the usual pings, pongs, and cracks of ice movement . . . but nothing else . . . Yes, there! A faint sound like an insect,* but my eyes could not stretch as far as my ears. I could see nothing but ice and snow for miles. Halifax bounded up beside me. I followed her gaze to an ice-boulder field three miles down Navy Board Inlet and well across the other side. "No way, Halifax—why would they be way over there?" I trained the binoculars on that spot. Around a block of ice I saw a small speck creeping forward. It seemed too small to be a snowmobile and sled. But it was just that the ice block was so large.

I paced the snow-covered tundra in excitement, watching them wind their way through this unfathomable scale and fantasizing our reunion a dozen ways until I settled on one I liked. Then I realized that if I did not head back to the boat quickly, they might beat me there to find an empty camp. I raced hard down the slope through the broken shore ice, tumbling head over heels. I sorted out the tangle and skied hard, but my skis felt glued to the ice. They were—I had forgotten to take off the climbing skins. I ripped them off and set out again, working up a real sweat, thinking, *How very un-Inuit of me. Well, today is special.* Halifax, lithe and light as a feather, passed me in a flash, streaked for the boat, and dove below.

A screaming snowmobile with a long sled in tow ripped past me as if I were invisible and slid to a stop between the emergency tent and the boat. I stopped to catch my breath and savor the sweet agony of the final seconds. But something was wrong. *No, wait! Besides the driver there are two, no three people getting off that sled. I expected only Diana and her guide. Is this the wrong sled . . . a different party?*

I raced up to the boat and stripped my skis. The visitors were clad from head to toe in traditional furs, and I could not see any faces under the hoods. But from their appearance and movements, I could detect no Westerner among them. My heart sank. I could hardly breathe. One huge person, wrapped round as a bear, waddled toward me. The high anorak hood extended so far out that it was impossible to see the face inside, but I wasn't trying, anyway. I was looking past the person, desperately trying to find Diana's nylon jacket and Western boots, some sign, any sign that she was finally here. It was no use, they were all native and nimbly unlashing walrus hide ropes from the sled. I held out my hand to the approaching Inuk in disappointed politeness.

I heard a sob from beneath the fur. "A handshake, Alvah?"

I pushed my face into the hood, and hidden deep within was my wife—brave, and beautiful, and home. I do not know how the Inuit feel about grown men crying. Five months of loneliness flowed out as we hugged desperately—or tried to, for she was too big a bundle for me in her beautifully crafted clothing. After a very long time I turned to the smiling faces around us. A gray-haired man, a very pretty young woman, and a handsome teenage boy beamed watching us as if they were sharing in this reunion—and indeed, they were. Diana introduced her guide, Limkee, a stocky man in his fifties with a wide, toothless grin. In my exuberance and gratitude for Diana's arriving home safely, I gave him a bear hug that nearly lifted him off the ground. Then Diana introduced Denise and Sam.

We rolled the drum of diesel off the sled and set it upright near the boat. I wasn't going to let this supply sink into the ice. I would decant it into five-gallon containers and store them on deck. I drove the furry lot of them below like a startled caribou herd. With parkas, gloves, and boots strewn around the cockpit, our guests sat around the table and marveled at the homey interior and all its gadgetry. I fed them heartily on spaghetti and smoked-meat sauce. I was torn between my need for time alone with Diana and my craving for all the human company I could gather around me. I suggested they stay for a day. Denise explained in English that they dare not waste the good weather and should return to the hunting camp soon. I was disappointed but understood that, up here, you make miles when the sun shines.

Outside, Limkee made the final adjustments to the hide sled lashings. I pulled out a stack of mail and a manuscript for *Cruising World* magazine and asked him if he would mail them in Pond Inlet. He readily agreed and slid the bundle beneath his anorak. We waved them off, watching as they vanished into the grand emptiness.

The fading hum of the snowmobile was a poignant reminder that we were once again alone in the wilderness. Until the thaw made travel unsafe, we might expect the rare hunting party, but still we were essentially on our own. Diana knew well how arduous were those miles from Pond Inlet.

What was by then the only world in which I could imagine being comfortable shocked Diana. In spite of my efforts, snows had reburied the boat and ice still clogged the interior. She immediately noticed the hull's alarming lean. The diesel she brought allowed us to turn up the heater to try to melt the interior ice. Soon, sooty rain dripped from the ceiling, making it impossible to keep anything dry. The boat became a sodden mess. You would have thought it too cold for mold to grow, but Diana's clothes emerged from their ice cubes green with slime.

Above all, Diana prizes cleanliness, and that means glorious amounts of hot water to splash, spill, and opulently waste. But water was not on tap here, and producing it took grueling labor. With a soup bowl for a bathtub, she cleaned herself in installments—here today, there tomorrow—calling her hurried sponge baths "a lick and a promise."

She tried to keep up a happy front, but it was plain that she was emotionally exhausted and needed caring for. She slid into her bag and slept long, but fitfully. I stared at her while she thrashed and talked aloud in her dreams, and I saw the stress of her father's passing etched into her face.

I heated the cabin until I was nauseous—to almost fifty degrees—but she felt cold. The food to which I'd become accustomed did not excite her palate after fresh New Zealand fruits and vegetables, fish, and meats. Still, I kept hot meals coming and kept talk to a minimum, letting her tell her sad saga as she saw fit. For two weeks she seldom went out, and then only for a few minutes. The cold shocked her, and she quickly retreated below to her sleeping bag and her kitten, who was now a cat. Because Diana smelled nice and settled territorial disputes through compromise, Halifax, the faithless hussy, immediately took to the bottom of Diana's bag.

I had consistently torn up my life with an obsessively active libido. Add to that five months of sexual abstinence, and Diana surely expected an overly eager advance. In her state of exhaustion, I did not want to burden her for the first few days—at least, that was what I told myself. The days rolled by, but still the moment never seemed just right. As the delay became obvious and inappropriate, she was confused, then hurt. I too was confused. I intended no cruelty, but even when I finally tried, my fumbling hands could not find her as a person. I turned away without explanation, because I simply could not find one.

The boat suddenly seemed smaller than ever. I had a difficult time adjusting to the idea that, when Diana chose to talk, I had to drop whatever I was thinking and listen, sometimes even answer. Just the month before, I could sit down with an idea and think about it for five or six hours uninterrupted. Now I couldn't find ten minutes of silence to sort a thing out. I faced a full-scale invasion of my privacy, and I rankled. Had I really lived like this once?

When Diana dozed off, I slipped out for long hikes. My nerves were raw and my thoughts repetitious. I gnashed away. *This is how women must have felt when their soldiers returned from World War Two: "With only one foot in the door, this stranger is already ruling the roost. On the first night he expects physical intimacy as if it were a switch to flip."*

I had things arranged the way I wanted them. Why must she change everything? I can't operate in my own galley. And when I'm writing, she asks me to hand her things that are closer to her than me, just to see me do her bidding. And now she has a work list for me to tend to! After all the cleaning I did, she says, "What this place needs is a good scrub." And she never stops worrying and talking about the boat's lean and problems with the breakup. What will happen will happen. There is little we'll be able to do about it then and certainly nothing we can do now. Sometimes I feel more alone than when nobody was here.

Diana's confidence had grown during the handling of her father's illness and affairs. She must have thought many things over, because she began to make definitive declarations about the direction in which she wanted her life to go—not ultimatums, exactly, but statements not to be taken lightly. Though we'd been apart only five months, our experiences during that time had profoundly changed us both. We had reorganized our worlds independently of each other and developed along unparallel lines. The atmosphere on board was not what we had both longed for those many months.

On March 19 Diana wrote in her diary:

The euphoria of my return has faded. I feel as if I'm infringing on Alvah's domain, a stranger in my own home. I feel trapped and too dependent on him. Wish I could walk alone over the tundra, but I just do not feel confident enough with the gun to protect myself from bears. Really should have practiced shooting more often.

Feeling isolated and penned below, Diana complained about many things. The ice explosions echoing through the boat unnerved her. She seemed to think that it was somehow my fault when the wind blew. Often, I felt I had to defend Tay Bay. One morning Diana snapped at me for some offense. I could hardly hold back an angry response, so I grabbed the gun and stormed off across the ice. She ran on deck and shouted, "How long will you be gone?" (A reasonable question out there, where lives depend on one another.)

"Two hours."

"Where are you going? I need to know."

"Well, I normally just play it by ear. Probably north, up the second valley at the glacier's base."

"This is the time that female bears come out of their dens. Don't you think it is too dangerous to go poking around those valleys?" she shouted as my skis carried me away.

"If I thought it was too dangerous, Diana, I would not be going."

I skied hard across Tay Bay, then turned toward the glacier's head. Three miles down the mountain base, I dropped off the sled and started traversing up and across the slope to intersect the valley that runs north out of Tay Bay. I climbed higher and higher, trying to exhaust myself and my anger. I stripped off my skis, lashed them to my backpack, and continued upward aggressively. An hour later, I found a rock outcrop, the first bit of actual land I had seen in months that was not snow or ice. Behind me was a clear view of Navy Board Inlet winding south. From an ice cap on the Borden Peninsula side spread five glaciers, out and down through steep valleys like fingers on a hand. Nothing I had ever read about glaciation explained it as well as this single view. The interior of Bylot Island rose, peak after sharp peak lined up as far as I could see. Not a jet trail, not a sound, not a scent. I felt really alone and happy for it.

From the corner of my eye I saw movement—something white. I jumped up and headed straight for it. Without trees for reference, it was difficult to gauge either the size of the object or its distance away. Given a choice, I wanted a bear, because fear helps me rearrange my priorities like nothing else. But as I rounded a boulder, I came upon an enormous arctic hare. This snow white buck had been living here all along, huddled in some warren through that terrible winter. Raven, Halifax, and I had not been alone. What breathless escapes had this hare made from toothed or taloned foe? The wind had stripped the ground bare of snow on these summits, and, although it was still bitterly cold, the sun was working its magic on the stunted black shrubs on the south-facing slopes. Emerging from their warrens, which can remain forty degrees warmer than the outside air, the hares come here to get a head start on the grazing season.

I lay down behind a rock. To pass through this world quickly is to pass through blind. By sitting still and counting my breaths to thirty, I adjusted to my surroundings and discovered fifteen to twenty more hares, crouched invisibly in the snow. I pulled a camera out of my backpack and photographed them slowly. My gun lay at my side, but even starved as I was for fresh meat, the thought never crossed my mind to harm them. They deserved a respite of peace before the snowy owls, foxes, wolves, wolverines, and bears began their predation. The hares relaxed, grazed, and chased each other about. They bounced around me, heavy muscles rippling under their fur. They touched noses, touching base after the lonely winter.

At first I was not privy to the secrets of their society, but as time passed, an atavistic understanding emerged. The largest hare on earth, weighing up to fifteen pounds, arctic hares are also the fastest, bounding like kangaroo on only their hind quarters. During the April rut, males box ferociously, slashing with sharp claws, contesting the plumpest mates. They collect in groups of thirty or more. On remote Arctic islands they hold national conventions of several thousand. They wheel like windvanes into cold gusts, letting their especially thick fur lie down as insulation. They squat down onto their thickly furred, long paws, which at rest insulate them from the ground but in flight can stay aloft over the lightest of snow. Their short ears reduce heat loss but remain keen detectors of the slightest sound. With their unusually strong and sharp claws, they paw through frozen ground in search of dwarf willow or sweet saxifrage. They use their long and delicate front teeth like tweezers to pull precious seeds from rock crevasses.

Through focused observation, I was transported into their speciel reality, but a thought surfaced, the spell was broken, and it was time to turn to my own special reality. I put my face down on the cold boulder and closed my eyes. I heard Raven in the distance, and I felt full. *I am here for this. We are here for this—not for the petty or trivial. I must recenter, get the big picture back. Think about what Diana has been through, how far she has come. Think about how terrifying the ice must be for her, the boat groaning in protest as it's pulled down, the unholy screech of the gales. I must go down there and tell her that I'm sorry. Tell her that I love her and I respect her. I must give her back her home, grant her a say in how it's run and how we face our common destiny. By trying to preserve what I have learned in the dark, I have somehow forgotten it. Remember, be an instrument of peace. Where there is sadness, sow joy.*

I had told Diana I would be gone for two hours. I looked up from my reverie and saw to my surprise that it was approaching twilight. That meant I had been gone over six hours already. She would be frantic with worry. I hiked down the mountain, slapped on the skis, and picked up the sled. I began my long skiing rhythm home—pole plant, kick and glide, pole plant, kick and glide . . . About a mile from the boat I saw marks in the snow—ski tracks I knew not to be mine, for I had memorized every old track and trail in the bay. These were new, but I couldn't believe Diana would be out alone; cold air aside, she had never come to terms with not being at the top of the food chain. I followed the trail around a large ice hummock, and there in a little scenic ice glen was Diana, her pretty face fringed in soft fur. She had spread a foam pad out on the ice. It lay there like a café table, covered with fresh-baked cookies, tea mugs, and a thermos. I staked down the sled with an ice screw and sat down with her on another foam cushion. She poured the tea with relaxed precision. I let the sweet, hot liquid warm my throat and energize my tired muscles.

We looked out on the dancing light, now grown purple near night. The ice, the mountains, the sky, even the silence shimmered and pulsed electrically like some transparent sea creature. With my eyes still fixed on the southern horizon, I unconsciously reached my hand out toward her, only to encounter her hand coming toward mine. At each shock-wave of light we hummed and murmured in unison, sharing the beauty to the center of our souls. We did not require even a single word to call off our boundary disputes, set aside our differences, and focus on our visceral connection to each other and to the land. *Like life on earth to that distant star, I am bound to this woman.*

We skied home in silence, where I said I was so sorry in a natural, wordless way, warm and fulfilling, intertwined, embraced, exchanging. Together again.

THIRTEEN

Tay Bay

APRIL 1995
18 HOURS DAYLIGHT

There is fear
In the longing for loneliness
When gathered with friends,
And longing to be alone.
Ah ya ya!
There is joy
In feeling the summer
Come to the great world,
And watching the sun
Follow its ancient way.
Ah ya ya!

—Ancient Inuit ah ya ya, recorded by Knud Rasmussen

IANA AND I WERE TOGETHER again, but we were not alone for long. In the first week of April, the Montana Team arrived in Pond Inlet, set up their tent on an ice-covered beach, and prepared the mountain of equipment and food for a possible fifteen days on the sea-ice. This, of course, attracted attention, not just because they were Kabloonahs but also because they were heading out without a guide and, worse than that, on foot! The Inuit, like the cowboys of the Old West, find walking somehow demeaning. Unlike their Cree and Chipewyan neighbors to the snowier south, they have no tradition of skiing or snowshoeing. Besides, they know this land and its demands. It is too big and is composed of either broken ice or soupy mud.

John and Phil mingled in the streets with the curious people of Pond Inlet. John, being six-foot-three, dark, deep voiced, and bearded, could have walked in right off a trapping line. Phil is slight of frame, but he runs twenty-six-mile marathons to *train* for "long" races. Together they had trudged every winter peak in Montana, slept in snow caves, and tested their gear and themselves.

They acclimated to the cold and the pulling strains of heavy sleds by visiting the caribou herds in the rolling hills behind Pond Inlet. At no other place on earth, except Africa, do animals collect in such colossal numbers. Herds of up to 100,000 animals move like muddy flood-waters over the landscape, in constant search of fresh grasses, sedges, lichens, mushrooms, and mosses. Caribou are among the most migratory animals on earth, and newborn calves must stand within thirty minutes, run within ninety, and be able to keep up with the herd within twenty-four hours. The caribou's is a life of peril, for they must swim swollen, cold rivers and navigate high mountain precipices, followed always by a host of fearsome predators. Men, wolves, grizzly bears, wolverines, lynx, and golden eagles compete for their tender, sweet flesh. *Tuktu*, as the Inuit call the caribou, has been woven into the fabric of their society through times of feast and famine, for the flow of the herds is fickle, and the fate of the inland people, especially, depends on which path the *Tuktu* choose.

The "Song of the Polar Inuit," recorded by Knud Rasmussen, best expresses their emotional ties to the great herds.

> Oh warmth of summer sweeping o'er the land!
> Not a breath of wind,
> Not a cloud,
> And among the mountains
> The grazing caribou
> The dear caribou
> In the blue distance!
> I lie upon the ground sobbing with joy.

John and Phil rented a radio from John Henderson, arranged a snow-mobile pickup for the end of April, and then headed out confidently to traverse those one hundred wilderness miles. They made it exactly four.

On their first night out, after unexpectedly hard going, they set up camp early. A tent that normally takes four minutes to pitch took a full hour, the fabric shrunken and stiff as sheet metal in the minus-forty-degree air. Shortly after crawling inside, they heard what sounded like an approaching train. The ground blizzard hit with a staggering blow. The tent shuddered, near collapse. The wind sucked the warmth out of them as they huddled together in the darkness. Had the blizzard hit an hour earlier, they would have been caught without shelter and would surely have struggled for survival.

The Arctic is officially a desert, receiving less than the benchmark ten inches of precipitation per year. John and Phil became extremely thirsty in the dry air, but they kept a firm safety policy of allowing no stoves in the tent, for to burn down that thin shield would expose them to the unleashed fury of Arctic winds. Phil crawled outside to the overhanging vestibule to melt the water in his hip flask. His headlamp could not pierce the steam from the hissing snow in the pot. Not seeing the water level as he placed his bottle upside down in the pot, he accidentally submerged his gloved fingers. When he pulled out his wet glove, the wind instantly freeze-dried four fingers. More dangerously, he did not know it, for he had lost feeling in his hands long before. When he crawled into the tent, pulled off his gloves, and saw the wooden whiteness by dim flashlight, he knew he was in trouble. He pulled off his boots and found that same dreaded whiteness on one heel. Things were going badly. The men acted quickly, alternately placing Phil's hands under John's armpits and his foot on John's stomach, warming the flesh slowly. Then the pain began.

At the scheduled radio time, I heard a very faint presence but could not decipher their message. Phil seemed to be screaming, and I was alarmed. Because Tay Bay was calm, I did not understand that he was shouting only to be heard over their local gale. The next morning's signal was equally weak, but I did manage to hear their recited latitude and longitude, which I plotted on my chart. I thought it must be wrong, for it placed them just outside Pond Inlet. Hoping they could copy me, I repeated three times another time and frequency at which to establish contact that evening. I contacted Peter, and he turned both his enormous radio knowledge and his antenna on that position.

It was a frustrating hour. The two men could receive Peter, but he could not receive them. I could receive John and Phil, but they could not read me. And even our limited communication was intermittent because their radio was malfunctioning, adding to the confusion and frustration. When I heard the word *frostbite,* I made an executive decision. I asked Peter to contact John Henderson in Pond Inlet.

In the middle of the night a piercing light and whining noise approached the men's tent. John Henderson and his Scottish friend David Reid had hauled themselves out of their warm beds and headed out onto the ice without hesitation, as the code of the North demands. They packed up the cold and grateful party and headed back to Pond Inlet.

While Phil and John recovered, David, who manages the Great Northern Store, offered them the use of his house. Dave disguises himself as a businessman, but given that all his assignments are far off the beaten track, and his house contains only kayaks, crampons, and climbing ropes, his cover is thin.

Phil and John were lounging inside when Dave dashed in to find the keys to his snowmobile. He shouted that a boy had been run over by a water truck and the only person with any medical background, a nurse's aid, was off caribou hunting. Phil jumped up. "I'm a registered nurse with ten years of emergency room experience, and John's a paramedic." Dave rushed them to the health center. The facilities were minimal. The town's emergency strategy was to hope a helicopter was available and the weather settled enough for the six-hour flight to proper facilities in Iqaluit, at Baffin's southern end.

The child was brought in. On a dare, the ten-year-old had tried to roll between the front and back wheels of the passing tanker truck as it delivered water to each house. The boy had gotten caught beneath the wheels. From across the village, women flooded into the nursing station. They wailed in a nerve-shattering trill. The eerie sound rose higher and higher, filling the room. Phil and John tried not to let the cacophony distract them from their work. They did everything possible, but the boy had been crushed to death, and not even the Mayo Clinic could have saved him. The two kept working away, more for the agonized crowd than with any real hope. After an hour, when the parents were slightly more prepared for the tragic news, Phil took them aside.

The town shut down in grief for several days. Shaken, frostbit, and delayed, Phil and John were forced to reassess their situation. Even if they could make the boat on skis, something they were no longer confident of, there would be no time left in Tay Bay. They decided to solicit local help.

They met their dogsled driver, Panoely Okango, on the beach one morning. He was short, dark, with high cheekbones framed with ebony bangs. He was as hard as stone, and just as silent. He saved his few sounds for his beloved dogs. Lined up in front of a twenty-foot wooden sled stood fifteen magnificent, brown-and-blue-eyed beasts, as wild as the wind and ready to blow.

In his heavy brogue, Dave said, "Listen carfoolee. Ya be on tha' sled way before ya think he's moving out, 'cause he's goin ta crack tha' whip with nary a word and leave ya behind. They're just like tha', ya've got ta know." As Dave was speaking, Panoely lifted his whip silently. John and Phil dove onto the sled, which was already moving out from under them. John's long body flew right over the sled and landed on the ice on the other side. He just managed to grab a seal thong and roll back aboard as the sled careened off through the ice upheavals. The lesson was clear: Panoely's job was to get the sled from Pond Inlet to Tay Bay; their job was to hang on or die in the dust.

To calculate what day they might arrive, I pulled out *The Noose of Laurels,* Wally Herbert's compelling book on Robert Peary's life. To this day, there is controversy concerning the Admiral's claim that he'd reached the North Pole in 1909. Through his last five-day dash, his diary recorded gains of fifteen to twenty-five miles per day, which many experts have declared impossible.

Phillip had a handheld GPS (Global Positioning System) and calculated to the yard that Panoely drove through fierce headwinds and rough ice for a spectacular forty-two miles the first day. On the second day out, after eight pounding hours, Panoely stopped the sled and fired up his Coleman stove. Feeling talkative, he explained, "Tea." On the trail again, bumping along for a further six hours, he turned to his half-frozen charges and, perhaps a bit late, asked, "Cold?" Panoely drove on for a stunning fifty-eight-mile second day to arrive in Tay Bay. While this doesn't prove Peary's claim, it does establish it as possible, for nothing has changed out there between man, dog, and ice.

Diana and I were below, not expecting Phil and John for days, when we heard a knock on the hatch. I slid it open to find two goggle-eyed, frost-rimmed characters straight out of a Jack London novel. When they crawled below, their bodies literally smoked from the cold. We hugged and danced in excitement, our words flying thirteen to the dozen.

When we returned outdoors to unload the sled, Panoely never

looked up from his work. Even if he should spare us the odd word, it would never be before tending to his dogs. He was not on this earth to chatter like a loon; he was here to drive sleds with athletic grace.

Diana drew John and Phil back below for hot drinks as I sat on the ice, watching Panoely's every move. With a small hatchet he chopped a foot-deep hole into the ice, chopped another two feet away, and then tunneled between the two, leaving the surface intact. This created a bar of ice to which he tied a chain. He attached the chain's far end to a similarly fashioned bar, then latched each dog to the chain with a lead short enough to prevent an all-out brawl.

Panoely pulled huge pink-and-gray frozen char from a sack, chopped them with a hatchet into approximately one-pound pieces, and divided them among the salivating dogs. As he fed each dog, he had a short eye-to-eye talk with it in hushed tones.

His huge fur mittens had long, stiff cuffs with wide, funneled openings that allowed him to slide one hand in or out easily without using the other hand. With a quick snap of both hands, Panoely's gloves fell to the ice for him to kneel on; then, task done, he easily slid both hands back in. It was a small thing, but imagine having two frozen hands and a pair of floppy gloves that require one working hand to get them on. Fingered gloves are unknown here because they restrict the circulation of warm air. The slightest inefficiencies can add up to dire consequences.

At regular intervals, Panoely flung off his high-peaked caribou anorak with a sweeping motion of his arms, the sleeves and waist being cut very full for just this reason. When he was cold again, he slipped it back on with a quick toss in the air and an arm tuck into the stiff fur. The anorak's full sleeves let him pull his arms inside and wrap them around his body, and the full cut promoted good air circulation. The purpose of these on-and-off, arms-in-and-out, air-always-moving features was to prevent *ever* sweating in the slightest, thereby avoiding any buildup of moisture. Panoely was acting out the ancient skills I had read about by the volume. As the light started to fade, the temperature fell rapidly. He paid no mind. His presence was like still, deep water, a reservoir of calm.

Panoely's pants were made of shiny, colored sealskin furs artistically arranged. His boots had calf-high uppers of seal fur, rimmed with folded-back inner socks embroidered with delicate flower patterns. Black, hooded-seal hide, durable and flexible at any temperature and so finely hand stitched as to be watertight, composed each boot top. An ankle-high outershoe made of coarse polar bear fur covered the boots. The combination of stiff outer and softer inner hairs created perfect traction over all types of ice and snow, and the soles' thickness efficiently insulated his feet from the ice. Besides being durable, the soles were silent, allowing him to stealthily approach seals; from beneath the white opaque ice, a seal could not see his foggy boot bottoms. Nothing in our technology has bettered this time-tested design, but even if it had, it would not be the same: We are in no way soulfully tied to synthetic rubber and nylon. What we wear, what we eat, and, increasingly, what we do, no longer connect us to our origins or the land in which we live.

When the heavy sled was empty, Panoely turned it over like a toy. The Inuit describe sled size by the number of boards lashed across the runners—four to six boards to train the children, ten to fifteen for quick trips, and this full-sized twenty-board model for long distances. Using a flattened tin can with nail holes punched in it, Panoely rasped smooth the chipped ice over the long wooden runners. He deftly fired up his Coleman stove and thawed a dented paint bucket full of blood. With a seal's paw for a brush, he carefully swabbed the length of each runner with blood to create a sticky surface to which new ice would strongly adhere. As he melted loose snow in an old pot, he stomped the ground snow, compressing it. Then he sawed it into blocks. He dipped slices of these blocks into the water, then pressed them down hard on each runner. As the water leeched out of the dense snow, his hand carefully formed a rounded rail, which froze immediately into concrete-hard and super-slick ice. In six-inch sections at a time, he painstakingly covered the rail. As time-consuming as this procedure was, Phil later told me that they had done this every several hours on their journey. Panoely felt ice runners so outperform nylon or steel that it was time well invested.

Phil and John appeared on deck with steaming mugs of soup. I helped them stash their quarter-ton of supplies in the emergency tent.

Panoely stood back for a final inspection of his work and then stripped his outer layer of clothing in the cockpit. Then we all crawled below.

Crowded around the salon table, I asked Phil, "Did you get my urgent message through Peter?"

"Oh, that, yeah. He said that there was an admission fee to enter Tay Bay. One bottle of whiskey per person. Locals get in free." He pulled a plastic bottle out of his day pack and set it on the table. John followed suit, but as a dedicated teetotaler, he first filed a protest concerning the additional two pounds he'd had to haul. It wasn't Jack Daniels, but in the Arctic, one must adapt.

I said phonetically to Panoely, "Some . . . time . . . you . . . drink . . . whis . . . key?"

He looked at me as if I were retarded and held out a glass.

Phil lifted his glass and said, "To Tierra del Fuego, wherever one finds it."

Diana and I served a big, fatty meat stew and a loaf of fresh bread. Our guests ate with gusto after fourteen hours of hard sledding. I eat enough for two, John can pack it in, and Phillip has to fuel the metabolism of a weasel, but Panoely polished off twice our best effort.

Stripped of his thick furs, Panoely was not a big man. Veins roped his taut muscles like fishnet. His broad shoulders tapered to a narrow waist. I had seen this same body type once on a friend in Borneo. Dahn was a Nepalese Gurkha, honed mentally and physically by constant outdoor work, not as cosmetically perfect as a designer-health-club body but inexhaustible during real-world use. There was in both these men an animal vitality and, beneath the soft smiles, not a little danger.

Halifax emerged from hiding. She sat transfixed by Panoely, and he by her. He petted her soft fur, inspected her retractable claws, tested her speed with some rough teasing, and paid with skin for that. He turned to me with a look of wonder.

He smiled. "First time."

Chatter filled the body-warmed cabin. Panoely must have wondered what there was in this world to throw this many words at. The weather? What is there to say? It is cold. The hunting? If it is good, our bellies are full of meat; if not, they stay empty.

When our family photos and gossip ran out, the fatigue of hard travel set in. Phil and John crawled outside and into their tent. I made up a berth for Panoely in the starboard cabin. Before he crawled in, he looked me straight in the eye.

He said, " Long time alone."

I nodded yes. He shook my hand hard. I knew exactly what that meant, and not a medal on my chest could have made me more proud. Panoely slid into bed and was asleep in a moment.

Sleep did not come as easily for me. I could hardly stand all the excitement, the people, and the talk. After that wore off, Halifax kept everybody awake by scratching the foil until I got up and let her out. Then I worried she would not understand the extreme danger those fifteen canine beasts posed. Should she wander near them, they would tear her to pieces. I felt nauseous at the thought, so I dressed and slipped out. Halifax stood just out of their range, engaged in a silent staring contest. When I picked her up, she purred with delight over her exciting game.

The dawn sky faded from flame reds to pastel oranges, rising to buffed blue overhead. The air was calm and crisp. A dusting of fresh snow lay on the rough surface. The dogs had not made a whimper throughout the night, but when Panoely appeared on deck, they leapt up in joy, shook off their snow coats, and betrayed with wild howls the wolf blood coursing through their veins. One by one, he brought them to their traces in a fan formation rather than the two-dog line used in tree country. Electric anticipation shivered through the pack.

But there was something he must remind them of first: who was master. Every day, every ride was a test of wills. If he slipped on the ice and was momentarily vulnerable, if his soft neck turned just so and triggered those fierce instincts, the pack could unite behind the lead dog and rip him apart. He cracked his long whip to the left of the pack, then to the right, then just above the ear of the lead dog. He walked around to the front and laid the whip on the ground in front of the leader and turned his back, daring the dog to make the slightest move without permission. No matter the animal's brute power, it had not become lead dog by being stupid, and to cross Panoely would be very stupid. The beast sat quiet as a mouse.

Panoely picked up the whip and, without a word or a backward glance, whispered, "Hup" and cracked his whip again above the lead dog's head. The team sprang forward. The sled's runners ripped free from the ice and hissed off in an accelerating cloud of snow. Soon they were a dark caterpillar inching along under the mountainous backdrop.

Tay Bay could not have shown itself to better advantage. Phil dubbed it a "solar bowler," referring to its knack for remaining bright and clear even while the other side of Navy Board Inlet was choked in dark clouds. So seductive were our immediate surroundings that, for the first few days, no one talked of serious expeditions afield. We lay on the cliffs for hours with a spotting scope, watching seals and their pups on the ice and hoping for bear. We hiked the five miles out to the iceberg from which I had fallen, and from there the view north toward Devon Island silenced our seldom-silent crowd.

Being naturally cautious, John became the de facto safety officer. I urged him to decide upon an epic trek. "It's been so long since you've had a real job," he said, "that you might not remember what this is, but I, sir, am on *vacation*." He carved a lounge chair out of a snowbank, lathered up his face with suntan lotion, put on his sunglasses, and laid back with a good book. The only thing missing was a mai-tai.

Diana and Phil hiked off toward the glacier at the head of the bay, a trip that appeared to be a ten-minute stroll but was actually over three miles long. They carried a handheld radio and a twelve-gauge magnum pump shotgun, which Phil planned to leave with me at the end of their stay. Included were a box of exploding cracker shells, which supposedly frighten bears, and a box of rubber bullets for closer encounters . . . but not too close, for they will wound a bear terribly but never stop it. There also was a box of rifled slugs for very close range and one of double-ought buckshot for absolute last-second, in-your-face-and-on-your-body range.

We had never exactly defined what would make our expedition a success, but I had decided that killing a bear would make it a sad failure. I was happy to now have a full range of response options for each unique bear encounter. The radios were abuzz this week with reports that a Japanese ski party attempting the magnetic pole had nervously shot at a sound through the wall of their tent. Daylight revealed a dead female bear and a terribly distressed cub. Completely unnerved by the incident, the group radioed Resolute for evacuation. Because two animals would now be unavailable for their annual quota, the local hamlet elders fined the skiers two thousand dollars, one thousand for the female and one thousand for the expected death of the cub. The Japanese paid the fine without complaint and flew home.

Diana and Phil had hiked on to the tidal plains, where an ice fissure cut the width of the bay and formed a four-foot-high rift. A female bear and two cubs tried to sneak behind them, using the natural terrain to their advantage, but their movement caught Diana's eye. She shouted to Phil, "Look at the arctic foxes!" (It was not until she read to me Knud Rasmussen's accounts of his often falling prey to this optical illusion that I stopped teasing her about this.) Knowing they had been spotted, the bears sprinted up a slope so steep that a human would have difficulty just climbing it.

In case Diana and Phil needed to get in touch, I was sitting below with our base radio on. Phillip knew well the protocols of radio usage: identify three times the party you are calling; identify yourself once; state the station or frequency. But in his exuberance, he lost control. Our radio blared, "Bear, bear, bear!"

To tease him, I returned, "Where, where, where?"

"There, there, there!" Diana told me later he actually pointed. I have never let him forget that, but in truth no one should ever be embarrassed by unabashed enthusiasm.

For a polar bear "experience," you must be out there, standing at eye level in their domain, with nowhere to run, nowhere to hide. Only then, as you feel the hair rise on the back of your neck, can you truly appreciate their speed, grace, and power. Should events take the slightest of turns—a wind shift, an unexpected cub bringing up the rear—all the bear's terrible traits will come to focus on you, as they just had the week before for yet another hiking party on Norway's Svalbard islands.

Two women had been hiking the hills behind a tourist camp. The lead hiker thought she saw movement in the snow ahead but on closer inspection dismissed it. She safely walked by the spot in question. Her friend was not as fortunate. As she passed, the snowdrift exploded. With lightning fury, a great paw crushed her with a single swat. The leader stood in numbed horror, watching the bear tear her friend limb from limb. She staggered backward, turned, and fled to the camp. The bear was subsequently destroyed, compounding the tragedy.

The glacier at Tay Bay's head blinked blue in the sunlight, calling to me like a siren. I had promised Diana I would not venture onto the glacier alone. Now I had company. With crampons, ropes, harnesses, and pitons, Phil, John, and I skied to the steep glacier curving in from the north. Roped together for safety, we wound our way up deep ice alleys to the base of vertical walls, where the thrill of defying gravity began. As Phillip paid out line through the system of icescrews and carabiners, I hung horizontally from a precipice, looking down a steep notch that opened into the interior of Bylot Island. My view was unobstructed for the sixty summit-spiked miles to Button Point on Bylot Island's southeastern tip. Rolling away in a rock-and-ice tumult lay a pristine wilderness, its spectacular beauty unsurpassed and seldom touched by humans.

The pragmatic Inuit seldom travel into the glaciated mountains, sticking mainly to the sea-ice and close to their food source. No doubt some intrepid Inuk ancestor entered Bylot's interior in search of a vision or a marvel, but history did not record a traverse until 1966, when the indomitable climber and author H.W. Tilman officially crossed Bylot Island for the first time. In dilapidated English Channel cutters, Colonel Bill Tilman scoured the world in search of little-known and yet-to-be-climbed peaks. His eight laconic books chronicle his many adventures and misadventures with assorted motley crews. As he aged (he was lost at sea on his eightieth birthday), the altitudes he achieved may have decreased, but never his delight with physical outdoor challenge. The Inuit, Tilman, and our little group were tied by common experience. We shared the gifts that come from being, as Peter Mathiessen wrote, "at play in the fields of the Lord."

Our appetites whetted, we discussed a more serious expedition. Diana did not feel up to extended ski camping, and there was Halifax to consider. She suggested we take a handheld radio and leave her alone for a few days. She practiced on the long-distance radio with Peter until she felt confident she had somewhere to turn in an emergency.

We skied off with John in the lead. One rope draped from his harness to a sled, then to me. Another rope led from my back to another sled, then to Phil as our anchorman. Should any one of us fall into one of the many crevasses on the Inussualuk Glacier, this system, in theory, left two anchor points to hold and eventually retrieve the individual. Even so, John warned me that when someone drops through a snowbridge into thin air, the forces of momentum develop so fast and furiously that we would be lucky not to lose the whole team. At unpredictable intervals, John faked a fall just to keep me on my toes and my ice ax at the ready.

For four days, we wound our way upward and into the interior of Bylot Island. Hauling a lurching sled up a long, steep glacier and sleeping on the ice at thirty below zero exposed the myth that my back had healed properly. I was concerned, not about facing the challenge of this outing, but how I might meet the physical demands of breakup and sailing, which we hoped was just a few months ahead. I thought I was masking my pain well. I voted to plunge farther into the interior, pushing to the edge of our supplies, ability, and nerve. Yet John and Phil seemed to pull up early and break camp late, as if intentionally making fewer miles per day than possible. I began to suspect they were holding back in fear that I would break down too far inland.

When they pulled up short again, I snapped, "Look, Phillip, I may have a bad back, but I still have balls."

"The worst possible combination," he said.

He was too right for me to waste another word, so the next day we headed down. While I was disappointed with curtailing our inland adventure, I was eager to see Diana, and my skis flew across the ice toward home camp. I skied right into her arms. Halifax jumped on our shoulders, completing our happy family.

April's end brought the day for our visitors' extraction. Hemmy Qaaraaq, a young but hardened North Pole veteran, had been commissioned for the job, but he did not appear. Anxious to keep to a tight and complicated travel schedule, reunite with their families, and return to their jobs as demanded, Phil and John looked at their watches, the horizon, and back at their watches. By late afternoon, John suggested for the third time that I radio Pond Inlet to be sure there was no mistake. Again, no mistake—Hemmy had left three days earlier. By evening, John had worn a deep rut in the snow where he paced back and forth.

To "catch the next plane" up here is not a matter of simply waiting a few hours—it could well be a few days. John threw his arms up in disgust. "It's over. We'll miss our flight."

Late the next day, Hemmy and a friend drove their snowmobile into camp as casual as you please. They had heard that Lancaster Sound's ice was now in motion and that a floe edge of open water had appeared. The hunting would be good, so they had taken a little side trip. It made perfect sense to them; after all, planes come and go, but a clean shot at a narwhal is a rare thing.

Hemmy cached two dead seals deep in the snow as a food supply for a dogsled team expected this way in the coming weeks. The Arctic was awakening, and the word was out: Our home was open to all. Inuit hunters felt free to drop in for a hot meal, a soft bed, and to see the now-famous Halifax, an animal strange and exotic to them. We would become a rendezvous point and forward base camp for the spring hunting season.

We unloaded the gasoline Hemmy had brought and loaded our garbage for proper disposal in Pond Inlet. Hemmy packed his frustrated charges onto the sled and buried them in bloody caribou hides. I thanked John and Phil for coming, and I meant it. Sharing the magic of Tay Bay had created a special bond between us. As Hemmy ripped off at full throttle, I ran alongside the sled holding Phil's hand until he was pulled free. I yelled, "Tell Mother that, if all goes well at breakup, we should make our way home within six months. Give my love to Roger, and Prue, Raoul, Sue, Carroll, and Kris . . ." my words trailed off, ". . . and tell them I miss them all terribly, and I promise to make myself a larger part of their lives."

Phil and John had underestimated young Mr. Hemmy Qaaraaq when they assumed he would have to stop for sleep. No, the winter night is for sleeping; the spring and summer are for work. The sled flew off the *sastrugi*, landing in bone-jarring, teeth-crunching, internal-organ-grinding force through his nonstop marathon run to Pond. His passengers made their plane and returned to their families. Alone once again, we returned to our wilderness home—our *sinking* wilderness home.

FOURTEEN

Tay Bay

MAY 1995
24 HOURS DAYLIGHT

The surge of life at the grass roots penetrates your soles, creeps up through your bones, your marrow, and right into your heart. You see it, you feel it, you smell it, you taste it in every breath you breathe. You partake of Spring. You are a part of it, even as you were a part of winter. Spring is all around you and in you, primal, simple as the plains themselves. Spring is and you know it.

—Hal Borland, *High, Wide and Lonesome*

T HE ARCTIC SPRING is a joy so pure that one forgets the nature of nature, where the great forces at play are largely indifferent to us. Diana and I were reminded, however, as the *Roger
Henry* continued sinking into apparently solid ice. In painfully slow motion, the bow rose farther while the stern sank until the deck was level with the surrounding ice. How could this be? What could we do? Our picks, shovels, and snow saws flew. We hauled heavy blocks away, excavating a wide, tiered pit around the boat. Ground blizzards filled our work. We dug our channel again, new snow filled it again, we dug again . . . Diana's shoulders ached from this grueling trench warfare. Slamming the long *tuuk* (ice chisel) into the resistant ice, hour after hour, inflamed my elbows. Most of May passed this way.

Eventually we chipped down through the six-foot-thick ice until we broke into an envelope of water surrounding the boat's midsection. Water flowed into the trench, creating a moat around the entire craft. When Diana passed between the low sun and the port side of the boat, her shadow cut through the dark waters beneath the keel, revealing that the keel was not held fast in ice. The *Roger Henry*'s bow was in the air. Its middle hull floated, sort of, yet the rudder, propeller, and propeller shaft remained locked in ice. The grip of that ice was pulling us down, overpowering the hull's natural buoyancy.

There is a theoretical point at which the bow can rise so high above the stern that the boat's weight can drive the stern under, flooding it. Like a great ship sinking, the *Roger Henry* was being pulled to the deep in slow motion.

My mistake was in thinking of ice as a solid. I would have better understood the dynamics had I thought of it as a semisolid, even a thick sap. Glaciers in every corner of my natural classroom could have instructed me in ice physics. There had been other clues, too, but I had not noticed. In the fall, I had leaned the heavy ice chisel against the boat and left it there for several weeks. Its own weight pressing down on the thin blade drove the chisel four feet straight down into the ice. Of course, then I needed the ice chisel to free the ice chisel. With a climbing ax, I had awkwardly made enough work out of retrieving the chisel that the lesson should have stuck.

The thick ice surface of Tay Bay was like the skin of a drum. The boat acted as a drift fence, attracting heavy snows. These snows pressed the elastic surface down. More snow filled the hollow. What looked flat was actually a snow-filled, deep depression. Our hull was captured in the sinking surface. Compounding this, pressure from expanding ice had pushed our slippery bow upward. The fins on the rudder, the propeller, and other horizontal surfaces near the stern resisted that rise. The bow's rise then added downward pressure on the stern. Surprisingly, even in ice that pressure created heat, which melted the ice to create a microscopic layer of water on the lower edges of the steel protrusions, allowing the stern to settle in small increments. This left tiny gaps on the protrusions' upper edges, which filled with water and instantly froze. Thus, we faced the unfathomable phenomenon of the *Roger Henry* sinking into a solid.

We did not need to understand the phenomenon, however, to understand its obvious outcome. Frantically we tried to cut the stern free, but cold water kept us from reaching deep enough under the fin-shaped rudder. I tried for an entire day to bail the water out of the ditch, but it seeped back in at a disheartening pace.

By the time the boat looked like a patriot missile ready to launch, it suddenly hit me that we had gone too far. If we continued to mine ice from under the hull's stern, the entire weight of the boat might suddenly yank the stern, rudder, shaft, or propeller up through the ice, quite possibly bending any or all. Damage to any one of the three appendages would leave us crippled far from help or home.

I tried to keep a calm and positive face, but I could not mask my worry. I stood back from the hull and hung my head.

Diana asked, "This is becoming rather serious, isn't it?"

It was no use softening the truth. "Yes, Di. I'm afraid it's very serious."

"Well, then, let's have a nice cup of tea." She laid a board on the snow, set up the camp stove, and put on the "billy," as she calls it. I have no doubt that the moment the news broke that England was entering World War II, the entire nation in unison went to their stoves and put on their billies. On our bleak afternoon, this ceremony (which, incidentally, mirrored the Inuit's calm reaction toward pending crisis) conjured some comfort and sense of continuity. We talked over our problem.

I explained that I saw no imminent physical danger. If we lost the boat now, we had perfect weather and sufficient equipment to make our way to Pond Inlet. However, we would not know if the boat was crippled until the thaw, and by then foot travel to Pond Inlet would be perilous.

Our Western inclination is always to *do* something, but in our predicament that approach might have already created more problems than it solved. What we now required was some of the Inuit's legendary patience. We poured soot into the water, hoping to warm the moat and accelerate the thaw, and we agreed to simply leave it alone for a while. We both knew it was most important not to let this crisis wear us down. We must not obsess about it every moment of our twenty-four-hour spring day—easier said than done, for constant reminders accosted us. Anything not flat rolled off our canted table. Diana marked the ten-degree spot on the inclinometer, and we agreed that when the little black ball inside the curved tube reached that point, we would move into the emergency tent. Each day, we watched the inclinometer like a television, and each day the ball sneaked closer to the "abandon ship" mark.

Hunting parties began to arrive in camp. While once I had tried to resist even radio contact, now I rushed out excited to meet someone new. The Inuit lashed large skiffs on some sleds and piled tents, stoves, and mountains of fuel cans on others. Occasionally, a sled carried a small, rough, plywood-and-Plexiglas house in which the children played. Wide-faced toddlers, lying on bloody caribou hides, happily played with inflated seal stomachs as their sled bumped and thumped deeper into the wilderness.

We never hesitated to put on the coffee pot and start up a stew. With my barrage of questions, I could coax something approaching chatter out of our guests. We were soon privy to the local gossip and hunting news: Eleven caribou had been shot in the hills behind Hatt Bay; a Kabloonah was fined for hunting (being married to an Inuk woman does not make you an Inuk); the char were filling nets, but the narwhal were late.

One man's name sounded familiar. "Oh yes," he said, "I am the brother of David Pitsulak."

I asked him to remind David that he promised he would come for a visit in the spring. "How is my friend Charlie Inoraaq?" I inquired. "I heard he was sick."

He said, "Charlie? Sick? No, he is too strong for sickness. He will live and then one day he will die, but sick? No."

"And Limkee? How was his trip back to Pond after he dropped Diana off?"

"You did not hear?"

The story was spellbinding. When Limkee left Tay Bay, he dropped Denise and Sam off at the hunting camp and set out for Pond Inlet alone. He ran out of gasoline, so he decided to leave his snowmobile and sled behind while he hiked back to the hunting camp. Halfway there he was beset by yet another blizzard. The wind tried to tear the very life out of him. Having no tools with which to fight back, he dug a snow cave by hand and huddled within it for two and a half days. To stay warm, he burned everything he had, including his gloves—everything, that is, except that which would have burned best: the mail and manuscript I had entrusted to him. These he kept dutifully protected against his side until a search party finally located him.

The company of these good people gave us back our spring. Their questions and concern about our boat did not keep our minds off the creeping disaster, but it seemed to spread our burden of worry. Their kindness, their notion that all problems are *our* problems, blurred the borders of individuality. I'd never known a race of people on this earth who so integrate the good of the individual with the good of the tribe.

Their belief that one should never draw attention directly to one's self is carried to such an extent that, when a hunter stands to leave the igloo, he says, "Someone is about to go hunting."

Handsome and hard, Leo Muktar walked around the boat, shaking his head and intaking breath sharply. In the Inuit's typically terse way, he summed up our chances, "Bad."

Our guests ate heartily, without shame. Inuit custom allows travelers to find food in whatever igloo or house is fortunate enough to contain some, eat until it is gone, and then move on to another. The hosts calmly watch their supplies dwindle, assuming that one day they will, without a knock, walk in the door of one of these guests and begin eating. What goes around, comes around. But for early Kabloonah expeditions, this often caused serious provisioning problems. To send the Inuit away would be rude and might spark hard feelings and dangerous outcomes. The cleverest of these past Kabloonah travelers found a subtle way around this by enthusiastically salting their food. Unaccustomed to the bitter taste, after a few bites the ever-polite Inuit would suddenly remember they had promised to rendezvous with ol' Qeeqag two days down the trail and excuse themselves. But Diana's five-month absence had left our larder fuller at this time than we'd planned, and we let our friends fill their bellies as they filled our home with warmth.

On one bright, blue day in late May, a sledding party stopped short of our boat. A big man got off, hidden in heavy furs and goggles. He stood well back from us and raised his hands in a "don't shoot" gesture.

"David?" I called.

His big smile gave him away. Accidentally being rude, I asked, "How was your first bear?"

He grinned sheepishly, "Still out there. Come, I want to show you something."

Diana and I followed him out to the vertical orange cliffs that form the mouth of the bay. Two magnificent white birds with scimitar wings soared along the cliff's length. We crouched behind a small berg locked in the ice. David whispered, "Gyrfalcons. They will nest near here. It is time. The ducks have returned to the floe edge. See, they are looking for the right spot." He pointed to a ledge on the sheer rock wall littered with a large old raven's nest and stained with guano. "There, I think, safe from the fox."

I looked not at the birds but at David, a full-grown man, tough as they come, who even after a lifetime out here whispered in awe at the sight of ghostlike raptors.

Just then we heard the high-pitched and haunting call of the world's largest and fastest falcon. Misty white and dappled with brown, the great hunters slashed the sky. Hardly a bird in the air is safe from this rocket. It does not have to dive in surprise from above; it simply chases down its prey and destroys it. Its shadow sent Halifax diving into a snow den at a berg's base. The falcon can pluck a heavy hare from the tundra; Halifax would be an easy lift.

Although gyrfalcons feed upon waterfowl, ptarmigan, small birds, and mammals, a breeding pair may develop a local specialty. Some are particularly adept at duck hunting; others soar the high slopes for hare. They are quite rare, but not endangered. If that sounds contradictory, consider humans part of the conundrum. Highly prized by sport falconers, the bird has been trapped and shipped to Europe and the Middle East regularly since before the Middle Ages. But because of the Arctic's remoteness and the birds' fortunate habit of choosing high, inaccessible nesting sights, they have endured. Their southern cousin, the peregrine falcon, on the other hand, has suffered a terrible population decline thanks to DDT-saturated prey. Those peregrines that remained north of the subarctic zone survived in greater numbers. Their eggs, now transplanted to the south, offer the only hope for the species's future.

The larger point is that, even though the earth's burgeoning population itself has not spilled over into the North, this vast but fragile ecosystem could collapse in an epic disaster if we do not immediately curtail spreading our deadly toxins there. Our waterborne pollutants will infect the plankton to be absorbed by the fish and, in turn, the seal. Even the seal-eating bear will not fall the final victim, for all the scavengers—fox, raven, gull—will pass the poison, one to the other.

We hiked back through deep snow to the boat. David pulled a box out of his sled, a gift from Peter. Below decks, Diana opened it and passed out the contents as if it were Christmas. For her, a pound of exotic chocolates. For Halifax, oat seeds to sprout for medicinal grasses.

For me, a little something from Lynchburg, Tennessee. Over a wee dram of Tennessee Tea and the obligatory crankcase coffee, David told us about the year in Pond Inlet.

Several more families had made the decision to move back across the land. Some were going south down the Baffin Island coast toward Clyde River, others up the Borden Peninsula. They would build cabins, net char in the spring and fall, hunt narwhal in the summer, and stalk caribou year-round. The children would collect the eggs of the snow goose, eider, and dovekie. More men had decided to go back to dog power, forsaking the pressure of monthly payments for flashy snowmobiles.

These were hard decisions: to leave the seductive cash and consumer economy behind, to tell the children, "No more expensive chips, Coke, candy. No more all-day video sessions." They chose this because they felt adrift—uncertain who they had become, where they were going, and why. To string nets beneath the ice; to harvest sweet, fatty fish; to dry the flesh for feeding the people and the dogs . . . these are good things. This is the Inuit way.

David spoke softly of the long-standing Inuit dream: a province of their own. It was finally going to happen in 1999. Canada would split the enormous province of Northwest Territory into two more governable and representative provinces. The old N.W.T. would be populated mostly by whites and Native American Gwich'in, Sahtu Dene, Metis, and Inuvialuit. To the east, 770,000 square miles (an area three times the size of Texas) would be set aside as a new province of mostly Inuit. In poignant simplicity, it was to be called Nunavut: "Our Land."

Nunavut's meager twenty-six thousand residents were making a brave decision, for even with a one-billion-dollar land-claim settlement due to them from central Canadian coffers, they would have to stand on their own as an equal and viable province of Canada. This would be no simple task, for they have cultural confusion, scarce jobs, limited social services, alcoholism, high despondency and suicide rates, a widening gap between youth and elders, the temptation of slipping into cronyism and corruption. But everything must be considered in its historical context. They are not confined on reservations in some corner of an unfamiliar land, as Chief Joseph and his people had been in the United States. They are not decimated in numbers as were the Yahgan, Alacaluf, Ona, and Tehuelches from the tip of South America. As we march north through history, tribe by tribe, how can we bear the length of this litany of injustice? But that march stopped just south of here. The Inuit have their land. Nunavut appeared a barren land, empty and frozen, but I found it rich. With wise management and an artful blend of old and modern ways, it will sustain them.

David's sled wound its way north toward Lancaster Sound. As Diana and I waved good-bye, we heard a rumpus high in the sky. Fifteen ravens flew overhead, spinning, diving, and raucously wrestling in the air. Like me, Raven had survived his vigil and was now joyfully immersed in the company of his own kind.

Not until much later did I learn that ravens often are found in flocks of many thousands. Rarely are they found alone, for they are as tied to the tribe as we. Why had this one bird broken a bond with his species to remain in Tay Bay? He never scavenged our camp. He simply sat, watching and waiting. Had I completely misunderstood the Raven's presence and purpose? Was he a witness, a messenger, a guardian?

After months of silence, the sky filled with chirps, honks, and shrieks as great flocks and their predators returned. What joy we found as the sweet music of songbirds filled the air! Black-and-white snow buntings twittered over every scrap of tundra. They tucked their little nests strategically in deep cracks in the rock cliffs, safe from all but the murderous ermine. Glaucous gulls formed a breeding colony at the far end of the thumb-shaped cliffs and posted thick-chested sentries at its borders. Another gull nest perched on the short cliffs just abeam the boat. Three speckled eggs were laid in a depression of rock only lightly lined with twigs and a few feathers. The season for meeting, mating, hatching, rearing, and escape south is too short for anyone to be overly house proud. On or near the nest sat the attentive female. Above whirled the ever-vigilant and combat-ready male with his subadult lieutenants. If Halifax, Di, or I so much as took a step in their direction, they would peel off in diving attack. They were fierce and brave. Not a single fox broke through their perimeter.

Snow geese flew high overhead in tight formation. Their haunting call of freedom stirred our souls. But that freedom is not found through selfishness. By working as a team they increase their flying range by seventy percent. The birds in the rear honk encouragement to the leader, and when the point bird tires, another takes the mantle and breaks trail through the thick air. If a bird drops out due to illness or old age, two others break formation and follow it down to the earth below, where they wait for days, keeping the bird company until its recovery or death. They mate for life; if one is killed, the partner never bonds again. Hundreds of geese chose the far tidal plains of Tay Bay for their nesting grounds, and we felt honored.

Six pairs of arctic loons drifted over, looking for freshwater lakes soon to thaw in the tundra's depressions. One loon remained without a lover and called out its loneliness constantly. Oldsquaws sat at the edges of ice leads squabbling among themselves. King eiders, their colored faces funny and fat, exploded into flight, beating the narrow lead of water into a froth.

Most glorious of all were the gyrfalcons, who chose the very spot David had predicted in which to lay their four precious eggs. If we moved as silently as fog, we could approach the nest from a rock ledge above and peer down upon the unsuspecting female.

The whole community of animals was on the move. Lemming trails etched the snow like fine embroidery. Foxes trotted across the bay and along the long, mountain slopes in search of opportunity. I told Diana how often Halifax had gone missing in the dark; how when I had followed her tracks by lantern light through the twisting icebergs and boulders, I found them crisscrossed with fresh fox prints; how I had worried myself sick that she would fall under their sharp teeth. In spite of all that, I could not bear to keep her locked below.

We were on the snow next to the boat, melting ice and doing camp chores while Halifax played close by. Because I always watched the cat as miners would their canaries for signs of imminent danger, I followed her stare far out onto the ice north of the boat. A large fox was heading straight for us at a full trot. I assumed it would stop short of the boat because of our presence, but it kept coming. I jumped up and shouted to Di that the fox was going to kill Halifax right under our noses. Just then Halifax puffed up in warning. The fox stopped, and the two locked eyes. An unearthly screech came out of Halifax as she sprang up and charged straight for the fox. I was too slow and would play no part in the outcome. The fox sat still until Halifax was upon it, then it whirled around and ran for its life with Halifax hot on its tail. They disappeared over the snow dunes. After an agonizing hour's wait, Halifax reappeared in camp, clearly pleased with her performance.

In late May a sled approached. Thomasee from Arctic Bay unloaded his Western cargo: a party of foreign journalists wrapped in caribou furs and in search of stories. They had heard of our wilderness vigil, pooled their resources, and hired Thomasee to drop them at our door. Again the stew pot boiled, coffee was poured around, and talk filled our home. Victor, an English photographer, charmed Diana with his curly dark hair, blue-blood good looks, and proper accent. He told us he was gathering material for a pictorial book on the Arctic, an ambitious affair. As an avid birdwatcher, he said his life's dream was to see a gyrfalcon. This was an easy dream to fulfill, considering we had befriended two, perched on that cliff not a five-minute hike from the boat.

Victor almost knocked himself out on our low ceiling when he jumped up, pleading with us to take him there. He seemed to share our deep love of the outdoors, wildlife, and adventure. We hit it off immediately, as if we belonged to some secret society. I trusted he would understand that, no matter the professional pressure he was under to return home with fine photos (and he had described that pressure to us in detail), if he was too aggressive he might drive the female off the nest. Temperatures still below freezing could harm the four frail, brown eggs in minutes. Diana and I had visited the nest many times, but we were always careful to leave several days between visits and move off immediately if the female showed any signs of stress. Victor understood, assuring me we would leave the moment I thought it necessary.

We all hiked to the cliffs. In spite of Victor's long lens, the female became nervous and lifted off too early. I insisted we leave. Everyone agreed, and boatward we went.

Victor was excited. He *needed* that photograph for his book, but his time was up. If we got a good photograph, he urged us to notify him. He gave me his business card, then in a hushed tone cautioned me to tell no one about the birds. He said there was a well-known standing offer of a quarter-million dollars per male gyrfalcon egg or chick delivered to the Crown Prince of Saudi Arabia. My mouth dropped. That was enough money to turn heads and twist thinking. I assured him we would do anything necessary to protect these glorious birds, and we said good-bye.

Several days later, Diana and I were below when Halifax came streaking down the steep stairs and dove into the forepeak. I jokingly asked her if she was being chased by a bear. The next morning I did my round of the boat and was shocked to see her little adventure written in the snow—Halifax's footprints moving ahead of a bear's, at first close together at a walk, then spaced widely on a run, then the last of her prints leaving the snow in a great arcing leap for the boat, and the bear sitting down a full three strides away, no doubt pondering the strange sight.

The standard joke in the high Arctic is that there are two seasons: August and winter. But we found the cold and clear of the long spring the best of all times. After one long hike, Diana and I fell deeply asleep in our bags in the aft cabin. She had developed the amazing ability to detect the slightest thing astir and wake instantly. She suddenly whispered, "Alvah, there's a noise on deck." When I did not respond, a sharp elbow emphasized the importance.

"Oh, Diana, it's probably just the wind. Let me sleep."

"There is no wind."

"Then it's Halifax." That settled, I rolled over for more glorious sleep.

"Halifax is in my sleeping bag."

My eyes snapped open. Above our heads, a steady sound moved as if something was being dragged across the deck. I jumped out onto the cold floor and pulled the insulating piece of foam out of the galley porthole. Ice and fog clouded my vision, so I rubbed it with my hand and put my eyes to the glass. A large, round, black object pressed against the glass. I simply could not figure it out, until it flared in breath. I leapt back stupidly. "My God, Di, it's a huge bear."

I dressed as quickly as I could between rushes back to the porthole. This time, I watched the underbelly of a female as she dragged the rubber dinghy off the cabintop. I was so excited that it took concentration to get my boots, hat, and gloves all on the corresponding body parts.

Grabbing my camera, I took a deep breath, then crawled out into the cockpit in slow motion. *If I can sneak my head around the corner of the tent without getting it smashed into pulp, I will have the ultimate "bear on board" photo.* Even as I thought it, I realized it rang hollow. The camera was a only a prop, a justification for coming close to the bear. Close, it had to be close, and I didn't know why. I spun around the tent flap and pushed the button. Nothing happened; the camera was not wound. The beast spun from the boat and, in two panther-quick bounds, was fifty feet away and chasing her two butterball cubs from danger. The cubs sprinted the best they could, but still she swatted their round rumps, urging them forward. This rolled them up into balls; they shot forward and then came out running, only to get tea-kettled again by their concerned mother. At two hundred feet away, she stopped and turned to investigate me. The excited cubs pounced on each other in mock battle. She sat down, content to let them play at this safe distance, but for an hour she kept a keen eye on us. The little culprits had hauled off an old caribou hide that had been dropped off during Diana's return. They killed it over and over, in every way known to bears: with stealth, brute force, pounces, clawing, and biting. Then they strutted in ferocious pride, daring it to move.

As the seamless days flowed on into June, the tundra shed its snowy mantle with amazing speed. We hiked with Halifax on the southern slopes, where a wide torrent of muddy meltwater tore down the mountainside, uprooting delicate plants and gouging away the mud. The frigid water was too dangerous to cross, so we decided to turn back. We had taken only a few steps when we heard a roar above us. Quickly we turned back to see a wall of muddy water crashing down the mountainside. Meltwater had formed a temporary lake, and the berm had just given way. We couldn't outrun it. Forced to flee back toward the first river, we sprinted to a rise of land, hoping it would protect us. We clambered to a high spot and stood stranded on a dwindling delta. Finally, the lake shot its load. Nervously, we picked our way home through shore leads and rotting ice. Spring held many hidden dangers for the inexperienced.

The softening brown mud on the shores of Tay Bay sprouted deep-purple saxifrage, then daffodil yellow arctic poppies, jungle green grasses, and a delicate rainbow of minute wildflowers. While the tundra lay fully exposed and rushed ahead in its short growing season, the sea-ice out on Navy Board Inlet remained unbroken and implacable. The dark lichens, dwarf willow, saxifrage, and other shrubbery had turned jet black just before the first snows in September. Now, lying beneath an opaque veil of snow, they absorbed the penetrating solar radiation. The dark plants, mud, and stones warmed at an impatient rate. Thus, the snow melted not from the sunshine down, but upward from the ground, where the heat was insulated from the still-frozen air. In contrast, the shiny sea-ice reflected away three-quarters of the sun's melting power. Whatever radiation penetrated the ice, the swirling waters below absorbed and dissipated. The real melt would have to wait until the multiyear pans, bergs, and sea-ice were pounded by rough seas and suffocated by warm airs.

The sun circled the horizon, rising slightly in the south, dipping slightly in the north, but never actually setting. Its heavy, golden rays swept around and around our bay. No matter how often we witnessed it, there remained something mystical about watching the sun at exactly midnight. Diana slipped out into the cockpit to catch a glimpse. She saw movement from behind the tent and excitedly called out, "Oh, look! A cute little bear."

The "cute little bear" lifted its head, focused hungry eyes on Diana, and charged headlong to the hatchway, growing less little with each bound. The bear hesitated at the aft deck piping, rigging wires, and antenna, giving Diana time to dive below. I jumped into the cockpit to grab the shotgun, which swung from the radar post in a tantalizing arc above the bear's head. Feeling exposed and defenseless, I joined Diana below.

We waited for the soft hatch cover to be torn away. Huddled there, I cursed my stupidity. The spare gun rested in the emergency tent. And in these close quarters the mace would do us more harm than him. If the bear burst below, we would have to resort to hand-to-paw combat. We waited for what seemed an eternity, trying to interpret the slightest sound, until I could wait no longer. I poked my head up to find the bear forty feet behind the boat, nosing around some fuel cans. I raced across the cockpit and grabbed the gun. The bear saw my motion. Without a second's hesitation, he charged again. He stopped at the bars and fixed his black eyes on me. We both stood frozen for a half minute, and something deep within me almost pulled me forward.

Storytellers say Davy Crockett could stare down a bear, but I could not fashion a look hideous enough to unnerve this creature. I shouted, hoping to startle him into retreat. He stepped back, but not in fright. He moved over a step to the gap in the aft bars and shot forward with lightning speed, right into the cockpit. Holding the gun, I stumbled backward toward the hatch. My foot found stairs behind me. There wasn't time to pump out the cracker shells or the rubber bullets to get to the lead rounds. I had thought of myself as quick, but by the time I could even lift the gun, the bear was upon me.

Perhaps I would have done better to club him with the gun, but I decided to shoot at his throat, hoping the paper wad might sting him into hesitation, giving me time to dive below. I was not relying on the explosion to frighten him off; these shells were designed for use at long range, and they would take three seconds to explode. Young as he was, this bear could completely rearrange me in three seconds. I squeezed off and tumbled backward down the companionway, expecting company.

Bears are curious creatures. He stopped to investigate the sizzle. To his surprise, it turned into a bang. He should have been terrorized, but when I poked my head up, he was ambling around the camp. He seemed pretty happy to me.

I crawled out and coaxed Diana up on deck. I told her that, since she was our official expedition photographer, and I was the gunnery sergeant, it was her duty to go out there to get good photographs. "I'll cover you," I assured her. Instead, she suddenly got the bright idea that, on occasion, we should exchange responsibilities to broaden our skills. Annie Oakley she is not, and the pictures I took could not exactly be called close-ups.

A majority of bear attacks are linked to juvenile males. This young male was in beautiful condition, with thick buttocks and wispy white hair trailing off his forelegs. He had probably been weaned earlier this season and, having a hard time in his inexperience, was hungry and aggressive.

Although not fully grown, he was still capable of killing and eating animals far larger than we. I decided it was best that we not engage in a rematch. From fifty feet I laid a cracker shell right underneath him. When he whirled around ready to crush any opponent, I hit him in the rump with another. That was enough for him. He rambled off indignantly.

TIME PASSED QUICKLY, and the Inuit's visits slowed. One afternoon, from the cockpit, Diana called to me below. Her tone frightened me, so I bounded on deck. She said nothing—just pointed to the cockpit and the aft deck, now disappearing under the ice. The surface water was rising rapidly, and the boat could not defend itself by buoyantly lifting above it. Water had begun flooding the cockpit through scupper holes and then freezing at night, twisting the steel with its irresistible force, the force that splits mountains into boulders and boulders into sand. The water level was now approaching the bridge-deck. Once it breached the bridge-deck summit, it would spill below through the hatch, start to fill the boat, and pull it down yet faster. A bent rudder or shaft was nothing compared with the loss of the entire boat.

"What can we do, Alvah?"

"Something, Di. I'll think of something."

I slammed the long chisel down for an hour, silently thanking Havilah Hawkins for his contribution, but I could not reach deep enough to undercut the rudder. My arms ached. My heart pounded. My head spun. *Think! Think, damn you. What can you do? We've come so far, too far to lose it all now. What would they do? No, not even the Inuit have any experience with this problem. They sled on it; they don't sail through it. Wait . . . sled on it . . . remember? In all the accounts you've read of navigating over ice, the Inuit always give wide berths to headlands, capes, and river mouths. Why? What is it about those places— the currents? Perhaps moving water beneath the ice weakens it, erodes it. But we have no current here, we can't just make a current . . . unless . . .*

Just off the starboard quarter I furiously chipped a shaft down into the ice next to the thin moat surrounding the hull. When the hole reached two feet in diameter and four feet deep, I drove two steel stakes into the ice on each side. I laid a two-by-six plank behind the stakes and clamped them together. Then I uncovered our little three-horsepower outboard engine, recommissioned it for use, dropped it into the water, and clamped it to the plank bracket. I pulled out the jerry cans of emergency fuel delivered by Hemmy Qaaraaq. The little engine and gasoline were supposed to serve as a backup, however pitiful, in the event our engine failed or the shaft and prop were damaged, but we'd have no need for backup power if our boat was swallowed whole. I started the engine, put it in gear, and watched the prop wash flow under the boat. I adjusted the angle until the bubbles bounced back off the ice wall beneath the rudder. Each hour I turned the engine slightly to the left and, after twelve hours, I turned it slightly to the right. If I could get the artificial current to cut the ice beneath the rudder like a laser beam, the boat could rip itself free and rise to safety.

Hour after hour we refilled the little gas tank, anxiously watching our supply dwindle. The ugly smoke and gurgle of the engine intruded on our clean and otherwise silent surroundings, but now they held our only hope. After two days I slumped in discouragement. Perhaps I had misunderstood what I'd read.

Then, as Di and I rested below, the *Roger Henry* groaned. Then the vessel moved. Then nothing. We leapt on deck to check the waterline and over the rail to look at our mark. "Did it move? Is the boat rising?" Diana asked hopefully.

"No. It's the same."

She groaned in disappointment. "Even if it breaks its grip, the ice has to part below the rudder." I said. "If it splits above, it will bend the shaft like a twig."

Halfway through June, which the Inuit call "the month when people do not sleep," we felt compelled to belatedly celebrate the one year anniversary of our expedition. Over a lavish char dinner, we tried to be festive—stiff upper lip and all that—but not even a surprise bottle of Diana's favorite wine pulled from its hiding place could overcome our depression. Diana cleaned up while I wandered out to stare for yet another hour at the alarming scene. I chipped around the rudder, coaxing the boat upward. The outboard was sucking up our dwindling fuel supply. Suddenly, a screech tore the air. The boat lurched. Diana shouted from below decks.

I yelled, "Lie down! Lie down! Things are happening out here."

I jumped back just as the stern leapt up and the bow slammed down. The *Roger Henry* shook like a dog coming out of a lake. A wave splashed out of the moat, drained back in, and disappeared into the clear ocean below. The boat bobbed and swayed like a proper yacht again. I wanted to whoop for joy, but first I pulled on a dive hood and mask and plunged my head into the frigid water. Safely encased in a brick of ice lay our propeller and shaft. I pulled my head out, throbbing from the cold. I wanted to tell Diana the good news, but I couldn't talk—the water had shocked my motor systems senseless. I could barely give her the thumbs-up sign.

Diana got the message. She beamed in relief and rushed to share the good news with Halifax. Surely more problems lay ahead. There was the recommissioning of the engine, the hope it would roar to life after its long slumber, the testing of the shaft for straightness. There was the crushing power of the breakup, the thousands of miles of ice and gales between us and our southern goal. But we had the *Roger Henry,* our "home sweet boat." We were ready for the rest.

FIFTEEN

Tay Bay

JUNE 1995
24 HOURS DAYLIGHT

Every part of this country is sacred to my people. Every hillside, every valley, every plain and grove has been hallowed by some fond memory, or some sad experience of my tribe. Even the rocks that seem to lie dumb as they swelter in the sun along the silent seashore in solemn grandeur, thrill with memories of events past.

—Chief Seattle, 1854

HEAVY GROUND SQUALLS buffeted the *Roger Henry*'s hull, which clanged and shuddered against the icy shores of its little pool. A year ago I might have cursed this weather, but now I understood its importance. This wind blew rotted snow clear of the ice, revealing a dark blue surface that absorbed those wonderful solar rays and accelerated the thaw. Walking on the translucent surface felt like walking on sky. Twigs, leaves, and any dark natural litter that lay there quickly warmed, bore tubes into the ice, and paused at different levels, where they rested like fire flecks within opal. Melt pools of lambent water stood an inch or a foot deep—there was no telling. They were magical but unsettling to walk through. We probed with our feet, searching for the real surface in this strata of illusion.

Also essential to our breakout were storms at sea, churned up by large, disturbed weather patterns. Powerful swells swept into our ice-covered waters, beating the edge of the pack ice into splinters, eroding it far faster than melting alone ever could.

We wandered the tundra, enthralled by sprouting life and color. With time to look, listen, and ponder the interconnected pattern of all things, we felt a keenly heightened sense of beauty. Diana and I had never felt so close to each other, bound to and by everything around us.

At the top of the finger cliffs, I stripped off my clothes and lay behind a rock. The temperature was still well below freezing, but the rock blocked even a hint of wind. If I lay perfectly still, solar radiation warmed my body. Sunshine caressed my skin, and I slept. We don't often describe the different types of sleep, beyond saying "deep" or "fitful." This was a light sleep, a lyrical sleep, a fun sleep. I soaked up the healing rays of our distant star. Lying on the tundra, in the wilderness, and buck naked, I was as happy as a person should ever be.

While exploring Antarctica, Australian Douglas Mawson lost his companions. One fell into a crevasse; the other succumbed to toxemia after eating a dog's liver. Mawson struggled through an unbelievable nightmare while trying to reach help. Both starving and freezing to death, he began to regularly strip off all his clothes to expose himself to the sun, in spite of horrendous air temperatures. He later swore this saved his life. He claimed he felt warmed and "fed"—that, in effect, he had drawn physical nourishment from the sun. Despite experts who dismissed the possibility, Mawson never changed his story. Little else could explain his miraculous survival, chronicled in the thrilling book *Mawson's Will*.

I woke up as Diana came near, picking flowers. With her glacier sunglasses and flowing hair, she looked like a movie star. I asked her, "Don't suppose I could interest you in . . ."

"Don't even think about it," she interrupted. "These clothes are staying on until we hit Savannah, Georgia—maybe the equator."

As I knew she would, Diana stooped over an orange, lichen-stained rock that framed an arctic poppy, a tuft of green grass, a tail feather from a glaucous gull, and the bleached bone of a small animal. The composition looked only slightly different from the other hundred tufts in the area, but we agreed that this one was perfect in every way, somehow balanced in the best textures and hues we had seen that day.

Diana cautioned, "Oh, but don't forget that purple we saw yesterday at midnight, just as the sun passed behind the mountain. Remember that purple?"

I did, and I still do. If I could have frozen time there, I would have. I loved this woman, loved watching her move that bleached bone one inch to the left, sighing, "There, now that is really perfect." We relished inventing names for these new colors. We stood still in awe, letting our bones reverberate the ecstatic sounds of the snow geese, so high in the sky that at first we'd thought we heard the soft voice of God, so numerous that on occasion we stood under snows of delicate white feathers. We might be found throwing our arms around a painted boulder to absorb its palpable power. We kept the world of ambition and exploitation far to our south. If only it could last forever.

We looked down the high slope onto Navy Board Inlet. The ice cover remained ten-tenths, but leads had fractured it and surface meltwater lakes had formed, mimicking the Minnesota landscape. Travel was precarious at best. We'd had no visitors for some time. Until the next spring, we expected the land and sea would lie silent again.

We spied movement on the ice—a small but definite dark spot moving north toward our bay. I dressed quickly and trained the binoculars on the mystery, which grew into a snowmobile and sled. We assumed these hardy travelers would round the finger cliffs into Tay Bay for a visit, as everyone before them had. Instead, the sled stopped and three small figures pitched camp on a dry patch of ice outside the cliffs and out of view of our camp. We returned to the boat, thinking surely they would visit on foot, for the Inuit prize politeness. Yet no one came. When I saw people on the cliff above the falcon nest, I decided it was time to take a walk.

I picked my way to land through twisting lakes and rivers flowing on the sea-ice, then scaled the slope toward the cliffs. Silhouetted on the cliff stood a large tripod. I shouted a greeting. From over the hill, heads appeared, familiar even from a distance. There was Victor, a long way from home, with Thomasee and someone I didn't recognize. Victor and I greeted like long-lost friends, but he obviously felt awkward for not having come to see us. I knew, and he knew that I knew, that he had stopped short of the boat, hoping to avoid my fluttering around acting as the birds' appointed guardian. He wanted those photos, and he would do whatever had to be done to get them.

By this time the four eggs had hatched. Three downy, pink chicks squawked incessantly at their mother for more and more food. The male streaked the fifteen miles north to open water, pulled down an oldsquaw or eider duck, and dragged the heavy booty home. As a lookout, he rested on the cliffs above the nest until the insatiable chicks started shrieking, when again he dutifully set off in search of prey. The nest was littered with slimy entrails, stripped arctic hare bones, and shiny duck bills. I knew that the female's being off the nest was not as dangerous now as it had been before the hatch, but I still advised caution. My warning went mostly unheeded for a day as Victor photographed the nest from every angle.

I tried another tack by asking Victor if he had ever seen a polar bear. His eyes lit up. I suggested I find him one and he spend a day on that page of his book.

"What? You think you can find one . . ." he snapped his fingers, ". . . just like that?"

"Well, not just like that. But I've been tracking them for some months now. I think I can turn one up."

The next morning I ascended the north slopes toward the valleys at the bay's head. I let my eyes relax and flow over the sea-ice. No odd shape or telltale off-white color halted my sweep, so I turned to the countless snow patches on the dark, rocky slopes. My eyes kept returning to the same two little white blotches miles down the bay, seemingly no different than the rest. I did not see but rather *sensed* slight movement.

I stayed under cover of the coastal cliffs to creep farther down the range until I lay beneath that point. I scrambled up the scree-and-sand embankment, tested the wind direction with a wetted finger, and only then lifted my head carefully, just enough to see. A gloriously large, clean, white female bear and a butterball cub dug in the thawing dirt. The mother's great paws ripped the earth like a diesel-driven machine. I couldn't see what the bears were after—perhaps a particular medicinal root or a den of lemmings they might swipe up and pop in their mouths as quickly as a cat would a mouse.

The mother lumbered in a tight circle on a flat spot on the slope and plopped her thick buttocks down. She called to her club with a gruff cough. The happy cub bounded over full-steam, tumbling into her lap. The mother cradled her infant in those great arms and put its mouth to her teat. As the cub suckled hungrily, its mother looked out serenely on her home. She felt content. Here a scientist might say, "You cannot know that. There is no data." But I know it as certainly as when I look into the beaming face of a human mother. I saw tenderness, pride, and deep happiness.

I slipped back under the cliffs and marched back down the bay. I ran

through the broken shore ice, jumping from floe to floe, balancing myself with the boathook. I hopped to shore and carried on up and over
the low saddle, down the outside cliffs, and up to Thomasee's tent.
Once I'd caught my breath, I called them out and explained our options. The bears would descend the north shore and turn toward us to
follow a long lead that split the bay's entrance. Ring seals had fre-
quented the lead in good numbers all week, and their scent would be
strong. Then the bears would turn right, under the cliffs, and walk
along them to the tip of the peninsula jutting into Navy Board Inlet,
then turn back down the peninsula's backside for half its distance before breaking off. We could sit on the falcon cliff and be sure of captur-
ing a photo, but it would not be *really* close. If Victor would trust me, I
could put him in a little box canyon on the peninsula's tip. There, if
Victor made not a whisper, the bears would walk right past him and
never know he was there.

We set out, hauling Victor's heavy tripod and large camera case.
Halfway down the high peninsula and across the bay entrance, the
female altered course directly down the lead as I had anticipated. But
Victor lost faith and decided to take the bird in the hand. He plopped his
tripod down on the cliff and set up for the approaching bears. My urging to move on went unheeded. I asked him to at least hold off with his
camera until I could get a photograph, for I had no lens even approaching his long-distance zooms. He assured me he would wait, but as the
bears approached, it seemed he couldn't help himself. He hit the button
as if he were firing a machine gun. His camera whirled in autowind.
When he'd shot that roll, he hit rewind, dropped the humming camera
on the tundra, and pulled out another of his seven Nikons. Now two
cameras ground away in mechanical protest.

Out on the sea-ice, the female lifted her head at the sound and then
swayed up on her two hind paws, her great nose probing the air for information. With a loud grunt she turned her cub around. The two fled
nonstop for five miles over the ice toward Lancaster Sound. Victor had
a glazed look as if coming out of a trance. Under his friendly, easygoing
veneer was a man driven to succeed. In the photography business, they
probably call it focus. He had some fine photos now.

At midnight we returned to the falcon nest. The three plump, fluffy

chicks held their mouths wide open in anticipation. No doubt beginning to sound a little boring, I suggested we leave and return together
the next morning before Victor's planned departure. We agreed to
share coffee at nine o'clock and then head for the cliffs.

At six the next morning, my eyes shot open. I peered out the porthole. No sign of life stirred in the tent Victor and his friends had moved
next to the boat. I dressed and went out. I saw movement. Someone actually stood *on* the cliff—not above, or below on the sea-ice, but *on* it.
Victor had beaten me to the punch. At seven, they returned. He explained that the light had been too good to resist, and he had not
wanted to wake me. I tried to swallow my anger as Diana, Victor, and I
ate breakfast together below. We talked for an hour while Thomasee
and his friend broke camp.

It was not until the sled was ready and handshakes exchanged all
around that Victor said, "I have some bad news." He hesitated and
shuffled in the snow. "Two of the gyrfalcons are gone, just gone. There
are no bodies, not a trace, not a feather. They are just gone. Maybe the
strong one ate the others . . . I don't know."

The hair stood up on my neck. Adrenaline surged through me. I
sprang forward. Instinctively, I turned to Thomasee. He would not
look at me. Their sled was wrapped in its tarp, so I could see nothing
beneath.

"No, this isn't right. What is happening here?" I demanded.

"What do you mean?" Victor asked.

My voice rose. "Those birds were safe last night. Now you tell me
they're just gone! Come on, Victor—what is this?"

"It's natural for the strongest chick to expel the others from the
nest."

"Between midnight and six this morning?"

"Well, I don't know what you're suggesting." He gestured to
Thomasee, who jumped on his snowmobile. Victor hopped on the sled.
"We have to go now. Good-bye."

My fist tightened. I wanted to pull them off, rip the sled apart, but
instead I stood stupidly still. I was confused. Why had Victor waited to
tell me? Why had he behaved so nervously? Why was someone *on* the
cliff? Could the birds have coincidentally died of natural causes? Could

his hesitation just be his guilty conscience—was he wondering whether his persistence did have a disturbing effect on the nesting sight? Could, *would* someone use me like that? He came all the way back here from England, for a photo, or for . . . They sped off, leaving me in absolute shock.

Diana sensed my near-murderous tension. She touched my arm and said, "No, it is just too much to believe. I'm sure it isn't what you think."

I hiked to the nest. Because people had been there in the morning, I did not want to further disturb it, but I had to see. I poked my head out over the cliff. My heart sank. Just as Victor had described, in the nest sat a single chick; not a trace of the others remained, not carcass, blood, feather, or bone.

The episode threw me off balance for weeks. We had come here to seek harmony with the land, the wildlife, and ourselves. We had adhered to the environmental adage: "Take nothing but photographs; leave nothing but footprints." We had carefully treated our waste, packaged our garbage. We had killed nothing. I had watched Halifax carefully, and I always followed her trails. No secrets can hide in the Arctic snows; she had killed nothing.

I played the scene over and over again in my mind. I sorted through every clue and came no closer to a firm conclusion. I finally resigned myself to the fact that I would never know what happened. I tell this story now reluctantly, for I do not want to wrongly malign a man's reputation. But herein lies a lesson so serious that only this story can tell it.

On a larger scale—be it our need for precious metals, hydroelectric power, or marine resources—we will all face the same decisions, feel under the same pressure to perform and produce. We will always be tempted to take a little more, push the land and its limits just a little bit harder. Do one or two birds matter? Will one more mineral mine or a few more drilling platforms alter the delicate balance? No, not on their own. But person by person, decision by decision, year by year, we will either nurture and protect this natural treasure for future generations, or we will not and our world will be profoundly diminished.

BY THE THIRD WEEK OF JUNE, the entire sheet of bay ice broke free from shore and began a slow revolution within the confines of the circular bay. For the moment we sat safe in our lagoon. As if we lived in a revolving restaurant, we woke each day to a new view through our portholes. The high dusty-brown ridges to the south gave way to the eastern glacier in Prussian blue, which slipped into the shiny, ebony northern slopes, and finally shifted to the west and the blinding whiteness of Navy Board Inlet.

Great rifts shot across the bay, dividing the surface into half-mile-long islands, bumping and turning to differing forces. I pulled the long wire antenna off the shifting ice and reverted back to the whip antenna on the aft deck. Peter had difficulty receiving us, so, sadly, our contact dwindled. Peter had been at my side through the dark, and I felt desperate to keep our experience whole, so night after night I called, "X N R 7 9, Whiskey, Charlie Gulf 4 3 7 7." The airwaves hissed and screeched, tortured by the aurora borealis, and his deep voice did not break through.

For all his support, we were able to give back to Peter only one gift: a memory. Some weeks earlier, we had been talking on the radio when my signal suddenly went dead. "Negative copy. Cannot read," he called. I ran outside to see a big polar bear tearing down the wire antenna. I quietly slipped the alligator clip back to the whip antenna on deck and crawled below to tell Peter what happened. He was beside himself with happiness. He swore that, in the history of amateur radio, no one had ever been cut off midsentence by a bear tearing down the antenna. He bubbled with anticipation of telling his radio buddies.

We struck the emergency tent, shrinking our world to within the gunwales of the *Roger Henry*. With our storm-tattered cockpit tent also stored, sunlight flooded the boat. We unbagged the sails and hanked them on their stays, ran the halyard and sheets, and consulted the barometer more frequently. We were ready to become sailors again.

There wasn't enough ice to support sledding to shore, nor enough water to dinghy there, making travel difficult and dangerous. I strapped on sharp crampons and danced across floating ice boulders like a lumberjack rolling logs.

The boat banged from ice edge to ice edge in its ever-enlarging pond.

With a sledgehammer, I drove two steel stakes into the sea-ice. I led ropes from the stern to these tiedowns and stretched a line to an anchor set into the ice off the bow. This held the vessel in place except when it was buffeted by especially gusty winds. A long plank with a rope handrail sloped from our aft deck, over the moat, and to the ice, like a castle drawbridge.

Diana was outside, stripping the hardware off the two sleds still staked to the ice. I was below, recommissioning the engine. Too many bloodied knuckles over the years have worn thin my patience with working blindly, upside down, in cramped spaces. To mask my inadvertent obscenities from Diana's ear, I turned up an Emmylou Harris tape. I rolled on down the desert highway, listening to that ol' eighteen-wheeler scream.

As Diana walked up the steep plank with her arms full of tools, the plank's end broke through the rotten ice and gave way beneath her. She plunged headlong into the frigid water. It jolted her like an electric shock. She tried to scream, but the cold sucked her breath away. She could utter but a desperate whimper.

I thought, *What was that? Hmmm. Must have been the song . . .* I went back to work. *Red wire is the alternator output and should go to the central battery switch . . .*

Diana paddled to the ice's edge and tried to pull herself out. She scratched desperately at the steep, slippery surface but could get no grip. She slid back into the smoking water, feeling her strength being sapped away. Her down-filled clothing soaked up heavy water and started to pull her down. Fighting the effect of the cold with all her strength, at last she screamed.

I tightened the electrical terminal. *There, again—what is that? I don't want to crawl out of here for nothing.* I went back to my work once more.

She flailed until her body no longer obeyed her commands. *This is it,* she thought. *Right here next to the boat, I'll sink under the ice and he won't even know what happened to me.* She started to drift off in a cold stupor. *They say the body doesn't decompose in cold water—no gases to make it buoyant. It sinks to the black depths and stays there forever.* Something in that thought snapped her back. She reached for a ramplike incline of ice and, hand over hand, inch by inch, scratching and struggling, she slid onto the pan. Her body quaked and her teeth chattered. Before she fell mute from shock, she screamed with the last of her energy.

What . . . My God, that's Diana! I rushed to the deck. She was not on board. I ran to one rail, saw nothing, then raced to the other. Separated from the boat by a wide moat, a sodden lump of freezing clothing lay on the ice. I yelled to her. She looked up and howled in fear. I jumped aft for the ramp, but it hung straight down into the water. I raced forward, grabbed the lower rigging wires, and stretched as far out as I could. *Almost. A little more!* But the boat drifted away.

I screamed, "Get up, Diana! Get up and give me your hand!"

She looked down at her hand, willing it to move, but it would not. I grabbed the long boathook and extended it to her. In slow motion, her stiff fingers curled around it. Using her as an anchor, I pulled the *Roger Henry* toward the ice and grabbed for her porcelain fingers. I pulled her almost to her feet, but she was too heavy to wrench up and over the high lifelines. The boat drifted away again. Diana dangled over the open moat as my grip slipped away. She screamed once more.

"You have to help me!" I yelled. "Put your foot up on the rail."

She just sobbed, staring at me blankly. Diana was not here with me; she had withdrawn into her cold body core, shocked numb. I used all my strength to yank her roughly over the steel lines and dropped her on the deck.

I stripped off her many layers of sodden clothing and helped her below. I toweled her off vigorously, put her in the thick sleeping bag, and threw Halifax in behind her to warm her slowly. I raced to put on the teapot, filled a hot-water bottle, and plied Diana with warm, herbal liquids. Then I crawled into the berth with her to share my body warmth. She shivered, and wept, and shivered, as did I when I realized how close I had come to losing her.

Diana lay in that bag for eighteen hours. She emerged no longer shaking, but we were both shaken. We both had been seduced, lulled into carelessness, by the beauty of an Arctic spring. It was still the Arctic after all—deadly and indifferent.

After this, Diana was hesitant to venture out onto the fast-rotting ice. Until we could launch the dinghy and reach shore safely, she busied herself with the many tasks of preparing our vessel for sailing.

I finished recommissioning the diesel engine. On June 30, the log-book reminded me in red letters that I must figure out a way to extract the foam plug from the engine water-intake valve. Our last wine was long gone, so I smashed the fancy plastic corkscrew with a hammer and epoxied its steel spiral into the end of a long and flexible fiberglass rod. This I slid down the curving hose until it reached the foam plug and, with a few twists, I secured the plug and slowly retracted it. Our hearts were in our throats when I turned the key. When the engine gave a mighty roar, we gave an equally mighty sigh of relief.

I had read horror story after horror story about ships being tossed about and crushed by the pressure of shifting ice during breakup. For months that fear had simmered in us like a low-grade fever. But while outside the bay the ice remained intact, inside, powerful forces of na-ture conspired in our favor. Dirty water thundered off the immense glacier and rumbled like a great river along the bay's north coast. The friction of this flow created a strong counterclockwise current in the bay, slowly spinning the surface ice like a pinwheel. The rough edges of the rotating ice plate scoured the banks of more and more mud, further darkening the bay waters. Darkness to capture heat, turbulence to agi-tate the ice—we could not have designed a better system for melting. This gentle and steady natural process graced us until the *Roger Henry* swung at anchor normally for the first time in ten months.

Once the larger pieces of bay ice broke into fairly harmless chunks, Diana and I could freely row away from the boat and wander the far valleys and slopes under the midnight sun. The often-said exasperation, "They're just aren't enough hours in the day," does not apply to an Arctic summer, for we enjoyed more sunlight hours than our senses could consume. With a dinghyful of jerry cans, we rowed to any one of a dozen temporary streams gushing down the mountainside. We gaily scooped up gallon after gallon of clean, fresh water. No more ice chunks to haul, chop, then chip. Now we were flooded with premelted water for cooking, bathing, drinking, and wasting with wild abandon. In our largest mixing bowl, Diana shampooed her hair in hot water, while I poured quart after quart of rinsewater over her. She smelled like wildflowers and smiled as brightly, for she is never happier than right out of a bath.

July wore on, as did our concerns about late breakup. Day after day I hiked out to Thinking Rock and anxiously looked up Navy Board Inlet toward Lancaster Sound, our shortest, and thus probable, escape route. For as far as I could see lay solid ice. My heart sank. It was mid-July, and counting. I mentally flipped back through the books, the Ice Atlas, the legends about cold years—the years when summer never occurred and the ice remained. I recalled that Peter told me his worst year in the Arctic was his second. The first was novel and exciting; the second was the real test. When that possibility approached the border of probability, I had to ask myself how we would fare.

Just about to sink into self-pity, I looked down on a twelve-foot circle of stones lying on the tundra cliffs overlooking Lancaster Sound. This tent ring, perhaps a thousand years old, once held down a *tupik,* the hide shelter of the nomadic predecessors of the Inuit. Perched here, they cast keen eyes over the sound, looking for seals, bear, and leads where narwhal might breach.

Like the snow blocks I'd cut out months before, this tent ring spoke to me. Chief Seattle said, "Even the rocks that seem to lie dumb as they swelter in the sun along the silent seashore in solemn grandeur thrill with memories of the past." How could I bemoan a second year equipped with food, steel tools, and electronics when faced with this reminder that, for millennia, the Inuit and their ancestors had struggled through this frozen land and kept the flame of human consciousness burning? They had no rifles nor radio, only skin tents and clothing, bone weapons and tools. But they had what this land calls for: inner strength and outer calm, as must we.

A few days later, Diana and I hiked into the primordial freshness of Bylot Island's interior. Beneath jagged peaks and precipitous glaciers, we slipped over moss-slickened boulders that flowed like a river out of the island's cavernous valleys. Glaciers had pulled the mountain down in slow motion, leaving in their receding wake this twisting road of round rocks. Grasses, flowers, and mosses had grown between the boulders, carpeting the canyon floor. We sat still for a moment, soaking up the silence. I told Diana that it was entirely possible this valley had never felt the foot of humankind.

She ran her hand over a lime green, spongy bed of caribou moss and said, "Perhaps not the foot, but it has felt our hand."

She was referring to radioactive fallout from the Chernobyl nuclear plant disaster, which settled here. Caribou lichen absorbed the strontium 90 in particularly high concentrations. Caribou eat the moss almost exclusively. The Inuit eat the caribou. Tests indicate that the Inuit now carry dangerously high levels of radioactivity. Through time immemorial the Arctic wind has blown deadly, and yet the Inuit and the animals have survived. But as clever and hardened as they are, what defense will they have against this insidious poison? In the sense that whatever we do in one part of our biosphere affects all others, there is no true wilderness.

Like a true tundra dweller, Halifax was unhappy with the summer season. No longer could she choose from countless deep footprints to squat over, then cover with snow. Annoyed, she scattered all over the bow the wet sand we had collected for her litter-box. Without the ice surrounding the boat, she could not get to shore unless we rowed her. When the dinghy drifted by the boat, she leapt in. It blew away to the end of its long tether, and she sat there for hours, mewing in protest, "Free Halifax! Free Halifax!" If I did not answer her calls, she jumped on passing ice floes and drifted off like a shipwrecked mariner. Time after time I had to search the bay for her ice rafts. When I found her, she jumped in the dinghy as if it were an ordered taxi, and I rowed her to shore, where I hiked her into exhaustion. She'd limp back to the beach but would suddenly find speed and energy when I tried to capture her and put her in the little boat.

During those hikes I checked in on each of our friends—gulls, hares, loons, and buntings. My mind could wander because my legs knew well the roll of the terrain, the best way to the high lookouts and clearest lakes. The lone young gyrfalcon grew at a stunning rate. His sharp ivory beak curved down to a powerful chest. He was fed to fatness on arctic hares, whose bloody leg bones littered the nest. He faced the north wind and let the air flow over his strengthening wings. If he caught us peering over the cliff, he shrieked fiercely, but not in terror— not this maturing master of the northern sky.

Eider ducklings and goslings paddled behind attentive mothers in the lakes and seawater. The three polka-dotted glaucous gull chicks grew huge and healthy. Their nest was directly south of the boat, and the finest of orange light bathed it at midnight. The gulls seemed always to look to the south, as if instinctively knowing that soon they must be ready for the long flight to escape the already approaching winter.

It's not quite true to say there are no trees in the Arctic, for the dwarf willow is a tree. It simply grows horizontally along the ground to protect itself from the frigid air. When any part of the plant senses contact with the ground, root structures grow and probe for another foothold against the tearing winds. A determined dwarf willow plant, while only an inch in diameter, can endure and prosper—if the Arctic allows such a word—for up to four hundred years.

Under the willow's leathery leaves, across the hot, black earth, crawls the black-and-orange-banded woolly bear caterpillar. This tenacious little animal grows slowly through the brief summer. Then it freezes, hibernating until the next short growing season. It thaws, freezes again, then thaws again. For fourteen years it inches its way toward its day of metamorphosis. Finally, with a light-winged flutter, it rises out of the mud for the skies, where it lives in glory for a meager two weeks before falling to the earth and dying.

The temperature climbed past thirty-two degrees, then to a balmy forty. The sun beat down relentlessly. Life was on the move. Water gushed off the mountains. Birds crisscrossed the sky. Day by day the ice split and shifted in Lancaster Sound.

On July 31 I climbed to the top of our lookout and trained my binoculars north. The iceberg that the bear had slept beneath and from which I had fallen was gone—a firmly fixed landmark, just gone. Bergs, pans, and brash still choked Navy Board Inlet, but it was all in motion and improving fast. The largest bergs, approaching a thousand feet deep, were powered by irresistible currents at the depths of Lancaster Sound. They crashed through the six-foot-thick sea-ice, carving a trail for our escape. I had to weigh the dangers of a gale rising while we sailed in this ice against the risk that perfect, safer conditions might not materialize. We might miss our one chance to slip out into Baffin Bay.

How can anyone *know* just what to do? I hiked slowly to the boat, hoping that, once again, the right choice would make itself clear to us. *Maybe we'll wait for a few days,* I thought. But I knew I was stalling.

I love this land, and I cannot let it go. I'm still steeped in the power of everything that has happened here. I was using the ice as an excuse to postpone our departure. I launched the dinghy and rowed back to a restless *Roger Henry* tugging on its tether. I consoled myself with the idea that, first and foremost, I am a sailor. Every sailor must sail away.

To exactly where we should sail remained a question, in my mind at least. I told Diana it was time. She smiled, eager yet anxious. She harbored no doubts as to what direction we should sail: east, along the leads on the north coast of Bylot Island, which would bring us into Baffin Bay, across to Melville Bay, down the long west coast of Greenland, and eventually, home.

In spite of her reasonable desires, I wanted to set our course for three-five-zero degrees, slightly west of north, away from home and directly toward Dundas Harbor on Devon Island, and then carry on for a second attempt on the Kane Basin, even though ice reports were rather discouraging. Eric's description of haunting beauty and abundant wildlife, coupled with my extreme frustration in having been denied access to both locations the year before, had elevated Dundas and the Kane Basin to near mythical proportions in my mind. Excitedly, I told Diana, "Musk ox—imagine! And Charlie said walrus, plenty of walrus. We haven't seen walrus yet."

She shook her head in disbelief. "Your time alone may have changed you, Alvah, but not completely." Her position concerning the Kane Basin was unambiguous: "No. Let me make that clearer. No! And that does not mean no, not with me. That means no, not with my boat, my home. No! We will go to Dundas only long enough for the ice to clear a bit more in Baffin Bay, and then . . . we . . . will . . . go . . . south."

She readied the sails as I tested all the mechanical and electrical systems. We rowed to shore for our final hike. We took Halifax far out over the tundra. For the last time we peeked over the cliff at the near-grown and high-spirited gyrfalcon. As we wished him well in soft tones, he shrieked insults back at us. Soon this fierce predator would soar over a Tay Bay with no *Roger Henry* in it—a thought I could hardly conceive. I stood on a rock with Diana and Halifax and turned slowly to the four corners of the compass, etching in my mind for the last time this glorious scene. This had been a year of raw nerves and intense emotion. Tears poured down my face. I couldn't help it. I took out a flask holding the last dregs of whiskey, which I poured on the rocky tundra as a libation to my sheltering host. Just as a Lakota Sioux once requested, "Bury my heart at Wounded Knee," I knew that here, overlooking this bay, I could happily make my final resting place. We rowed back to the boat and readied ourselves.

As we wound our way out of the entrance, a thick fog rolled in. I was grateful for that, because the part of me that is not nomad could not bear to look back.

SIXTEEN

Tay Bay

AUGUST 1995

20 HOURS DAYLIGHT

Yearly with tent and rifle, our careless white men go

By the Pass called Muttianee, to shoot in the vale below

Yearly by Muttianee he follows our white men in

Matun, the old blind beggar, bandaged from brow to chin

Eyeless, noseless, and lipless—toothless, broken of speech

Seeking a dole at the doorway he mumbles his tale to each;

Over and over the story, ending as he began:

"Make ye no truce with Adam-Zad—the bear that walks like a man!

Sudden, silent, searing as flames the blow—faceless I fell before his feet,

fifty summers ago."

—Rudyard Kipling, *The Truce of the Bear*

GHOSTING NORTH through Navy Board Inlet, we bounced off and between large ice floes in the fog. I started the engine, that wonderful engine, and motored carefully through the misty maze. We wound our way through ice pans, some as big as football fields, and motored six miles to make good one mile.

The bow almost slammed dead into one floe. Through the opaque veil I saw crimson splashed across the ice. On the next floe sprawled a bloody seal skeleton. August or not, the chill seeped into our bones, and Diana dropped below to fix a hot drink. She looked out the galley porthole into the steamy wall of white. It swirled clear for a moment, and there stood a bloody-muzzled bear staring back at her. She dropped her cup and yelled to me. The bear dove in the water and swam to another pan in front of us. He hauled himself out, shook like a dog, and turned toward us. I hit reverse for all it was worth, but our ten-ton momentum took us forward, right up to the pan. Polar bears can leap like leopards. For a moment, it could have gone either way. Then the bear whirled, sprinted across the ice pan, and did a magnificent swan dive into the water.

I started to laugh. Diana banged me on the arm, "Stop laughing. This is *not* funny!" She looked to the sky for support. "Crickey Dicks, he has me sailing amongst bears now." We passed them with such frequency that she was not exaggerating. Huge males, identifiable by their thicker snouts, patrolled the ice edges as we slid silently past.

Nature keeps its system of politics and borders invisible to us. Here, ten miles north of Tay Bay, nearing Lancaster Sound, a confluence of strong currents and active ice movement created ideal sealing grounds. The air was awash with ivory gulls and arctic terns drawn to the same abundance of fish as were the seals. South of this point we had seen mostly female bears, cubs, and juvenile males, wisely staying clear of the dangerous adult males, who lay claim to these prime hunting grounds.

The ice drifted into mile-thick bands. Between them lay beautifully open water. The wind came up strong out of the east, and we sailed hard, the boat heeling in the gusts. Cold water sprayed over the bow and stung our faces. Halifax and I were both seasick, having been landlubbers too long. When another ice band blocked our way, we dropped sail and pushed our way slowly through to clear water under engine alone.

We were thirty miles out into Lancaster Sound doing five knots, when an enormous polar bear passed us. He swam with powerful strokes of his forelegs, his back legs trailing, streamlined and still. Stamped in his keen memory was a precise map of where these currents would deposit this congestion of ice. As we followed him toward Dundas Harbor, I missed the message.

Near Devon Island, the wind weakened. Fog blanketed the narrow entrance to Dundas Harbor, just as Charlie had predicted it would. The radar was useless, its screen pockmarked with signals from heavy ice. This land has never been charted with sufficient accuracy for the GPS to be of any help. I shut down the engine and tuned my ears to the grumbling ice. Wafting on the cold fog, soft bellows emerged from our port side. I started the engine and veered to the left. The sound intensified. Moving so slowly that we barely had steerage, we followed our ears and noses. We heard belching and harumphing and splashing, and then suddenly a rock appeared just off the bow. I turned hard to starboard and slid just past a wall of agitated flesh and tusk. We dropped our anchor in deep water. I have never felt prouder of a landfall, because I had depended on ears, eyes, nose, and head, not electrical substitutes. We took turns standing ice-watch while the other dove gratefully into a berth.

When the fog cleared, we stumbled on deck and were treated to one of the Arctic's most dramatic scenes, the uninhabited expanse of Devon Island. Great layered mesas fell vertically to open rolling plains that stretched inland for ten miles. Thick grasses blew in the wind like an Oklahoma prairie. Deep water glistened blue-black and was speckled with crenated-crystal bergs, steep and majestic. A gargantuan glacier curved elegantly inland to an expanse of ice cap six thousand feet high, dominating the center of the island. Devon Island stretches 350 miles east to west and a hundred north to south. In its majestic entirety of 21,000 square miles, not a single human being dwells.

This awesome scale may have been good for the soul, but not for my back. Trouble began at once. That ice cap generated winds that ripped across the five-mile-long, thumb-shaped bay. Our anchor skated across a rocky, fouled bottom. The shoreline fell almost vertically into unanchorable depths, and we searched in circles for the rare ledge or pinnacle on which to drop our hook. When we finally found and fastened to one, the bay inhaled a billion tons of ice, which bore down on us like an avalanche. We quickly hauled anchor and sneaked behind a rocky hook to let the thickest of it pass, only to have the tide exhale the ice. I felt as if we had been purse seined when we were forced out into Lancaster Sound. We slipped back in at slack water, but the ice soon followed.

After two days, the lesson was clear: I'd cursed my bad luck for not making it here the year before, but if we had made it then we would have fought for our lives through every day of the past year. Tay Bay had been benign, even serene, compared to this. Good luck? No, all too often now it had proved to be more. A hidden hand had cradled us, and its work was not yet done.

Walrus huffed and puffed around the boat, their fishy breath thick on the air. I rowed to shore, my eyes sweeping the surface for trouble, for these creatures are aggressive. Walrus can capsize a dinghy with the slightest push and are armed with enormous tusks. On MacMillan's Crocker Land Expedition alone, three hunters were lost to walrus.

I took the handheld radio and headed toward the western shore.

Diana agreed to call me every hour or in the event of ice trouble. After our first contact established that she was confident and happy, I set out up the long valley.

The radio squeaked, and I cringed at its loudness. Had it really been a whole hour?

Her normally soft voice boomed, "*Roger Henry* Mobile, this is base. How copy?"

I whispered, "Base, this is Mobile. Go ahead, but speak softly."

In her excitement, she ignored that. "With the binoculars I can see a herd of musk ox on the tundra to the west. Ten, twenty of them, *huge,* with giant horns. Where are you?"

Very faintly I responded, "Train your binoculars on that rock in the middle of the herd. Got it?"

"Yes, I see . . . Oh no, Alvah—it's you!"

I had seen the telltale black specks on a mountain slope and slinked down the tundra. Using every depression, rock, and ridge for cover, I worked my way downwind of and close to the herd, then slithered into the open on my stomach in such slow motion that even when they looked at me they saw nothing out of the ordinary. They grazed even closer, and I took some photographs. They grazed up to me and soon surrounded me. I lay there with several tons of wild meat, hard hooves, and sharp horns chomping and stomping happily around me. I was trapped. If I moved . . . well, I didn't want to move. I was happy there among a herd of the far North's most enduring creatures, the *umingmak* ("the bearded ones").

A strong stench saturated the breeze. During the rut, which begins in July, the breeding-age males urinate on themselves. Although the animal has no musk glands, early European explorers mistook this smell for musk, and the misnomer persists to this day. Any moment, another male could rise over a hill and challenge the mighty harem-holder to battle. They would square off, lower those great, horned heads, and slam into each other with neck-breaking force. The hills would echo their collision as they reared back and crashed again. The bigger or the braver would overcome the interloper and then nimbly chase him away. The loser would have a whole year to nurse his wounds and wounded pride, and then he would try again.

As the genus name *Ovibos* suggests, the musk ox is a mixture of both ox and ram. It is the size of an ox, with males reaching a half-ton, and has great oxlike horns sloping downward from its head boss. But it is ramlike in its pointed ears, hairy muzzle, and special hooves that splay out into a huge dish for use over tundra bogs, yet fold into pointed climbing hooves enabling them to scamper on the highest precipices. Its sweet meat and its warm hide have contributed to the extreme hunting pressure on the species from time immemorial.

Ironically, their near-demise was a result of a defense strategy that had stood them well for millennia, until they faced *Homo sapien* hunters whose rifles spit hot lead at two thousand feet per second. When threatened, the herd does not flee. Rather, they rush together to form a rump-to-rump circle or wall, depending on the number of attackers. The young and old huddle in the middle, trusting their protectors' sharp horns and flashing hooves. These same tools of battle can throw a wolf high into the air and then trample it to death.

Account after account by European explorers, from the early Parry and Ross parties to the more recent Otto Sverdrup, Robert Peary, and Donald MacMillan expeditions, casually detail the slaughter. Because the herds numbered from ten to one hundred animals and wandered no more than sixty miles from their summer to winter ranges in search of sedge, grass, and willow, they were easy to locate and dispatch. Diminished to dangerously low numbers, they found sanctuary only in the extreme northern islands. Still, because they seem impervious to the cold and require only one-sixth the food to sustain themselves as cattle of the same weight, they prospered there on the scant willow their hooves could uncover. Their numbers are on the rise, but numbers alone do not tell their plight, for danger lurks when a species becomes too concentrated. On these islands a rare warm spell might melt the snow cover. The return of blistering cold air can refreeze the slush into an impenetrable ice barrier. Although musk ox are masters of energy conservation, driven by hunger they have no choice but to exert themselves heavily in pawing through the barrier, thus burning more fuel than the scraggly underbrush can replenish. The starving beasts perish in droves. As a species, they must spread out into areas wide enough that no single catastrophic weather event can seal their collective fate.

After Diana's radio call, a feisty little calf split off from the herd and wound its way behind me. Instinctively I knew I was breaking one of the hard-and-fast rules of nature: Never get between a mother and its child. I made a quick decision and stood up. The herd shuddered in protest, then whirled, kicking up dust. The calf dashed past me back to its mother's side. All the cows and the big bull bunched together, forming a wall of horns that wheeled toward me and then stopped thirty feet away. In spite of the danger, I was thrilled to see their instinctive strategy in action.

The calf huddled behind the fortress of adults. I stood perfectly still. There was nowhere to run, anyway, for they are very swift—if they charged, I was done for. An amazing bull stepped out from the herd. Very slowly, almost ceremoniously, he turned sideways so I might see his muscular majesty. The message was obvious: If you want trouble, begin here. Then he turned to me and snorted, and my bones rang hollow. He pawed at the earth with great swipes and shook his thick horns. I took a half-step backward. He relaxed and began to graze. I stepped forward. Instantly he whirled again and bellowed deeply. I stepped back, and he grazed serenely. He was drawing the line. I had a simple choice—cross it and die, or respect it and we could all enjoy this lovely summer sunshine.

We stood like this for nearly an hour, my heart racing and my head filled with images of their lives. I felt them relaxing with me. With time the wall might have dispersed and I might have been accepted, but it was not to be. Again the radio crackled for my help as ice entered the bay.

I backed away slowly and double-timed the miles to the dinghy. We moved the *Roger Henry* to a small bight on the east side of Dundas Harbor, just inside the walrus rock. Our careful observations of ice movement uncovered a small patch of water less often assaulted. On the outgoing tide, the bay cleared, and we rowed to the eastern shore. We hiked the spongy tundra to the cliffs overlooking Walrus Rock. Perfectly concealed, we lolled about on the shelf above and watched the walrus lolling about below. They, too, were enjoying quiet moments in the warm sun.

For an aquatic marine mammal, walrus spend an inordinate amount of time out of the water. They are a very social, even if grumpy, lot. They sprawl all over each other in crowded colonies sometimes numbering up to two thousand. This band totaled about thirty. The dominant males claimed the center of the colony for more warmth, while the small infants and their mothers stayed to the fringes, avoiding trouble. And big trouble it could be, for males are armed with three-foot tusks and can reach weights of nearly a ton here and a ton and a half in the Pacific.

We watched the males slam their tusks into each other's necks with violent force, doing gruesome damage to one another's thick, blubbery hides. Walrus are clumsy and hideous, but what is ponderous on land is poetic in the water, and they glide with grace and beauty in their other world. They travel at fifteen miles per hour and dive to three hundred feet for up to half an hour, rubbing their sensitive whiskers over the sea bottom in search of clams and other mollusks. Their mouths have a specially dome-shaped roof that allows them to vacuum-shuck up to one hundred pounds of shellfish a day. They often sleep hanging vertically in the open sea by inflating a neck sack like a life preserver. Living forty years or longer, they develop strong ties to one another. If one is wounded, others will first help it onto the ice and then turn with a fury on the attacker. They fear only the orca, polar bear, and humans, but little is known of their attrition to predation other than Inuit subsistence hunting. One can hardly overstate the role this animal played in the traditional Inuit life, for its meat could feed an entire village's people and dogs, its tusks formed sled runners and hard tools, and its hide made pliable ropes, tents, and boats. The early Inuit rendered its blubber into a fine burning oil and with its intestines made translucent windows for their igloos, and flexible rain gear.

The lapping of the waves on the rock and the walruses' deep-throated rumbles put me to sleep. In the rocky cliffs behind me, Diana collected *quiviut*, the soft underhair that the musk ox shed and scrape on rocks this time of year. I woke to the screech of an arctic tern and began helping Diana pull little tufts from the grass, clear off the twigs and manure, and stuff the precious wool into plastic bags for later spinning and weaving.

Again the next day the ice allowed us long hours on shore, and again we dashed out on the tundra to collect wispy spiderweb-like patches of gossamer hair. We shouted to each other to help mine rich veins. It was a wonderful excuse to wander the tundra in pretense of work. Autumn colors reminded us winter was on its way. Arctic hares sprinted away in white flashes. A fox slinked over the hill. Ptarmigan, now a mottled brown, cooed to each other.

We came upon a sod house ruin overlooking Lancaster Sound. Massive, petrified whale bones formed struts and supports. Smaller ribbone lathes lined the dirt walls. A huge skull with jaws agape may have served as an entrance tunnel. We later learned that these ruins are believed to be from the predecessors of both the Dorset and Thule cultures, the Small Tool People. Such ruins have been dated from one thousand to four thousand years old. The residents had chosen the perfect perch from which to look out on the ice—always the ice. Because the Arctic waters are frozen solid for ten months of the year, we often forget that the Inuit are a true sea people in that much of their sustenance comes directly from its depths.

Over the long hill separating Dundas Harbor from Johnson Bay rested ruins of a much more modern nature. On an open stone beach huddled a dilapidated little wooden town of five or six buildings. Rusted diesel drums sat scattered across the tundra. Refuse lay piled beneath a lone signal tower, and eclectic graffiti painted the rotting walls: *Manasi was here 1987*, scrawled near a charcoal stick-figure sporting an enormous phallus. Across a standing drum the word *Rum* had been painted. I fell for the joke, having to open it and see. We poked through the vandalized scene. No doubt we felt so forlorn because we were familiar with its sad history.

In the mid-1930s the United States showed no inclination to recognize Canada's claim over the Northwest Passage as a sovereign waterway. The Canadian government felt that, if they could establish a permanent population on the islands bordering Lancaster Sound, their claim would carry more weight in international courts.

With this in mind, the government induced Inuit families from Baffin Island to relocate in Dundas Harbor, a spot picked by deskbound bureaucrats from Ottawa who had never been north of their backyards. Assured that this was a land of milk and honey, a happy hunting ground crawling with game, the Inuit also were promised, "Besides, you can leave anytime you want." These claims did not prove true on any count.

Devon Island was deserted for good reason. The ice cap generated winds ferocious enough to literally sweep people up off the beach and blow them out to sea. Johnson Bay and Dundas Harbor, where ships were supposed to make regular resupply stops, were constantly choked with ice and dangerous to enter (as we were discovering). The ice on the sound in winter was in constant flux and was too dangerous for regular crossing by dogsled, completing the homesteaders' isolation. The years wore on. Semistarvation, disease, and loss of contact with their larger families to the south took their toll. They pleaded to be relocated, but no evacuation occurred.

Only after many years did the government finally admit the experiment was a sad failure. In 1953 the M.V. *Nascopie* loaded up the last of the people and took them away to Grise Fjord in Jones Sound. The front doors of the wooden huts were locked. Not long after the ship was out of sight, bears began tearing great holes through the walls, eventually destroying all that was left. What remained was a blight on the landscape.

Diana and I strolled through the remnants that rust in peace. We wandered up the slope behind the village to view a small burial plot where villagers' remains rest in peace. Enclosed by a collapsing picket fence lay the graves of two Royal Canadian Mounted Police. One had slipped and fallen between two pieces of rolling ice and was crushed to death. The other had put a pistol to one side of his head and blown out the other side the mind that, no doubt, had tortured him through his winter ordeal. Both had died of elemental Arctic forces.

Somberly, we made our way back to our boat, pondering darkest moments of the past year, both thinking "here but for the grace of God go we." Suddenly, the low-level flyover of a Twin Otter, the workhorse of the Arctic, shattered our reflection. The high-winged aircraft banked over the slope toward Johnson Bay and then, with the engine throttled back, settled toward the boulder beach for a landing. At the last second, it roared back up into the sky, wheeling around for another attempt. We could hardly believe anyone would fly this far off the beaten track, much less risk a touchdown. After five failed attempts, the airplane peeled off across Dundas Harbor and landed safely on a long stretch of flat tundra to the west. Through binoculars I watched people and equipment offload. Then, much to our surprise, as the tiny figures stood on the tundra, the Twin Otter took off and disappeared over the southern horizon.

I was at once both repelled and attracted by the presence of people in our wilderness. We could only assume they composed a party of scientists. If so, the last thing they would want was privateers wandering into their camp, so we stayed at our anchorage.

The next day a fire sent smoke spiraling into the sky. While it might not be a distress signal, the Code of the Sea said it must be answered. We pulled anchor and threaded our way toward the other side of the bay. A small inflatable dinghy carrying two Inuit approached our boat. They pulled alongside and scrambled on board. One was perhaps forty-five, moustached and lean. The other was a grizzly, gray-headed man, stiffened by too many nights sleeping on the ice but with the sharp look of the hunter yet in his eyes.

The younger man, Elijah Panipakoocho, from Pond Inlet, introduced himself in English and explained their situation. As a belated form of apology, the Canadian government had decided to round up what survivors of the Dundas days could be found and fly them to their childhood home in search of a sense of closure. The chartered airplane could not land safely at Johnson Bay, so they were forced to settle for the nearest flat ground. Because of enormous expense, the airplane could not stay. Its scheduled pickup was in one week. That left mostly elderly people stranded across open water, with only an inflatable dinghy as transport. Better than anyone, these two knew that elderly people in a small inflatable, crossing waters boiling with ice, walrus, and bears, was a foolhardy mission. Discovering the presence of the *Roger Henry* renewed their hopes for a successful reunion with the land.

Perhaps our presence was an accident, but Diana and I preferred to think not. Instead, we felt we were granted an opportunity to repay the Inuit for their year of kindness and support. The *Roger Henry* would serve as a floating base camp for the next several days. We ferried aboard Mr. and Mrs. Qaaraaq (Hemmy's parents), Elijah's cousin Rita, and several others.

The *Roger Henry* motored across the bay, and then we all rowed to the western shore. The group walked through the buildings in hushed solemnity, whispering the names of those now gone: "That bunk was Uncle's, and that one Father's." They laughed outside at the memories of childhood pranks. They set out on long hikes over the tundra with absolutely everything they needed—a teapot, because they love their "mug ups," and a rifle, because the Inuit think of a .303 cartridge as the most concentrated form of protein on earth.

I felt an immediate connection with Elijah. He displayed a gentle smile, a soft voice, and a directness that let me into his life. To make his living, he balanced hunting, fishing, and construction work in Pond Inlet with leading tourist trips to the floe edge. In my preparations for this journey, I had clipped every article on the Arctic that *National Geographic* had run in the last fifteen years. As I spread them out on the salon table, he shyly pointed to several photographs of himself. Elijah was outward looking and very curious about our travels and the native cultures we had encountered. We talked for hours about Solomon Islanders, Polynesians, and Zulus.

He asked me how we support ourselves. I explained how little money we actually make, that we had designed our lives around action and ideas, finding our happiness in nature, not in things, and our security in a good outlook and good health, not pension plans.

He said, "You would make a good Inuk."

I hoped he was right, because hidden beneath all my admiration and respect for the Inuit was a growing envy. He had heard of our Tay Bay adventure and was intensely interested in my reaction to the dark and solitude. I described it as best I could. We hiked over to the barracks, where he helped me siphon fifty-year-old diesel fuel out of rusty drums into jerry cans. We lashed these to our backpacks and humped them the two miles back to the boat, trip after trip, to top off our already dwindling fuel supplies.

Through the next few sunny August days, Elijah talked of his childhood in this place, hunting walrus on that same rock; where the best trout lakes were; how the fox population collapsed and left them in grinding poverty with almost nothing to trade to the Hudson Bay company for canned milk and coffee. Life had been hard, but as a child he had known nothing else. "Yes," he said looking around wistfully, "This is a good land, but those were hard days."

In the afternoons we motored the *Roger Henry* out into the thick ice in Lancaster Sound. Elijah's elderly uncle pulled an old-fashioned brass telescope from under his anorak and swept the ice tumble for bear. He babbled in delight. They were everywhere, more than when he was young! At one time we spied seven at once, which thrilled me but made Elijah nervous. He cautioned me that bears could explode from beneath the water and mount the boat in an instant.

One bear, full of fresh seal fat, leapt up from an ice pan and sprinted away from us, his belly so huge it swung under him to its own rhythm. Casually, Elijah said he was probably *only* sixteen hundred pounds. He'd seen bigger. Old Uncle counted on his fingers each of the forty-three bears he spotted in three days, recording some specific feature of each to memory. Each time we saw another, he counted on his fingers and recited the entire list first, etching this sacred scroll into his memory before adding the new information. No doubt when the hamlet gathers over coffee to reminisce, they turn to him to supply the minute detail of stories from long ago and far away.

Elijah and Rita visited the graves above the village. Lying unmarked and outside the cemetery fence lay the grave of her little nephew who perished, probably from influenza, just before the last relief ship arrived. As they laid flowers on the site, Rita talked in hushed tones with Elijah about that memorable day when the M.V. *Nascopie* steamed into the bay. I could understand the Inuit's bittersweet parting with their land, having so recently made my own parting.

Rita asked Elijah if he remembered that her father and the Mountie had buried a can atop a steep hill overlooking the sound. It contained messages, photographs, and other items, as was the custom in the Arctic in the old days, for this was the mail and telegraph system until radios came into general use. The next ship to pass through would see the flag on the manmade cairns of rock, stop to retrieve the messages, then leave the date of their ship's arrival and details about when the next vessel would pass.

They wondered if the can might still be there and set off up the hill. An hour later they returned to the boat. Once below, they laid the rusty

can, untouched these many decades, on the salon table. We opened it
and spread out its contents. The old people crowded in to see and
hummed in excited unison at what lay before them. A curled brown
photograph showed all of them lined up in front of a white wall tent.
Behind the children stood their fur-clad parents, the innocence that led
them to Dundas still reflected in their faces. Like the photograph, this
outlook had withered with time. Standing head and shoulder above
them was a muscular Mountie in full uniformed regalia. A piece of
lined school paper was covered with a strange text. As Elijah read this
list of Inuit names, the cabin fell silent. Another piece of paper listed
only numbers; the government had found their names too hard to pro-
nounce and so had mandated by law that every Eskimo in the Arctic be
assigned an identity number. I read aloud a letter in English that out-
lined the Hudson Bay Trading Company's charter. Another had given
The Royal Canadian Mounted Police their standing orders.

A personal letter was addressed from a policeman to "The Finder of
This Letter." It read: "I would very much appreciate if you could contact me at the below address. I should like to know on what date the
next person stood upon this God-forsaken hill."

Thoughtfully included in the can were a clean sheet of paper and a
pencil, a cigarette and a box of matches, a live .303 cartridge should
the finder still have the health and will to hunt, and, in case he or she
was beyond hunting, a 9-mm. pistol round.

I pulled out a handheld tape recorder, wanting to preserve the moment for them. Elijah gave me a look that said, "Now you are being a
white man." Embarrassed, I put it away.

Crowded around the salon table, sipping strong coffee, we talked for
hours. Mrs. Qaaraaq told me a story about her husband. Mr. Qaaraaq,
so barrel chested he could barely clasp his two hands in his lap, sat there
silently, staring above our heads, as if not really there at all. A traditional Inuk and a particularly prideful man, he would never tell a story
about himself. As a young, powerful, and skilled hunter, Mr. Qaaraaq
had chased a bear up a mountainside. He could have shot his quarry
from a safe distance, but that is not their way. He wanted to approach
more closely as a matter of respect. Closer and closer he came, but he
did not fire. He walked right up to the bear. Before he could even lift his

rifle, the beast twisted around in a blur and hit him with both paws on the chest with such force it knocked him off the mountainside. He landed with his back broken but still managed to crawl to his rifle and shoot the bear dead. His wife told us that he had limped since that day but was, nonetheless, the most respected hunter in the high Arctic.

With my jaw agape, I sat staring, spellbound, at Mr. Qaaraaq, wondering what kind of man could stand toe to toe with the great bear. What was he thinking? What compelled him? What drew him toward those slashing claws and dripping jaws of death?

To face a life in these extremes, these men must live to a code of machismo that would wither the men of many cultures. Is it somehow required that, to hold your head high as a man among men, you must treat your life with such casual abandon? Or, I wondered, is it more than that? Is it tied to their overall spiritual view of life? By walking the thin line cast by the shadow of death, do they come to know life with an intimacy that the timid cannot?

The next morning I hiked east down the Lancaster Sound coast to think over what I had learned from the Inuit. I was deep in thought when a huge bear rambled out in front of me. I stood downwind, and he did not see me. I could have ducked behind a boulder and then safely slipped away. But I did not. My journey was nearing its end. I had come far, learned much, and survived sufficient episodes to "authenticate" my adventure, yet I knew it was incomplete, and now I knew why.

I had come here specifically to experience life as the Inuit do. I had come to the Arctic to intimately understand their land and animals before I could even pretend to understand the people. I had endured the dark, the cold, and an aloneness that perhaps only a handful of human beings have ever known. But I had not stood before the Ice Bear. Each time I felt myself inexplicably drawn forward I had pulled back, wisely perhaps, but this had left me just short of the defining, quintessential experience of Inuit manhood. As the Masai must face the lion, as the Pacific Islander must face the tiger shark, I had to face the Great Bear. I had to declare with my body, "I may not have Inuit blood in my veins, but I have their spirit in my heart."

I crouched and slid in step behind the beast, trying to time my footfalls with his. Steadily I closed the gap between myself and the ambling giant. When I was right behind him, when his smell filled my nostrils, I turned to look once more at the sun-drenched, flower-sprinkled tundra, the diamond-faceted ice grinding by in indigo blue waters, the great flock of snow geese cutting across the high, clean sky. Then I called out his name, "Nanook."

The bear whirled and locked his eyes on me. He let out a deep huff. I thought the sound alone might blow me away. A flash flood of fear thundered through me. He stretched his powerful neck toward me. We stared at each other for a lifetime, black eyes probing blue.

I slowly laid my gun on the ground and stepped toward the bear. That first step, over perhaps only three feet of earth, was actually my final step in a very long journey. I had scoured the earth, skies, and seas to find this. I'd unwittingly passed a hundred moments as ripe with potential as this, but as the mythologist Joseph Campbell said, "We have the adventure for which we are ready." And finally, I was ready. My time alone in the darkness had been but preparation for this. Here, as if it was etched in the delicate tundra grasses, was my line, my edge, my Ultima Thule, where a man meets his moment, where the fear passes through him and still he stands, open to every consequence of living and dying.

I took one more step. The bear grunted and rocked forward. I opened my arms, turning my palms to the heavens. The bear stepped toward me. He rose above me, a horrible mountain of fang and claw, crushing power, and lightning speed.

The moment hung in its own eternity. And then the bear spun around and slid away in great strides over the tundra. I stood stunned and faint, my soul indelibly embossed with the bear's message: "Here, I give you back your life. It has been washed pure by your fear. Enjoy it deeply, learn from it daily, and use it wisely, for there is a purpose larger than yourself."

Smells grew stronger and colors more vivid. The slightest breeze sweetly caressed my skin. I dropped to my knees on the tundra. Perhaps as much to my father as myself I said, *"It's done. No more doubts. No more tests. I have much left to do, but nothing left to prove."* I stood up, turned, and headed back toward my wife and home.

SEVENTEEN

Dundas Harbor

AUGUST 1995

18 HOURS DAYLIGHT

We shall not cease from exploration
And the end of all our exploring
Will be to arrive where we started
And know the place for the first time.

—T.S. Eliot, "Little Gidding"

OWN DEEP, unspoken but not unfelt, perhaps I harbored a
slight smugness for having stood before the bear. If so, my next
lesson was designed to remind me, forcefully, of my true status
in the overall nature of things. The next day, after our Inuit friends had
been picked up by the Twin Otter, ice swept into the bay and once again
bore down on the boat. We quickly hauled the dinghy on board, pulled
up the anchor, and tried for the entrance. It was choked, sealing us inside
a fast-filling bay. Resorting to the trick we learned in the Kane Basin
storm, we found a hundred-yard-long pan with a deep bay scalloped into
it. We tucked deep into the cul-de-sac and tied up to one wall. However,
an ice floor rested only one fathom beneath us. I hiked out to a freshwater pool lying on the pan surface and began filling jerry cans. Halifax
romped happily from one end of our ice island to the other. Diana called
us back, worried the ice might split with us on it. I called back, "Sure it's
gotta break up sometime, but what are the chances of it splitting during
the few hours we're hiding in it?"

Soon we did head back, and all went below. Bubbles caressed the hull.
Suddenly, shockingly, eerie shrieks and groans surrounded us. They gave
way to thunder, then a roar. The monster we had just been walking on
shuddered, shattered, and rolled, lifting the *Roger Henry* from the water.
Diana and I stumbled into the cockpit, into a tempest of sound. A wall of
ice flashed by. The anchor held fast to a large mass of rolling ice, tearing
the chain off the bollard. The chain streamed out, hissing at deadly whip-
saw speed. Had it not given, the ice would have pitchpoled our home in a
judo hip-slam. Sharpened ice shards weighing many tons rose from the
boiling surface and crawled on board. A tower of ice loomed above,
threatening to fall and smash us, but the monster rolled forward instead.

We ducked, thinking this pinnacle would rip the mast and rigging away, but its tip just missed the wires as it crashed on the bow. The boat shuddered and lurched forward. Like retreating hands of an ice god, our attacker withdrew into the sea, leaving our steel rails smashed to the deck. During the sixty seconds of this hissing death dance, we just stood dumbly watching. The sea and the ice settled as the *Roger Henry* rocked violently to the reflex waves. Then everything fell perfectly quiet. It was over as if it had not happened at all.

I turned to Diana and said, "Let's go home."

It took several days to jack the rails off the headstay so we could hoist the headsail. When we were ready to sail, the entrance to Dundas was closed tight as a drum in a three-mile-wide band of ice. It was August 9, and as each day ticked by with us sealed behind this drifting brash, our fears that we would be trapped for another winter mounted. We needed one more bit of good fortune—a strong southwesterly wind. Only this would both blow the ice free from the Dundas entrance and force open a lead along the steep cliffs of northern Bylot Island, forming an escape route into Baffin Bay. Each hour that we waited seemed like a day, and each day a week. The constant infiltration of ice required a continuous anchor watch. It was tiring and trying.

August 11: The ice remained and the wind was calm. August 12: More ice and a southeasterly. August 13: No change. August 14: We looked at each other and waited. Over and over, I chastised myself, *You had your chance; you could have gone two weeks ago, but no . . .*

At last, on August 15 a strong southwesterly wind blew. By the next day, it had forced the ice back from the entrance. We slipped out into Lancaster Sound. With all sails set and our precious fuel pouring into the engine, we raced in a long curve around the ice edge. We pushed through steep, cold seas mined with ice, all the way to Bylot's northern edge, only to find ice jammed tight against the cliffs.

Now with growing darkness to consider and no bay to shelter in, we turned down Navy Board Inlet and fled for the only protection we knew of, Tay Bay. It was wonderful to see it again. Only after our constant troubles at Dundas could we fully appreciate Tay's sublime beauty and natural protection. But our stay was short. The worst possible mistake would be to linger in hesitation and then set out into the open ocean too late and get caught in an early freeze. We slept fitfully and tried again early the next day.

We slashed up Navy Board Inlet, rounding the tip of Bylot to find one long lead just a slim half-mile wide. I looked at Diana. She nodded and sheeted the main tight. The narrowing lead forced us right under the vertical cliffs. For sixty long miles we watched the sky for the slightest sign of change. A northerly wind could close this lead in minutes and seal our fate as sixty miles of pack pressure drove us up against vertical granite walls.

A roar sent us spinning in every direction, looking for the approaching danger. But it seemed to come from above. *What now? Avalanche, flash flood, what?*

"It's birds!" Diana said, "Look, at the rock wall, it's made of birds." Perched shoulder to shoulder, clinging to every crack and indent in the sheer wall, hundreds of thousands of dovekies, thick-billed murres, and black-legged kittiwakes swirled above us like storm clouds. The shattered air was electric, exciting. Above us soared a rare density of life, one of earth's largest bird rookeries. From all over the world they come to breed on these vertical cliffs, safe from the predation of fox and humans.

While entire species rally and rely on this one lonely spot for their very survival, in boardrooms to the south there is a different noise— the talk of oil-drilling platforms just off these cliffs. The smallest oil spill could have cataclysmic repercussions on the fragile balance of life. Waters remain open only briefly, and the Arctic grants no second chances. The tens of thousands of murre chicks clinging to these cliffs must get an early start on their escape south, so much so that they can't even wait for their bodies to develop the capacity for flight. Instead, in an unbelievable burst of courage, these tiny prefledglings hurl themselves off the high cliffs. With weak, untried wings, they glide desperately, clawing inch by inch out past the rocky shore for the dark waters below. Once there, those that have survived this first terrible test must swim all the way to Greenland. A single ribbon of oil would seal the fate of an entire year's population.

AS IF DIRECTED BY SCRIPT, the southwesterly wind died just as we cleared the coast of Bylot. We headed into a Baffin Bay congested with ice but calm. The setting sun lit the entire seascape in a burnt-orange burst. For three days we motored in a long arc toward the Cape York cliffs at the north end of Melville Bay. Then we turned south, following the eastern edge of the central pack ice down a long sweeping alley of clear water through Melville Bay.

Fatigue and relief battled in us as we approached the mouth of Upernavik's harbor, one year to the day since we had left there. Two massive icebergs had grounded just outside the breakwater. We crept past them respectfully, then dashed in for shelter and sleep. We tied up alongside a supply barge moored near the outer harbor.

When I woke I rowed quickly to shore, thinking I would be glutinous for supermarket delicacies, eager for the bustle of unlimited human company. But even little Upernavik was too much, too soon. Within an hour I returned to the boat. I told Diana, "This town is too big. We have to go."

Although we'd planned a longer stay, we took on fuel and fresh supplies and the next morning departed, rounding the breakwater, sneaking past the mountainous icebergs, and starting the second leg of our long journey home. Later that morning, one of the icebergs at Upernavik's mouth exploded. This conjured a wave—the second of this century—so powerful that it overwhelmed the seawall, sank all the boats, drowned the staked-out dogs, and injured many unsuspecting villagers.

On learning this, I had to sit down. The pattern was clear and the conclusion too obvious to avoid any longer. Once again, a hidden hand had swept us from harm's way. The skeptic may immediately claim coincidence, but for me coincidence no longer existed. From the very start, our adventure seemed aligned with purposeful good fortune. Selling our wooden boat, changing dinghies, our preparation, reprieves, narrow escapes, even my apparent mistakes—all now appeared mere props meant to maneuver us toward specific lessons, some brutal, some gentle, some physical, some psychological or spiritual, but all timely and essential to our safety and growth. I looked up at Diana. Without words, I heard her asking herself the same questions as I. If we even began to accept the notion that our lives were not totally our own, then we had to wonder to where and for what purpose we were being led.

We fled south with winter winds nipping at our heels. We split from the Greenland coast into Davis Strait at Sukkertoppen. Gale-force winds and horribly high seas pushed us past Ungava Point at Labrador's northern tip. Cold water crashed onto the boat. Gray winds seemed bent on our destruction. In spite of our desperate need to reach warm, safe waters, we did not hesitate to let nature dictate the rhythms to which we sailed.

If we were too cautious, it was with the feeling *Make no mistakes now*. We coasted through Labrador's rocky "tickles and rattles" by day, anchored by night, and sat out autumn's increasing gales. As we entered the Strait of Belle Isle, we looked back on the last iceberg we would see. Then, with the relief that only release from long hardship and genuine danger may bring, on October 20, 1995, we laid our lines on the same dock in Maine from which we had begun seventeen months and eight thousand miles earlier.

EPILOGUE

Tenants Harbor, Maine

MARCH 1998

12 HOURS DAYLIGHT

It is a commonplace of all religious thought, even the most primitive, that the man seeking visions and insight must go apart from his fellows and live for a time in the wilderness. If he is of the proper sort, he will return with a message. It may not be a message from the god he set out to seek, but even if he has failed in that particular, he will have had a vision or seen a marvel, and these are always worth listening to and thinking about.

—Loren Eiseley, *The Immense Journey*

A S I SCRATCH THE LAST LINES of this long work, Halifax scratches at the front door of our rented home on the wooded shores of Penobscot Bay. She is full grown now—perhaps too full grown, for we cannot deny her a single treat after all we put her through.

Ever industrious, Diana is at the boat shed in Camden putting the final touches on the new deck paint. For over a year we have pounded out the dents, straightened the rails, sandblasted and painted the hull. Soon we'll launch the *Roger Henry,* and once again it will eagerly tug on its tether.

Diana hopes to sail soon for New Zealand. I hope she'll agree to a quick detour into the primitive islands off Burma, now called Myanmar, before the civil strife there ends and tourist hotels line the beaches. For now she is just happy to be here. Her loom is set up, and exotic yarns are scattered about our living room. The wood pile is stacked high, and we have lots of hot water and no bears—pure paradise.

I know it is important to look ahead and live from this day forward, but often I catch myself drifting back into the Arctic mist. I did not escape the Arctic unscathed, and I have daily reminders—my back injury appears permanent, and my eyes have been damaged. A small price to pay, really.

In standard terms, it is difficult to measure the success of our expedition, for we sought nor set no records. Nevertheless, by living out our wildest dreams, we did accomplish three things. We went far beyond the limits of our physical, intellectual, and emotional skills and, in doing so, extended them substantially. We came to know the Inuit with an intimacy that only shared hardships can create. We placed ourselves subservient to a cruel nature for one full cycle of seasons. Only through this did the Arctic unfold its intricacies, share its secrets, and in spite of its demanding nature, shelter us for the most powerful year of our lives.

The marvel we saw, the splendor of which no prose could ever adequately describe, is the Arctic itself. It is a land of sublime beauty, humbling terror, and natural wonder. If not there, what place in our world will we dedicate to silence and solitude? It is the Arctic's very emptiness that makes it so fulfilling. To look upon or even only consider those vast horizons stretches both the imagination and the soul.

Like no other people we've met during decades of wandering the globe, our Inuit friends have proven that we all are born of this earth, that we are shaped both materially and mentally by its terrain, weather, flora, and fauna as surely as we now shape it. A storehouse of knowledge and wisdom resides in the hearts and minds of the world's native peoples, many of whom we have nearly destroyed and continue to dismiss. They have taught us how we are bound to every rock, river, and ravine, how we are inextricably tied to every animal of the earth, sea, and sky, and how every man, woman, and child is woven into the true fabric of life on earth.

And what vision or insight can I share from my solo sojourn into the darkness? It is a small thought, perhaps not relevant beyond the borders of my own life: All hope lies in one's openness to experience and ability to change.

I hope I found the Inuit way, that I can still be bold but no longer brash. After such an ordeal I hope I will be profoundly confident but never cocky. For many have survived the Arctic but no one has beaten it. I entered the abyss in many ways a stranger to myself and emerged intimately familiar with the inner man. I searched the edges of darkness and plumbed the depths of my soul, faced my fears, learned my strengths, and uncovered my weaknesses. In isolation from humanity, I discovered the true essence of my humanness. I briefly and lightly touched the face of God. I cannot define it, I cannot defend it, but I can flatly state that I am here because my spirit protector was there. With that support and the help of history, nature, the Inuit, and my beloved

Diana, I did something else, something of some importance, at least to me—I survived.

Diana and I followed our dreams deep into the landscape of our imaginations. And while our presence only momentarily changed the Arctic, the Arctic forever changed us in an elemental way. Earth, wind, and water combined to create fire in our souls, in that wilderness of Arctic ice.

ACKNOWLEDGMENTS

T HERE LIES AFFILIATED with this expedition no long list of corporate sponsors. Those that helped us did so for no personal gain other than the knowledge that each person who ultimately achieves his or her dream does so in part for us all.

First and foremost, I would like to thank the Inuit, past and present. Their undaunted courage inspired us, their ingenuity guided us, and their land sustained us.

Via his radio, Peter Semotiuk stood by my side through the dark time. His kindness and support leave me forever in his debt. My mother, Mary Alice Simon, has known too much loss yet kept her fears to herself lest they undermine our confidence. And when our world fell apart, it was our New Zealand family that helped gather the pieces. Thank you, Mike, Joan, George, Beth, Gavin, and the Golden Girls. Phil Simon and John Bleicher, you were hearty and happy trail companions.

Surviving the darkness, the bears, and the ice, however, was the easy part. It was writing about it that I found most perilous. In that humbling attempt I must first thank Kathy Massimini for her early guidance and straight-shooting, double-barreled opinions. Her husband, Steven Callahan, whose own survival story, *Adrift,* makes our adventure seem like a walk in the park, first brought our story to public attention as our editor at *Cruising World*. We are grateful for their support, both professional and personal. Thanks to my editors Jon Eaton and Kate

Mallien, who persevered through my wounded-wolverine responses to their editorial guidance. The Writer's Roundtable of Camden suffered patiently through the early drafts, and when I began to stall around chapter eight, Mary Carver's 95-year-old mother sent word that I had damn well better finish this book before she died. I have, Ma, and I'm touched that you like it. And finally, inexpressible thanks to Halifax the Cat. It is entirely possible that I owe her my life, and that's always worth an extra can of tuna.

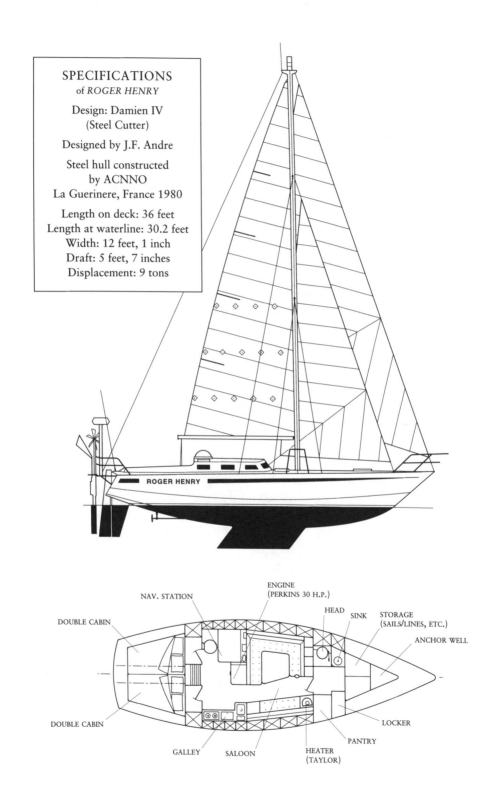

SPECIFICATIONS
of *ROGER HENRY*

Design: Damien IV
(Steel Cutter)

Designed by J.F. Andre

Steel hull constructed
by ACNNO
La Guerinere, France 1980

Length on deck: 36 feet
Length at waterline: 30.2 feet
Width: 12 feet, 1 inch
Draft: 5 feet, 7 inches
Displacement: 9 tons

ROGER HENRY

NAV. STATION

ENGINE
(PERKINS 30 H.P.)

HEAD   SINK   STORAGE
(SAILS/LINES, ETC.)

DOUBLE CABIN

ANCHOR WELL

DOUBLE CABIN

LOCKER

GALLEY   SALOON   HEATER
(TAYLOR)   PANTRY

ABOUT THE AUTHOR

A NATIVE OF UPSTATE NEW YORK and the fourth of nine children, Alvah Simon made a slow migration westward through his younger years. After bouncing out of nearly every school he attended, he did social work in a Chicago ghetto, operated heavy equipment in a Nebraska grain elevator, and taught skydiving in Montana. Eventually he ran out of continent, and in the late 1970s, in his late twenties, he set sail from Key West in a leaky little sloop, with no money and few prospects.

Over the next thirteen years, Simon circled the world, sustaining himself by stripping logs, selling opals, laying underwater pipe off the coast of Papua New Guinea, working in shipyards, and opening a marina. In Borneo's jungles, Africa's deserts, and Cape Horn's ship graveyards he found the adventures he craved—and something else. The world's native peoples invited him into their huts and shared their ways of life and spiritual insights. He left each village humbled by the growing awareness that these people, so easily dismissed as primitive, have a wealth of knowledge to contribute to the modern world. Eventually this certainty and his longtime fascination with the Arctic propelled Simon and his wife, Diana, a New Zealander, to undertake the unique small-boat odyssey to the land of the Inuit that is described in *North to the Night*.

For this and other sailing accomplishments, the Simons received the 1997 *Cruising World* Award for Outstanding Seamanship. Alvah's chronicle of their Arctic adventure won the 1996 International Boating Writers Contest. The Simons have appeared across North America on television and radio and in newspapers. They live aboard their 36-foot cutter *Roger Henry*.

Byam Martin Mountains

No Name Glacier

Inussualuk Glacier

Hareline Ridge

Snowgoose Camp

Moguls

Glacier Moraine

The Trails

Ptarmigan Hills

Roger Henry

Emergency Tent

Raven's Rock

Valley of Mosses

Tundra

Gyrfalcon Cliff

Bergy Bits

Upwelling

Gravel Plain

Pond

Pond

Thinking Rock

Glaucous Gull Colony

Bear Alley

The Thumb

Tundra

Lancaster Sound
15 miles

Navy Board Inlet

Pond Inlet
100 miles

Raven's View
of Tay Bay

N

Borden Peninsula, Baffin Island